PREACHING
THE
PSALMS

PREACHING
THE
PSALMS

UNLOCKING THE UNSEARCHABLE
RICHES OF DAVID'S TREASURY

STEVEN J. LAWSON

 BOOKS

British Library Cataloguing in Publication Data
A record for this book is available from the British Library

Unless otherwise indicated, Scripture quotations are taken from the NEW AMERICAN STANDARD BIBLE®, Copyright © 1960, 1962, 1963, 1968, 1971, 1972, 1973, 1975, 1977, 1995 by The Lockman Foundation. Used by permission.

ISBN: 978-1-78397-017-9

Printed in Denmark

Evangelical Press, an imprint of 10Publishing
Unit C, Tomlinson Road, Leyland, PR25 2DY, England

Email: epbooks@10ofthose.com
Website: www.epbooks.org

———————————

To a new generation of
Reformed pastors,
who must passionately preach
the glorious truths of David's treasury
and Israel's ancient hymn book — the Psalms.
Through such fervent proclamation,
may we see the dawning of
a new Reformation.

———————————

CONTENTS

A RECOVERY OF THE PSALMS

I n the first decade of the twenty-first century we are beginning to witness a revival of preaching in the worship of the
Christian church. In the work before us, Steven Lawson will
surely help shape this biblical resurgence in the pulpit.

It was in 1985 that I set my hand to the writing of a history of
Christian preaching.[1] Up to that time, I had for almost twenty
years preached Sunday by Sunday through a good portion of both
the Old Testament and the New Testament. God had blessed this
ministry. It was, therefore, surprising to hear that many of my
colleagues were admitting that they were disappointed with the
meager harvest of their own preaching ministry. One frequently
heard the denominational leaders complain that the era of preaching was over. It was a time when churchgoers were looking for
something more engaging.

James I. McCord, at that time president of Princeton Theological Seminary, told me that he was greatly concerned by the inconsequential preaching issuing from so many American pulpits. He even said at one point that the church was embarrassed to discover that it could not fill its major pulpits with worthy successors. Famed preachers such as George Buttrick, Peter Marshall, and Donald Barnhouse had seemingly left no heirs.

If at the end of the twentieth century there was a widespread breakdown of the American pulpit, it is even more regrettable that the devotional life of American Protestantism seems to be drying up. The major churches of our land seem to offer very little leadership in public prayer. Our ministers have given little time to developing a devotional life. They fall back on prayer books and liturgical formularies. Even worse, they give it little attention on Sunday morning — five minutes, perhaps, but rarely more.

Surely one of the most interesting facets of Steven Lawson's work is his realization that the Book of Psalms is the wellspring of the devotional life of the Christian church today. One needs only to look to church history to witness that the great awakenings and continent-altering reformations were always marked by a return to the Holy Scriptures, especially the Psalms. Lawson specifically points to the importance of the Psalms in the devotional life of the renowned German Reformer, Martin Luther. Luther's lectures on the Psalms at the University of Wittenberg were the first-fruits of his preaching ministry and, in many ways, the impetus behind *sola scriptura*. Moreover, and for centuries, the Psalms have held a central place in the life of the church, whether preached, read, or sung. Since the time of the sixteenth-century Protestant Reformation, several great Psalters have even been produced such as the *Huguenot Psalter*, the *Scottish Psalter*, and the *Massachusetts Bay Psalter*.

Another thing is very clear about the message of our author. He is a great believer in preaching the *lectio continua*, the sequential verse-by-verse exposition of Scripture. I would love to have heard his long series of sermons on the Book of Psalms. Noticeably and strongly influenced by Charles Haddon Spurgeon's magnum opus, *The Treasury of David*, Lawson preached more than two hundred sermons on the Psalms in all. I myself, in over fifty years of ministry, have preached four or five series on the Psalms, giving great attention to the various psalm genres. But never have I attempted to preach through the whole book from beginning to end. To find such a rare preaching feat, one could go back almost a hundred years to them time when Alexander Whyte did so at St. Georges West in Edinburgh over the span of three years.

This rediscovery of the *lectio continua* is certainly one of the vital keys to the preaching revival we are beginning to experience. We find preachers today rediscovering this discipline, taking up the pulpit mantle that has been passed down by nineteenth-century sequential expositors such as Alexander Maclaren, Joseph Parker, and B. H. Carroll. From J. Vernon McGee and his *Thru the Bible* radio program, to James Montgomery Boice and the famed pulpit at Tenth Presbyterian Church in Philadelphia, the twentieth century has been witness to swelling tides of revival in the pulpits across the globe. Such waves of reformation have thus served to strongly influence a new generation of expository preachers in this present hour.

Arguably, one of the most successful *lectio continua* preachers of the twentieth century was London's John Stott. Stott was an evangelical Anglican who, without question, took his Bible very seriously. Just as enthusiastic in his use of the *lectio continua* is Kim Sang Bok in Korea, and still another is Africa's Conrad Mbewe in Zambia. Last, but a long way from the least, we have John MacArthur, who has labored in preaching sequentially through the Bible for over forty years in one pulpit at Grace Community Church in Los Angeles, California. When one looks at this list, one cannot overlook the importance of systematic, expository preaching.

We want to listen very carefully to what Steven Lawson has to say about how the preacher goes about sequential, expository preaching. Simply put, there are ways to do it and ways not to do it. The key is the careful study of the Holy Scriptures as the authoritative Word of God. It is when the preacher begins to hear the Word in his study that the preacher becomes powerful in his message. This is precisely what has happened in this revival of preaching. The Word of God is rightly elevated to its place of pre-eminence in the pulpit.

One of the best things about Lawson's work is the way he balances the theology of grace, which he finds in Romans, and spiritual discipline, which he finds in the Psalms. Without the life of prayer, the speculations of theology are all in vain. Lawson is vigilant in respecting both.

Steven Lawson has given us a thorough manual for preaching the Psalms, a very important book which combines the devotional life with its emphasis on praise and prayer with the truths of the gospel. We would do well to read it carefully.

Hughes Oliphant Old[1]
Erskine Theological Seminary
Christmas, 2011

PSALMS FOR
A NEW REFORMATION

In critical periods of the church, certain books of the Bible have played a pivotal role in shaping the spiritual direction of those history-altering eras. These key biblical books have been used by God to launch reformations and spark revivals. They have strategically defined epochs and birthed movements in the church. One such book is the New Testament epistle of Romans. Another is Israel's ancient hymn book, the Old Testament book of Psalms. These two monumental books of Scripture — Romans and Psalms — uniquely came together in the life of one pivotal figure in church history. Such a man was Martin Luther.

Since the time of the Protestant Reformation in the sixteenth century, this famed German Reformer has been largely identified with the book of Romans. In particular, one specific verse,

Romans 1:17 — 'The just shall live by faith' (KJV) — is the text that God used in the conversion of Luther. In his famous 'tower experience,' this passage contained the truth that revolutionized his life and subsequently launched the Reformation. This verse became the theological cornerstone for this mighty movement. This doctrine, known as justification by faith alone, defined the very substance of the gospel in this historic movement. In short, *sola fide* is the means by which an unholy sinner may be right before a holy God.

LUTHER'S FIRST BOOK TAUGHT

However, it is often forgotten that before Luther was converted through his reading of the book of Romans, he first taught the book of Psalms. As Professor of Bible at the University of Wittenberg, he began expounding this inspired book of praise in the classroom on 16 August 1513. Later, in 1517, Luther published his first book, an exposition of seven penitential psalms. To be sure, the study of the Psalms infused his inner man with a transcendent view of God so great that, once converted, this German Reformer was fortified to stand against the world, if need be, for the message of the gospel of grace.

It was these two strategic books — Psalms and Romans — that Luther was predominantly studying and teaching in the years preceding his posting of the Ninety-five Theses.[1] It was these two books of Scripture that radically affected Luther and changed the course of human history. While Romans would principally formulate his doctrine, it was the Psalms that dramatically emboldened him to proclaim God's message to the world. In other words, Romans gave Luther his *theology*, but it was the Psalms that gave him his *thunder*. The Psalms gave Luther a towering view of God, so much so that in preaching the gospel, he was ready to fight the devil himself. In so doing, these two biblical books laid the scriptural foundation for the Protestant Reformation.[2]

THE BIBLE IN MINIATURE

On 31 October 1517, Luther posted his historic Ninety-five Theses, launching his defiant protest against the vile perversions and grave abuses of the church in Rome. This decisive act became the hinge upon which history turned. And at the very core of this Protestant movement were the Psalms, which continued to play a defining role throughout Luther's life and ministry. While being hidden by supporters in Wartburg Castle, the German Reformer translated the Bible into the German language. Included in this work were the Psalms, which Luther referred to as 'the Bible in miniature'.

In future years, Luther would repeatedly turn to the Psalms for solace and strength. With the continent of Europe in upheaval, he found great comfort in the soul-lifting truths of the Psalms. Specifically, in 1527, Luther faced one of the greatest difficulties of his life as the Black Plague swept across Germany and much of the European continent. During this time, Luther's son almost died and his own body was fainting under the mounting pressure. In the midst of this personal conflict, Luther found himself contemplating the promises of Psalm 46, an encouraging psalm of trust in the invincibility of the Lord.

Gaining new strength from this old song, Luther composed what is arguably his most famous hymn, 'A Mighty Fortress'. Amid such adversity, this embattled stalwart found God to be his 'bulwark never failing'. Though he had previously taught and even translated the Psalms, Luther now found himself living them as never before. Many times during this dark and tumultuous period, when terribly discouraged, he would turn to his co-worker, Philipp Melanchthon, and say, 'Come, Philipp, let us sing the forty-sixth Psalm.' Together, they would sing:

> A sure stronghold our God is He,
> A timely shield and weapon;
> Our helper He will be and set us free
> From every ill can happen.[3]

Against the Gates of Hell

With unshakable confidence in God, Luther reflected upon and drew strength from this choice psalm:

> We sing this psalm to the praise of God, because He is with us and powerfully and miraculously preserves and defends His church and His word against all fanatical spirits, against the gates of hell, against the implacable hatred of the devil, and against all the assaults of the world, the flesh, and sin.[4]

Despite Luther's intense inner turmoil, this valiant Reformer clung to the rock-solid truths of Israel's ancient hymn book. Four years before he died, he wrote in his Bible the text of Psalm 119:92: 'If Your Law had not been my delight, then I would have perished in my affliction.' Such biblical truth empowered this spiritual leader and enabled him to persevere in the midst of his many struggles to reform the church. To the very end, this daring leader of the Reformation tenaciously held to the glorious revelations of the Psalms.

The Call for a New Reformation

Down throughout the centuries, this has been the strengthening experience of countless believers. The unfailing, unchanging truths of the Psalms have been their greatest source of strength in such hours of difficulty. It is, unquestionably, the divinely inspired Psalter that brings courage and comfort, support and stability to our lives in times of greatest need. This canonical book of praise has ministered abundant grace to untold numbers over the centuries and has proven to be an immovable rock in the times of greatest advance for the church.

If the church is to see another reformation in this present day, there must be, first, a reformation of the modern-day pulpit. It is not merely more preaching that is needed. Rather, there is a certain kind of preaching that must be restored, namely *expository* preaching. In this systematic approach to the pulpit, the preacher primarily reads, explains and applies what the Bible teaches, all in a persuasive way. In true preaching, Philip Ryken notes, 'The main points of his [a preacher's] sermon are the points made by a particular text in the Bible. The ministry not only begins with Scripture, but also allows the Scripture to establish the context and content for his entire sermon.'[5] In its purest sense, expository preaching is biblical preaching that is God-exalting and life-altering.

Such a reformation in preaching is precisely what took place in Luther's day. Scripture alone — *sola scriptura* — became the battle cry of the Protestant movement. If a new reformation is to come in this present hour, it will most certainly be preceded by a return to the unvarnished preaching of the Scriptures. Such a heaven-sent revival would see men of God once again preaching the unsearchable riches of God's inspired Word, which would surely showcase the Psalms. With the renewed fervor of past generations, expositors today should once again commit themselves to expounding the sacred writings of the ancient psalmists. In this generation, pastors should passionately preach and teach the much-loved book of Psalms with increasing confidence and bold conviction.

PREACHING THROUGH THE PSALMS

But the question begs to be asked: How many preachers know *how* to preach the Psalms? It must be admitted that noticeable differences exist between the Psalms and the narrative sections of Scripture. Further, obvious distinctives exist between the Psalms and the four Gospel accounts, as well as between them and the New Testament epistles. These literary variations pose real challenges to every expositor. As a result, the Psalms, tragically, remain a neglected book in many pulpits. That is to say, the book of Psalms is often read, but rarely exposited. Therefore, this book is an attempt to provide a helpful key to unlock the inexhaustible riches of this vast storehouse of truths that Spurgeon once called 'the treasury of David'.

One of the most rewarding experiences of my pulpit ministry has been the privilege of preaching consecutively through the entire Psalter. In all, this expository series took six years to complete, each week working psalm by psalm, verse by verse, phrase by phrase, line by line. Upon completing this series, I had the additional joy of writing a two-volume commentary on the Psalms, as a part of the *Holman Old Testament Commentary Series*.[6] This project afforded me the added opportunity to re-study, re-explain and re-apply each of these worship songs. Producing these two volumes required studying each psalm again, with care and precision, examining the central thrust of each. In this study, I gave even more attention to the Psalms, studying their truths and contemplating their beauties. Further, I have preached many of these psalms in other churches and conferences around the world, affording me yet further exposure to them.

Surveying the Entire Process

As a result of preaching the Psalms and writing a two-volume commentary on this towering portion of Scripture, I want to provide a useful guide for preaching through this transcendent worship book. I want to survey the entire process of preparing and delivering expository sermons on the Psalms. From the study to pulpit, I want to examine the entire expository method, with the result being to make the exposition of the Psalms an integral part of one's preaching and teaching ministry.

I first taught this material in the 'Distinguished Lecture Series' at the Master's Seminary in Sun Valley, California. Since then, I have further developed this material while teaching through it multiple times in Samara, Russia, at the Samara Bible Institute and Samara Preachers' Institute. It is my stated desire here to lay out a strategy for preaching this highly-prized book. Moreover, it is my hope that, through this study, God would give a new generation of preachers a love for the Psalms, specifically for *preaching* the Psalms.

May this book spark a new reformation in the church today. May it be so with you in your ministry.

Steven J. Lawson
Mobile, Alabama
February, 2012

1

PREPARE
THE HEART

Humble yourself before God,
who illumines the mind and ignites the heart

M artyn Lloyd-Jones, the noted expositor of Westminster
Chapel in London, was correct when he stated, 'The
work of preaching is the highest and the greatest and
the most glorious calling to which anyone can ever be called.'[1]
This *is* true, not because there is anything special about the
messenger, but because there is everything glorious about the
Sovereign Lord who summons and sends forth His messen-
gers to preach the Word. Because the Bible is what it claims to
be, namely, the inspired, inerrant, and infallible Word of God,

the call to proclaim the Word is the highest calling known to man. As heralds of the sacred Scripture, expositors have been entrusted with the greatest responsibility of all, being mouth-pieces through whom God has chosen to speak. Therefore, all who preach must be firmly committed to rightly interpreting and properly applying His Word.

As the expositor approaches the Psalms, he is like a mountain climber, poised at the base of a towering summit, ready to scale its lofty heights. The formidable challenge that lies ahead is daunting. But the demanding ascent is well worth the effort. The book of Psalms is the Mount Everest of Scripture, the largest book in the Bible. Despite this challenge, it is my personal con-viction that an average preacher becomes a good preacher, and a good preacher becomes a great preacher, when he learns to preach this book. The fact is that he becomes, I believe, a better preacher of other books in the Bible when he learns to preach the Psalms. The expositor's skills are, arguably, significantly enhanced when he digs deep into these transcendent truths, magnificent literature, and vivid language.

The Place to Begin

The specific focus of this book is upon how to preach the Psalms. Where do we begin such a monumental study? We start at the most basic level — with the preacher himself. A strategic grasp of the Psalms commences *before* the expositor even opens this inspired Psalter. Before the man of God launches his exegesis and sermon preparation, some initial steps must be taken in ordering his own life so that his journey arrives at the right des-tination. Regarding the personal life of the preacher, the place to begin is with the following requirements.

PERSONALLY CONVERTED

First, those who would preach the Psalms must be personally

converted to Jesus Christ. The primary prerequisite for preaching the Word is the saving knowledge of Christ. The preacher must be regenerated by God's Spirit in order to be effectively used by God in His service. He must be one who has truly believed upon Jesus Christ. Before he can call others to repent and believe, he himself must have done the same. The apostle Paul told Timothy, 'Pay close attention to yourself and to your teaching; persevere in these things, for as you do this you will ensure salvation both for yourself and for those who hear you' (1 Tim. 4:16). In other words, every preacher *must* first pay attention to his own salvation and be assured of his right standing before God.

GRACE IN THE SOUL

In his classic work *The Reformed Pastor*, the Puritan Richard Baxter addressed the ministers of his day in seventeenth-century England, many of whom were unconverted.[2] Baxter began his urgent appeal by calling his fellow pastors to make certain that they are born again:

> See that the work of saving grace be thoroughly wrought in your own souls. Take heed to yourselves, lest you be void of that saving grace of God which you offer to others, and be strangers to the effectual working of that gospel which you preach; and lest, while you proclaim to the world the necessity of a Saviour, your own hearts should neglect him, and you should miss of an interest in Him and His saving benefits. Take heed to yourselves, lest you perish, while you call upon others to take heed of perishing.[3]

In this quote, Baxter is warning that an unconverted minister is the ultimate hypocrite. Such a man calls others to the springs of living water, yet he himself never drinks. He invites others to eat of the bread of life, but he himself never partakes. He attempts to share what he himself does not possess. He tries to lead people where he himself has not gone. Tragically, an unconverted preacher endeavors to teach that which he has not experienced. He preaches without the aid of the Holy Spirit, certainly a vain endeavor.

Of such futility, Charles Spurgeon writes:

> A graceless pastor is a blind man elected to a professorship
> of optics, philosophizing upon light and vision, discours-
> ing upon … the nice shades and delicate blendings of the
> prismatic colours, while he himself is absolutely in the
> dark! He is a dumb man elevated to the chair of music; a
> deaf man fluent upon symphonies and harmonies! He is a
> mole professing to educate eaglets.[4]

THE JUST LIVE BY FAITH

Most notably, Martin Luther exemplified this sobering reality. The great German Reformer was a professor of Bible at the
University of Wittenberg, yet unconverted. While translating
the Psalms in 1519, line by line and word by word, Luther himself remained unsaved. In Luther's own words, we read:

> In that same year, 1519, I had begun interpreting the
> Psalms once again… I had conceived a burning desire to
> understand what Paul meant in his Letter to the Romans,
> but thus far there had stood in my way, not the cold blood
> around my heart, but that one word which is in chapter
> one: 'The justice of God is revealed in it.' I hated that word,
> 'justice of God', which, by the use and custom of all my
> teachers, I had been taught to understand philosophically
> as referring to formal or active justice, as they call it, i.e.,
> that justice by which God is just and by which He pun-
> ishes sinners and the unjust… I meditated night and day
> on those words until at last, by the mercy of God, I paid
> attention to their context: 'The justice of God is revealed in
> it, as it is written: "The just person lives by faith."' I began
> to understand that in this verse the justice of God is that
> by which the just person lives by a gift of God, that is by
> faith. I began to understand that this verse means that the

justice of God is revealed through the Gospel, but it is a passive justice, i.e. that by which the merciful God justifies us by faith, as it is written: 'The just person lives by faith.' All at once I felt that I had been born again and entered into paradise itself through open gates.[5]

Every expositor must have this saving reality in his own soul. In Luther's words, he must have already 'entered into paradise itself'. Let me ask you a personal question: Are *you* personally converted to Jesus Christ? Have *you* died to yourself that He might live within you? Have *you* repented of your sin and submitted your life to Jesus Christ the Lord?[6] No one can be an effective expositor unless he is in a converted state of grace.

SOVEREIGNLY CALLED

Second, the one who would exposit the Psalms must be sovereignly chosen and called by God to do so. This sacred call is a divine appointment by which one is separated from one's mother's womb to preach the Scriptures. Such a sovereign commission was the experience of the prophet Jeremiah (Jer. 1:5), John the Baptist (Luke 1:15), and the apostle Paul (Gal. 1:15-16). Before they were born, each of these men was marked out by God to preach His Word. So it is with all of God's preachers. This divine summons to preach is, as James M. Garretson writes, 'the special work of God's Spirit in the heart, specifically calling the man into the ministry'.[7] In issuing this effectual call to preach, 'God communicates His intentions to the men who He calls into His service.'[8] By divine leading, a man must be deeply persuaded that God is calling him into the ministry. No man should take this position to himself. Instead, God must be the one who sets a man apart to preach His Word.

DISTINGUISHING MARKS OF A CALL

How can one know whether God has called one to preach? In

Lectures to My Students,[9] Charles Haddon Spurgeon outlines the distinguishing marks of a true call into the ministry. Each chapter in this book was given as one of the Friday afternoon lectures that Spurgeon issued to the students in his Pastors' College, regarding the work of the ministry. In a chapter with the title 'The Call to the Ministry', Spurgeon states there must be the following elements:

1. Compulsion

Foremost, there must be what Spurgeon called 'an intense, all-absorbing desire for the work'.[10] There must be 'an irresistible, overwhelming craving and raging thirst'[11] to speak God's Word. This intense desire is not a sudden impulse that comes quickly and then soon leaves. Rather, this inward compulsion to preach deepens with time. The man of God feels what Paul felt when he declared: '…woe is me if I do not preach the gospel' (1 Cor. 9:16).

2. Competency

Further, Spurgeon argued that there must be 'an aptness to teach and some measure of the other qualities needful for the office of a public instructor'.[12] This includes a personal self-awareness that a man is gifted to teach Scripture.

3. Conversions

Moreover, Spurgeon maintained there must be conversions. The prince of preachers asserted, 'He must see a measure of conversion-work going on under his efforts'.[13] The fruit of conversions must be seen in a man's ministry if he is to know that he has been called to preach. God will validate his call with souls brought to Christ. Spurgeon further argued, 'As a man to be set apart to the ministry, his commission is without seals until souls are won by his instrumentality to the knowledge of Jesus'.[14]

4. Confirmation

Finally, Spurgeon insisted, 'Your preaching should be acceptable to the people of God'.[15] This is to say, the body of Christ will confirm the man who is set apart and sent from God. Concerning those truly called by God, Spurgeon explained, 'The sheep will know the God-sent shepherd; the porter of the fold will open to you, and the flock will know your voice.'[16] Others must confirm this divine calling.

SOVEREIGNLY ENLISTED TO PREACH

To be sure, no preacher should be self-appointed. The pulpit is not to be manned by a volunteer army. Rather, it is reserved for those men who are sovereignly enlisted by God Himself. Only these divinely appointed ambassadors are permitted to represent Him. In the ultimate sense, no school, no denomination, and no church can make a preacher — only God can make a preacher. Ministerial training and biblical education can certainly provide the necessary tools to preach. But it is God *alone* who calls and appoints men to be heralds of divine revelation. With this in mind, all those whom He calls into the ministry of the proclamation of Scripture, He supernaturally gifts with the abilities to teach and preach His Word. Every preacher should ask himself this question: Has God set *me* apart for the purpose of preaching? Has He set His hand upon *me* to lead me into this ministry of Bible exposition?

WHOLLY CONSECRATED

Third, the one who would preach the Psalms must be fully consecrated to God. His life must be presented as a living and holy sacrifice (Rom. 12:1). He must be one who is engaged in the personal pursuit of holiness. Accompanying every preacher's giftedness must be his own godliness (1 Tim. 3:1-7; Titus 1:5-9). This progress in spiritual maturity should be evident to all (1 Tim. 4:16). Paul writes, 'I discipline my body and make it my slave, so that, after I have preached to others, I myself will not be disqualified' (1 Cor. 9:27). That is to say, a failure to discipline one's spiritual life brings a disqualification from the pulpit. Simply put, the spirituality of the expositor is the sturdy platform upon which he stands to preach.

MODELLING THE MESSAGE

The godliness of the expositor means 'a habit of mind, heart, and will which seeks to love God with all of one's being'.[17] This is the Christlikeness that the preacher must pursue, namely, 'that disposition of spirit whereby the child of God seeks to walk in the obedience of faith, in the fear of the Lord, growing in the grace and knowledge of Christ'.[18] Archibald Alexander, founding president of Princeton Seminary, writes that such personal piety 'is always wrought in the heart of him who is inwardly called of God and those who have no satisfactory evidences that they have been the subjects of renewing grace may rest assured that they have no call to preach'.[19] Such blameless character must be present in all who would preach the Word. The preacher *must* model the message.

Personal godliness, at its heart, is rooted in one's love for Christ. The preacher must have deep affections for the God of the Word before he can preach the Word of God. Speaking to this very point, Alexander stated:

> Love to Christ — supreme love to Christ — is the most important qualification of a pastor of Christ's flock… Nothing but the love of Christ can make a truly faithful pastor, or evangelist, assiduous in all his services, and indefatigable in the most private and self-denying duties of his office. Other motives may lead a man to great diligence in preparing for his labours in the pulpit, where splendid eloquence wins as much applause as anywhere else. Other motives also may stimulate a minister to great public exertion, and give him all the appearance of fervent zeal and devotedness to God, in the eyes of men; but if supreme love to Christ be wanting, he is, after all, nothing; or, at best, a mere 'sounding brass or tinkling cymbal'. Genius, learning, eloquence, zeal, public exertion, and great sacrifices, even if it should be of all our goods, and of our lives themselves, will be accounted of no value, in the eyes of the Lord, if love to Christ be wanting.[20]

Prioritizing this spiritual virtue, Baxter further comments in *The Reformed Pastor* regarding every preacher's need for godliness:

> Content not yourselves with being in a state of grace, but be also careful that your graces are kept in vigorous and lively exercise, and that you preach to yourselves the sermons which you study, before you preach them to others... O brethren, watch therefore over your own hearts: keep out lusts and passions, and worldly inclinations; keep up the life of faith, and love, and zeal: be much at home, and be much with God. If it be not your daily business to study your own hearts, and to subdue corruption, and to walk with God — if you make not this a work to which you constantly attend, all will go wrong, and you will starve your hearers.[21]

THE NEED FOR PERSONAL GODLINESS

No preacher can advance beyond his own personal devotion to Jesus Christ. No matter how well one studies, the message must flow out of the man. Every expositor must cultivate his own heart for God. With this in mind, John Owen, the noted English Puritan, writes, 'A minister may fill his pews, his communion roll, the mouths of the public, but what that minister is on his knees in secret before God Almighty, that he is and no more.'[22] Or as Robert Murray M'Cheyne once remarked, 'My people's greatest need is my personal holiness.'[23] In other words, what one is in the pulpit can never exceed what one is in private before God. This is the expositor's need for personal godliness.

Regarding this heart preparation of every preacher of the Word, Spurgeon wrote:

> It will be in vain for me to stock my library ... if I neglect the culture of myself; for books .... are only remotely the instruments of my holy calling; my own spirit, soul, and body are my nearest machinery for sacred service; my

spiritual facilities and my inner life are my battle axe and weapons of war.[24]

To be sure, the pursuit of individual holiness is of the utmost importance in preaching.

BIBLICALLY SATURATED

Fourth, every preacher of the Psalms must be thoroughly saturated with a working knowledge of the entire Bible. No other book requires such an understanding of the whole Bible as do the Psalms. To this end, Paul charged Timothy, 'Be diligent to present yourself approved to God as a workman who does not need to be ashamed, accurately handling the word of truth' (2 Tim. 2:15). So it must be with every preacher of the Psalms. He must cut it straight with the Word, making precise incisions in interpreting the biblical text.

A COMPREHENSIVE GRASP OF TRUTH

This comprehensive grasp of Scripture encompasses a wide understanding of its major movements and doctrinal truths. The expositor must be well studied and well grounded in the full counsel of God (Acts 20:27). John Stott commented, 'Because the Christian pastor is primarily called to the ministry of the Word, the study of Scripture is one of his foremost responsibilities.'[25] His knowledge of God's Word must be comprehensive. Affirming that the preacher must possess a command of the Scripture, Stott states:

> The systematic preaching of the Word is impossible without the systematic study of it. It will not be enough to skim through a few verses in daily Bible reading, nor to study a passage only when we have to preach from it. No. We must daily soak ourselves in the Scriptures. We must not just study, as through a microscope, the linguistic minutiae

of a few verses, but take our telescope and scan the wide expanses of God's Word, assimilating its grand theme of divine sovereignty in the redemption of mankind.[26]

In order to master the Scriptures, Martyn Lloyd-Jones notes that there must be the regular reading of the entire Scripture, from cover to cover:

> Read your Bibles systematically… I cannot emphasize too strongly the vital importance of reading the whole Bible… Then, having done that, you can decide to work your way through one particular book, with commentaries or any aids that you may choose to employ… Do not read the Bible to find texts for sermons; read it because it is the food that God has provided for your soul, because it is the Word of God, because it is the means whereby you can get to know God. Read it because it is the bread of life, the manna provided for your soul's nourishment and well-being.[27]

BEING SATURATED WITH SCRIPTURE

If a man is to preach the Psalms with power, his very thoughts and words must be those of Scripture. He must be absorbed in the Word. C. H. Spurgeon wrote, 'It is blessed to eat into the very soul of the Bible until, at last, you come to talk in Scriptural language, and your very style is fashioned upon Scripture models, and what is better still, your spirit is flavoured with the words of the Lord.'[28] So it is for the one who would preach the Psalms. He must be saturated with biblical truth throughout the whole of the Bible.

Martin Luther, a great preacher himself, became an ardent student of the Word of God. This occurred not only in his preparation to lecture on the Bible in the classroom, but also in his own personal study in preparation to preach and write. Luther wrote, 'For a number of years I have now annually read through the

Bible twice. If the Bible was a large, mighty tree and all its words were little branches, I have tapped at all the branches, eager to know what was there and what it had to offer.'[29] Therefore, the German Reformer concluded, 'He who is well acquainted with the text of Scripture is a distinguished theologian. For a Bible passage or text is of more value than the comments of four authors.'[30] Such hunger for the Word must mark every expositor.

Nevertheless, Luther plainly understood the dire need for the Holy Spirit to be his infallible Teacher amidst his personal study of Scripture. This God-given insight into the Word must continue as the man of God stands in the pulpit to preach. To this end, Luther asserts, 'Be assured that no one will make a doctor of the Holy Scripture save only the Holy Ghost from heaven.'[31] In the pulpit, the Spirit further illumines the heart and mind of the preacher as he stands in front of an open Bible.

THIS SURE FOUNDATION

This opening chapter is making the claim that the personal life of the preacher — his spirituality and godliness — is the very foundation upon which his public preaching stands. His maturity must be established before his message can be effective. If God is to speak through a man, that messenger must be converted, called, consecrated, and consumed with Scripture. Only in his pursuit of personal holiness can he come to his study and rightly understand the Word. And only in that same spiritual state can he ascend into the pulpit and rightly deliver a biblical message in the power of the Holy Spirit.

The expositor's spirituality is indispensably foundational to his preaching. As the famed English Puritan Thomas Watson maintained, 'There are two things in every minister of Christ that are much exercised: his head, and his heart. His head with labor, and his heart with love.'[32] This is to say, expository preaching involves both the preacher's head and his heart, both his labor and his love. In particular, it is the expositor's love for Christ that propels his labor in the Word. Everything stands or falls according to his personal relationship with Christ. His own godliness, in the final analysis, is the necessary foundation upon which his giftedness rests.

George Whitefield, the renowned eighteenth-century English evangelist, once said:

> As God can send a nation or people no greater blessing than to give them faithful, sincere, and upright ministers, so the greatest curse that God can possibly send upon a people in this world, is to give them over to blind, unregenerate, carnal, lukewarm and unskilled guides.[33]

Whitefield is right. There is no greater blessing that can fall upon any people than for them to be led by spiritual men who are growing in personal godliness. At the same time, there is no greater curse upon a land than for it to be subjected to religious leaders who are 'blind leaders of the blind'.

In this hour, may Jesus Christ give to His church godly men who are holy instruments in the hand of the Master, expositors fit for every good work.

EMBRACE
THE TASK

*Commit yourself entirely to being
an expository preacher of the Psalms*

Having established the necessary prerequisites for the
preacher's personal life, our focus now shifts to what
expository preaching actually is. Many talk about expository preaching, but few understand what it entails. Still fewer
practise it. So many ministers resort to little more than philosophizing in the pulpit, yet others to moralizing, politicizing, and
even storytelling. And the reason is quite simple — either they
do not know what God requires of them in preaching His Word,
or else they know, but have lost confidence in the power of the

Word to perform its work. Where either situation exists, Philip Ryken warns, 'Their congregations rarely hear the voice of God's Spirit speaking in Scripture. The post-Christian church no longer believes in the power of biblical preaching, plain and simple.'[1] In a day in which biblical preaching is a lost practice, it is important, if it is to be recovered, that we clarify what it actually is.

What, then, is expository preaching? The word 'expository' is an adjective that describes a certain kind of preaching — expository preaching. The word itself means that which 'explains or interprets,' or what is a 'commentary,' or is 'explanatory.'[2] That is to say, expository preaching is chiefly *explanatory* preaching, or the kind of pulpit ministry that interprets a biblical passage. It is Bible-based preaching that gives a careful explanation of a text of Scripture, correctly interpreting the passage and presenting it in a compelling way with relevant application. This approach to the pulpit is distinctly *biblical*.

A Commitment to Scripture

Expository preaching presents a moving commentary on a biblical text, laced with its practical application, which seeks to move the listener to glorify God and pursue a particular course of action. Such preaching gives the meaning of a passage of Scripture that God intends in a life-changing manner. To put it simply, every preacher, as Martyn Lloyd-Jones says, 'must always be expository. *Always* expository.'[3]

Having clarified what 'expository' is, let us now consider what it is *not*. There are many misconceptions about expository preaching that need to be repudiated. To be sure, expository preaching is not a 'data dump' that is overflowing with disconnected observations from Scripture, lacking a central theme or compelling appeal. It is not a 'barrage' of rambling comments on a biblical passage, devoid of logical order and sequential thought. Nor is it a 'digest' of exegetical findings that omits compelling interest and powerful persuasion.

Neither is expository preaching a 'string' of word studies and cross references without any discernible movement or central theme and lacking powerful motivation. Expository preaching is not a 'sequence' of independent headings, missing a unifying thrust and final summation. It is not a religious 'pep talk' without biblical moorings or an exegetical foundation. Nor is it a 'devotional chat,' bankrupt of theological content. Expository preaching is none of these things.

WHAT EXPOSITORY PREACHING IS

Expository preaching is preaching that gives the sound interpretation of a biblical text, presenting the proper meaning of a passage in a logical, unifying manner and showing its practical relevance for daily living. This kind of preaching is Trinitarian — that is to say, it is centred upon the glory of God, magnifies the supremacy of His Son, Jesus Christ, and is empowered by the Holy Spirit. It is preaching that arranges and presents its truths in an orderly sequence of thought and is related to the everyday life of the listener. The one who would be an expositor must be committed to these basic essentials in pulpit presentation.

In short, true expository preaching is biblically grounded, God-centred, and practically relevant, coming through a man who is passionate for God and who is sovereignly enflamed by the Holy Spirit. To this point, Lloyd-Jones writes, 'What is preaching? Logic on fire! ... It is theology on fire. And a theology which does not take fire, I maintain, is a defective theology... Preaching is theology coming through a man who is on fire.'[4] Using this same imagery, the Puritans stated that expository preaching builds a fire in the pulpit. John Owen, writes, 'The word is like the sun in the firmament,' yielding 'spiritual light and heat.'[5] This is to say, a pulpit fire yields both light and heat — the light of instruction and illumination combined with the heat of conviction and transformation.

This chapter will set forth what is involved in this disciplined approach to the pulpit. What are the component parts of

expository preaching? We must understand the six basic elements that constitute true expository preaching.

BIBLE-BASED EXPOSITION

First, expository preaching is, principally, *biblical* preaching. It is
preaching that primarily expounds and explains a text of Scripture.
In this approach, the expositor is simply a mouthpiece for a text
from the Psalms. He says what the psalm says. The message arises
out of the biblical text itself. He goes where the psalm takes him.

THE GENIUS OF EXPOSITION

Regarding this commitment to Scripture, Merrill Unger writes
that expository preaching 'is emphatically not preaching about
the Bible, but preaching the Bible. "What saith the Lord" is the
alpha and the omega of expository preaching. It begins in the
Bible and ends in the Bible and all that intervenes springs from
the Bible. In other words, expository preaching is Bible-centred
preaching.'[6] This is the genius of expository preaching. It does
not begin with a human need and then work backwards to find
a biblical text to support one's ideas. On the contrary, expository
preaching begins with a text of Scripture, works through that
text, and applies it to the lives of believers.

Expository preaching is to be uniquely distinguished from all
other approaches to the pulpit. Walter C. Kaiser, Jr., writes:

> What separates topical preaching from expository
> preaching … is that expository preaching and teaching
> unwaveringly begins and remains with the biblical text
> throughout the whole sermon. Rather than beginning
> with a human need or concern as the impetus for the
> sermon, the expository sermon deliberately reverses
> the action and has the sermon originate in the exposi-
> tion of the Biblical text itself. Exposition starts with the

Biblical text and holds fast to that text throughout the sermon.[7]

In other words, expository preaching is, as J. I. Packer notes, quite simply, 'letting texts talk'.[8] It says what Scripture says — nothing more, nothing less. It is based upon the fundamental belief that when the Bible speaks, *God* speaks.

THE INSPIRATION OF SCRIPTURE

All expository preaching of the Psalms is based upon an unwavering commitment that Scripture *is* what it claims to be. The doctrine of the divine inspiration of Scripture is why we preach the Psalms. We do so because it is the written word of the living God. In preaching the Psalms, the substance of the sermon is derived from the text of a psalm. The book of Psalms makes this very claim for itself — that the entire Psalter is from God. That is to say, it is the Word of God Himself. This fundamental belief is the bedrock of expository preaching — the inspiration of Scripture.

To be sure, the Scripture is described as coming not from man, but from God Himself. Although recorded by human authors, there is, nevertheless, only one primary Author, the Lord God. God superintended the authors of Scripture — including the psalmists — so that, using their own individual personalities, they composed and recorded without error His word for man. Thus, the Bible is 'the law *of the* LORD' (1:2), not the law of man. The ultimate source is the Lord. It is the law that has been issued by God. The Scripture is the written record of God's truth and wisdom. Expository preaching is rooted and grounded in this fact.

THE INERRANCY OF SCRIPTURE

Because the Bible is divinely inspired, it is absolutely pure, without any error. It is perfectly reliable in all that it affirms. The flawless purity of God's own character ensures the perfect purity of His Word. Thus, inerrancy means the Scripture is:

1. Absolutely Pure

God's words are purified as silver refined in a furnace seven times. Seven is the number of completeness and perfection. Scripture is, therefore, flawless, like perfectly refined silver. All dross of error has been removed. The psalmist writes, 'The words of the LORD are pure words; as silver tried in a furnace on the earth, refined seven times' (12:6). Again, 'The word of the LORD is tried' (18:30) and 'The sum of Your word is truth' (119:160). Only the pure truth of God is contained in His Word. God is without sin, and His Word is without any impurities.

2. Perfectly True

Because the Bible is absolutely pure. Thus, every preacher has a divine mandate to preach its truths. The psalmist writes, 'I have seen a limit to all perfection; Your commandment is exceedingly broad' (119:96). That is to say, everything in this world falls short of perfection except the full revelation of God's Word. The psalmist asserts, 'Your law is truth' (119:142). Again, '…all Your commandments are truth' (119:151). That the Bible is truth, as the psalmist maintains, means that it tells it like it is. Whenever God says anything, it is what it is. Truth is reality. It is the way things really are. Sin is whatever God says it is. Salvation is whatever God says it is. Heaven and hell are whatever God says they are. All that the Bible affirms is truth.

THE AUTHORITY OF SCRIPTURE

Moreover, Scripture is the authoritative word of God to man. It does not contain mere options for, or suggestions to, man. Rather, it contains God's directive commandments that are binding upon the conscience of every human life. To disbelieve or disobey any word of Scripture is to disbelieve or disobey God Himself. In the book of Psalms, there are various synonyms for God's Word, each revealing the many-sided perfections of divine revelation. Among these synonyms are:

1. God's Law
This is the chief term for God's Word. The 'law' (*torah*) of the Lord comes from a Hebrew root meaning 'to project,' 'teach,' or 'direct'. This word refers to any direction or instruction flowing from the Word of God that points out, or indicates, God's will to man. It can refer to a single command, or to the entire teaching, instruction, or doctrine of Scripture. 'Law' reminds us that divine revelation is not simply for man's interest, but for his obedience.

2. God's Testimonies
The word for the 'testimonies' (*edut*) of the Lord is derived from a root meaning 'to bear witness' and, thus, testifies to its divine Author. This refers to the outspokenness of Scripture, with its high standards and frank warnings. It is a solemn attestation, a declaration of the will of God, the ordinances that became God's standard of conduct. To put it plainly, this word for Scripture means that it contains truth that is attested by God Himself. It is a term for His covenant declarations. Thus, it was used of the two stone tablets summarizing the law, the Ten Commandments, that were placed in the ark as a witness to the holy character of God. David states that Scripture is 'the law of the LORD' — which is to say, it contains God's perfect teaching on the many issues of life and eternity.

3. God's Statutes
The word 'statutes' (*huqqim*) indicates the eternal stability of Scripture. These irrevocable laws of the Lord are 'engraved' or 'inscribed,' as though etched in stone. This synonym for God's Word speaks of its immutable character, binding force, and fixed permanence. In other words, His statutes endure forever and will never be rescinded, removed, or replaced.

4. God's Precepts
The term 'precepts' (*piqqudim*) is a poetical word for divine injunctions that is found only in the Psalms. It is drawn from the

sphere of an officer, or overseer, a man who is responsible to look closely at a situation and take precise action. In like manner, this word points to the particular instructions of the Lord, as one who cares about compliance with the details of His will. Literally, it refers to an authoritative charge, or order that is binding upon the recipient. In this instance, it is the divine Word from the sovereign Lord of the universe, directing, and ruling people.

5. God's Commands
The word 'commands' (*miswa*) signifies a definite, authoritative command, or anything ordained by the Lord. It emphasizes the straight authority of what God says. It conveys not merely the power to convince or persuade, but the right to order His people. It designates the general body of imperative commands contained in God's law. God's Word is never to be taken as a suggestion, or an option laid before His people. Rather, it should always be received as a divine command placed upon the conscience.

6. God's Ordinances
The word for 'ordinances' (*mishpat*) represents a judicial decision that constitutes legal and moral precedence. It indicates the higher decisions of the all-wise Judge regarding human situations. It denotes divinely ordered judicial decisions on all kinds of issues in what might be called 'case law' that makes applications to specific situations of human life. In short, it is the divine standard given to man. In the Pentateuch, this term referred to the ordinances of the civil and ceremonial law. The word can also mean God's judgmental acts on the wicked.

7. God's Fear
The 'fear' (*yira*) of the Lord refers to the parts of God's law that especially evoke fear and reverence. This includes passages that reveal God's holiness and awesome judgments. This term is a synonym for the law, since its purpose was to put a healthy fear into human hearts (Deut. 4:10). Thus, the Scripture is God's manual for worship. It should lead those who read it to reverence God, holding Him in the strictest awe. The Word of God

also pronounces divine judgment on those who disobey its message, depicting God as angry at sin. Such passages should inspire the proper fear of God.

THE SUFFICIENCY OF SCRIPTURE

Further, biblical preaching of the Psalms is built upon the absolute sufficiency of Scripture. When accompanied by the ministry of the Holy Spirit, the Bible is entirely able to accomplish all that God desires to do upon the earth (Isa. 55:10-11). The truth of the sufficiency of Scripture forms one of the key cornerstones of biblical preaching. It is clearly seen in Psalm 19:7-9, where we find six descriptions of His Word — 'perfect,' 'sure,' 'right,' 'pure,' 'clean,' 'true' — along with the effects produced in the one who receives it — 'restoring,' 'making wise,' 'rejoicing,' 'enlightening,' and creating the 'fear of the LORD.' These verses describe the many-faceted nature of the all-sufficient Scripture. Here is what the Psalms are able to perform.

1. Restoring the Soul
Scripture is 'perfect' — that is, whole, complete, comprehensive, and sufficient. The effect of the Word, when explained and brought to bear upon one's life, is seen in its supernatural ability, 'restoring the soul' (19:7a). Scripture is so powerful, David writes, that it converts and transforms the entire inner person. This radical change works from the inside out, restoring man at the deepest level of his existence.

2. Instructing the Simple
Scripture is represented as the 'testimony of the LORD' (19:7b), meaning that it contains God's outspoken witness to man. The Bible speaks frankly, openly and directly. The Word is 'sure,' indicating that it is absolutely reliable, trustworthy, unwavering, and immovable. The Scripture is always 'making wise the simple.' In other words, it provides God-given insight to those whose understanding and judgment have not yet matured: 'Your commandments make me wiser than my enemies, for they

are ever mine. I have more insight than all my teachers, for Your testimonies are my meditation. I understand more than the aged, because I have observed Your precepts' (119:98-100).

Scripture makes one wise beyond one's years, causing one to be skilled in godly living.

3. Rejoicing the Heart
The Word is 'right,' meaning that it makes known the right and proper path to take in life. Its effect is 'rejoicing the heart,' producing great gladness (19:8a). The scriptural truth is so all-sufficient that it even causes the fearful or depressed heart to be glad. It gives true happiness and lasting contentment, which only God can give.

4. Enlightening the Eyes
These commands of the Lord are 'pure,' meaning that they are illuminating. They make the dark things of life come to light, bringing eternal realities into focus. Scripture gives light to those who are in darkness concerning the ways of God. The psalmist writes, 'Your word is a lamp to my feet and a light to my path' (119:105). 'I have chosen the faithful way; I have placed Your ordinances before me' (119:30). God guides His people by His light-giving Word.

5. Enduring Forever
The law is 'clean,' without any impurity, devoid of any flaw. Every facet of Scripture is 'enduring forever,' meaning that it is permanent and eternal, lasting throughout time and the ages to come. 'Forever, O LORD, Your Word is settled in heaven' (119:89). 'Of old I have known from Your testimonies that You have founded them forever' (119:152). 'Every one of Your righteous ordinances is everlasting' (119:160).

6. Righteous Altogether
Scripture is 'righteous altogether,' containing the revelation of divine righteousness to man and producing righteousness in those who obey it: 'Your righteousness is an everlasting

righteousness, and Your law is truth' (119:142). The Scripture *is* right, *speaks* what is right, and *produces* what is right.

These sterling qualities of the Psalms — their inspiration, inerrancy, authority, and sufficiency — lay the bedrock upon which all expository preaching of this sacred book rests. The preaching of the Psalms is public proclamation that explains a psalm by laying it open before the listener, clearly setting forth its meaning, while making relevant application. True preaching is always *biblical* preaching, always giving the God-intended meaning of the Word and always relating it to everyday life. Regarding the Psalms, such preaching opens up the meaning of a psalm — stanza by stanza, verse by verse, line by line, even at times word by word — as a unit of divinely inspired literature, allowing God to speak through His Word.

GOD-EXALTING PROCLAMATION

Second, expository preaching of the Psalms is God-exalting preaching that magnifies the greatness and glory of God. The pulpit proclamation of a psalm elevates a supreme vision of God before the listeners. It lifts high *God* in His awesome holiness, *God* in unrivalled majesty, and *God* in infinite splendor. It is biblical preaching that is exaltational exposition, focusing upon the greatness of God. John Piper describes such preaching when he writes:

> My burden is to plead for the supremacy of God in preaching — that the dominant note of preaching be the freedom of God's sovereign grace, the unifying theme be the zeal that God has for His own glory, the grand object of preaching be the infinite and inexhaustible being of God, and the pervasive atmosphere be the holiness of God.[9]

This is the thunder and lightning of all expository preaching of the Psalms, namely, the magnification of God.

Such God-centred proclamation is certainly the kind of expository preaching that Martyn Lloyd-Jones demonstrated at Westminster Chapel in London in the twentieth century. On hearing Lloyd-Jones preach, J. I. Packer commented: 'I have never heard another preacher with so much of God about him... The thrust of Lloyd-Jones' sermons is always to show man small and God great.'[10] Of this preaching, Iain Murray concludes, 'The ultimate impression was not of the preacher, but of *God* Himself.'[11] Lloyd-Jones viewed preaching as being 'much more than the teaching of orthodox statements. As he saw it, preaching required the sense and experience of God both in the preacher and, if hearers were to be saved, in the pew. The presence and power of God Himself must be there.'[12] So it is to be in preaching the Psalms.

PROCLAIMING GOD'S ATTRIBUTES

The Psalms display the vast array of God's attributes, which are the divine perfections of His character and essence that distinguish Him as God. The sum total of God's glorious being may be expressed in the many divine attributes that He possesses. With this in mind, the expositor's preaching should be a direct reflection of his view of God. As it was said of the Puritans, 'How they saw God determined how they saw themselves in their pulpits.'[13] These divine characteristics are the intrinsic qualities that identify, distinguish, and reveal His glory to man. Consider the following attributes of God, which are revealed in the Psalms.[14]

1. Eternal
As the self-existent One, the Psalms declare, God has no beginning and no end. He is the uncreated Creator of the universe, who precedes time and endures for all time: 'Before the mountains were born or You gave birth to the earth and the world, even from everlasting to everlasting, You are God' (90:2; cf. 102:25-27; 106:48).

2. Goodness
God's moral character is such that He is marked by steadfast love and by kindness that remains faithful towards His people

forever: 'Surely goodness and lovingkindness will follow me all the days of my life, and I will dwell in the house of the LORD forever' (23:6; cf. 25:8; 31:19; 33:5; 34:8; 52:1; 65:4; 68:10; 86:5; 104:24; 107:8; 119:68; 145:9).

3. Gracious
God's dealings with man are not on the basis of what is deserved, but are in terms of His generosity: 'Gracious is the LORD, and righteous; yes, our God is compassionate' (116:5).

4. Holy
God is transcendent and majestic, separated from sin, morally perfect in His being, actions and words. He is morally blameless and without any flaw in His totally pure being: 'Yet You are holy, O You who are enthroned upon the praises of Israel' (22:3; cf. 30:4; 47:8; 48:1; 60:6; 68:17; 89:35; 93:5; 99:3, 5, 9; 145:17).

5. Immutable
God is unchanging in His being, attributes, purposes, and promises. It is impossible for God to change either for the better or for the worse. He is forever the same: 'Even they will perish, but You endure; and all of them will wear out like a garment; like clothing You will change them and they will be changed. But You are the same, and Your years will not come to an end' (102:26, 27).

6. Just
God always acts in accordance with what is right, administering perfect justice and equity. He both punishes the wicked and rewards the righteous: 'Against You, You only, I have sinned and done what is evil in Your sight, so that You are justified when You speak and blameless when You judge' (51:4; cf. 89:14; 98:9; 99:3-4).

7. Lovingkindness
God considers the fallen condition of mankind and is moved to extend unconditional love towards those who are undeserving. This is God's faithful and persistent covenant love towards His people: 'Wondrously show Your lovingkindness, O Savior of those who take refuge at Your right hand from those who rise

up against them' (17:7; cf. 23:6; 25:6; 26:3; 31:21; 36:7, 10; 40:10, 11; 42:8; 48:9; 63:3; 89:33, 49; 92:2; 103:4; 107:43; 117:2; 119:76, 88, 149; 138:2; 143:8).

8. Long-suffering
God is slow to anger and patient towards His creatures. He is abounding in lovingkindness that endures forever: 'But You, O Lord, are a God merciful and gracious, slow to anger and abundant in lovingkindness and truth' (86:15; cf. 78:38).

9. Merciful
God is compassionate towards His people. He is tender-hearted in His treatment of the needy: 'The LORD is gracious and merciful; slow to anger and great in lovingkindness. The LORD is good to all, and His mercies are over all His works' (145:8-9; cf. 6:2, 4; 25:6; 31:7; 32:5; 36:5; 51:1; 52:8; 62:12; 86:5, 15; 89:28; 103:4, 8, 11, 17; 106:1; 107:1; 115:1; 118:1-4; 119:64; 130:7; 147:11).

10. Omnipresent
God is everywhere present with His whole being. There is no place in which the fullness of God is not present: 'Where can I go from Your Spirit? Or where can I flee from Your presence?' (139:7).

11. Omniscient
God is all-knowing, fully aware of Himself, and He knows all things actual and possible. He sees through the outward façade of situations and people, and gazes with penetrating insight into the hearts of all men: 'O LORD, You have searched me and known me. You know when I sit down and when I rise up; You understand my thought from afar. You scrutinize my path and my lying down, and are intimately acquainted with all my ways. Even before there is a word on my tongue, behold, O Lord, You know it all' (139:1-4; cf. 44:21; 139:12; 142:3; 147:5).

12. Omnipotent
God is all-powerful, able to accomplish all things according to His infinite might. Nothing is impossible to God, who is able to carry out all His good pleasure: 'Be exalted, O LORD, in Your

strength; we will sing and praise Your power' (21:13; cf. 29:4-5; 37:17; 62:11; 63:1-2; 65:6; 66:7; 68:33, 35; 79:11-16; 89:8, 13; 106:8; 136:12).

13. Righteous

God is the perfect standard by which all things and people are measured. He rewards conformity to His will and punishes all lack of compliance with His Word: 'O Lord, lead me in Your righteousness because of my foes; make Your way straight before me' (5:8; cf. 7:9, 17; 11:7; 19:9; 22:31; 31:1; 35:24, 28; 36:6, 10; 40:10; 48:10; 50:6, 51:14; 69:27; 71:2, 15, 16, 19, 24; 73:12-17; 85:10; 96:13; 97:2, 6; 98:2, 9; 103:17; 111:3; 116:5; 119:7, 40, 62, 123, 137, 138, 142, 144, 172; 143:1, 11; 145:7, 17).

14. Sovereign

God possesses and exercises all authority over everything that He has created. By His supreme control, He governs over all. He does whatever He pleases, whenever He pleases, to whomever He pleases: 'The Lord has established His throne in the heavens, and His sovereignty rules over all' (103:19; cf. 2:4-5; 47:2, 8; 93:1; 96:10; 97:1; 99:1; 115:3; 135:6).

15. Truth

God is unwavering in His truthfulness as He always represents things as they actually are. All God's knowledge is true and His words are the final measure of reality: 'All the paths of the Lord are lovingkindness and truth to those who keep His covenant and His testimonies' (25:10; cf. 31:5; 33:4; 57:3, 10; 71:22; 85:10; 86:15; 89:14, 49; 96:13; 98:3; 100:5; 119:160; 139:2; 146:6).

16. Wise

God is all-wise and always acts with full knowledge. He perfectly knows the best path to pursue in order to attain the highest end: 'O Lord, how many are Your works! In wisdom You have made them all; the earth is full of Your possessions' (104:24; cf. 136:5).

17. Wrathful

God intensely hates all evil and inflicts perfect vengeance upon the wicked who violate His Word. His wrath is demonstrated in eternal judgment and divine punishment: 'Do homage to the Son, that He not become angry, and you perish in the way, for His wrath may soon be kindled. How blessed are all who take refuge in Him! (2:12; cf. 6:1; 7:11-12; 21:8-9; 30:5; 38:1; 39:10; 58:10-11; 74:1-2; 76:6-7; 78:21-22, 49-51, 58-59; 79:5; 80:4; 89:30-32; 90:7-9, 11; 99:8; 102:9-10).

PROCLAIMING GOD'S NAMES

The book of Psalms also expresses God's greatness through His different names. Each conveys a unique facet of His infinite greatness. Every one of these divine names reveals a unique truth about His supreme character. Here are His own self-descriptions that make known particular aspects of His divine being. Even the 'name' of the Lord (8:1, 9; 18:49) is intended to reveal His holy character. A divine name stands for His character, who He is, and what He is. God's names are synonymous with the sum and substance of His divine perfections. Among the divine names found in Psalms are the following:

1. Elohim
The name *Elohim* comes from a root that means 'strong', emphasizing the power of God. At times, the word is used as a general term for deity (86:8) and angels (8:5; 97:7), but most often it identifies the one true God (7:10). It should be noted that *Elohim* is plural and, specifically, a majestic plural, revealing the exponential greatness of God's power. God is the Strong One, the God of unlimited greatness and supremacy.

2. Elyon
Another divine name, *Elyon,* means 'the Most High', and emphasizes God's sovereignty and supremacy over all persons, beings and events. David states: 'I will be glad and exult in You; I will sing praise to Your name, O Most High [*Elyon*]' (9:2). All peoples, angelic hosts, nations, and circumstances are under the authority and control of *Elyon*.

3. El Olam

Yet another name, *El Olam*, means 'the Everlasting God,' coming from an original Hebrew form meaning 'the God of eternity'. The psalmist proclaims, 'For the LORD [*El Olam*] *is* good; His loving-kindness is everlasting (100:5). This name for God emphasizes His unchangeableness throughout all generations. He is forever the same.

4. Yahweh

The most common name for God in the Psalms, as well as in the entire Old Testament, is Yahweh. It occurs 6,823 times in the Old Testament. This name, literally YHWH (probably pro-nounced Yahweh), relates closely to the Hebrew verb meaning 'to be' (Exod. 3:14). David writes, 'O LORD [*Yahweh*], our Lord, how majestic is Your name in all the earth' (8:1). This name means that He is the active, self-existent One. He is the absolutely immutable One, who is independent and autonomous. He is the One who is dependent upon no one, yet all are dependent upon Him.

5. Adonai

The divine name *Adonai* is also a plural of majesty. The singu-lar form means 'lord,' 'master,' or 'owner'. The plural intensifies its force when addressing God, signifying the idea of supreme master, absolute authority, and unrivalled sovereignty. Thus the psalmist asserts, 'He who sits in the heavens laughs, the Lord [*Adonai*] scoffs at them' (2:4).

PROCLAIMING GOD'S IMAGES

The psalmists use many images for God, each intended to reveal a different aspect of His person and work. A picture *is* worth a thousand words. Rich in imagery, each of these pictures of God communicates a particular aspect of His worth and works. Some of these are listed below.[15]

1. Shield

Israel's musicians often depicted God as a shield, who protects

His people from the harm of encroaching enemies and threatening dangers: 'But You, O LORD, are a shield about me, my glory, and the One who lifts my head' (3:3; cf. 28:7; 119:114).

2. King
The ancient poets also pictured God as King, sovereignly ruling over the works of His hands. That is, He is the one upon His throne, exercising authority, governing all people, events and circumstances for His glory and the good of His people: 'Heed the sound of my cry for help, my King and my God, for to You I pray' (5:2; cf. 44:4; 74:12).

3. Judge
Many psalms portray God as the righteous Judge, who presides in judgment over every human life. Every created being is directly accountable to Him and will surely come under His all-discerning assessment. Surely God will punish all wrong and reward all good: 'God is a righteous judge, and a God who has indignation every day' (7:11; cf. 50:6).

4. Rock
This divine emblem represents God as the believer's sure and impregnable defence, unshakable in shifting times, a base of unwavering strength and solid protection: 'The LORD is my rock and my fortress and my deliverer, my God, my rock, in whom I take refuge; My shield and the horn of my salvation, my stronghold' (18:2; cf. 18:31, 46; 28:1; 31:3; 42:9; 71:3; 78:35).

5. Shepherd
A very common figure in ancient Israel, this image communicates God's gentle leadership and heroic protection of believers: 'The LORD is my shepherd, I shall not want' (23:1; cf. 80:1).

6. Fortress
Here, the psalmists present God as a high place of protection from harm. As David found protection in the Judean mountains, God was his ultimate stronghold. This emblem conveys a position of superior advantage over one's enemies which all believers have in

God: 'For You are my rock and my fortress; for Your name's sake You will lead me and guide me' (31:3; cf. 18:2; 71:3; 144:2).

7. Refuge

Many psalms picture God as a shelter from danger, a hiding place and a place of rest: 'You would put to shame the counsel of the afflicted, but the LORD is his refuge' (14:6; cf. 46:1; 61:3; 62:7-8; 71:7; 73:28; 91:2, 9).

8. Horn

The horns of an animal symbolized strength, and later depicted human beings, especially rulers: 'And He has lifted up a horn for His people, praise for all His godly ones; even for the sons of Israel, a people near to Him. Praise the Lord!' (148:14; cf. 18:2). This pictures the forceful strength of God's rulership.

CHRIST-CENTRED PREACHING

Third, expository preaching of the Psalms is distinctly Christ-centred, elevating the person and work of the Lord Jesus. The heart of both the Old and New Testaments is the Son of God. This certainly is true of the Psalms. Thus, a Christ-centred focus should be true of the one who preaches the Psalms. It would be a mistaken assumption to conclude that Christ is not revealed in the Psalter. On the contrary, the authentic preaching of the Psalms uniquely expounds the majestic glory of God's Son. Expounding this book assigns Him His rightful position of unrivalled pre-eminence over all creation. Proclaiming the Psalms finds its highest expression in declaring the excellencies of Jesus Christ, the *only* Saviour of the world. The expositor will unveil the perfections of Christ in the Psalms in the following ways.

MESSIANIC PROPHECIES

Throughout the Psalms, there are many prophecies that point ahead to the coming of Christ. This is not to say that these texts were known to be prophetic at the time they were written. But when New Testament writers referred to these statements in the Psalms, it became clear that they enlarged, or extended, those statements beyond their original historical setting to refer to Christ. The situation recorded in the Psalms was heightened in the New Testament to speak of Christ. The New Testament references did not contradict the passages quoted from the Psalms but were expressions of related truths.

PROPHECY	PSALM	FULFILLMENT
God will announce Christ to be His Son	2:7	Matt. 3:17; Acts 13:33; Heb. 1:5
Christ will be praised by children	8:2	Matt. 21:16
All things will be put under Christ's feet	8:6	Mark 12:36; 1 Cor. 15:27; Eph. 1:22; Heb. 2:8
Christ will be resurrected from the grave	16:8-11	Mark 16:6-7; Acts 2:25-28; 13:35
God will forsake Christ in His moment of agony	22:1	Matt. 27:46; Mark 15:34
Christ will be scorned and ridiculed	22:7, 8	Matt. 27:39-43; Luke 23:35
Christ's hands and feet will be pierced	22:16	John 20:25, 27; Acts 2:23
Others will gamble for Christ's clothes	22:18	Matt. 27:35-36
Christ will have many spiritual brothers	22:22	Acts 4:11; Heb. 2:12
Christ will commit His Spirit to the Father	31:5	Luke 23:46
Not one of Christ's bones will be broken	34:20	John 19:32-33, 36
Christ will be hated unjustly	35:19	John 15:25
Christ will come to do God's will	40:7-8;	Heb. 10:7

PROPHECY	PSALM	FULFILLMENT
Christ will be betrayed by a friend	41:9	John 13:18
Christ's throne will be eternal	45:6-7	Heb. 1:8-9
Christ will ascend to heaven	68:18	Eph. 4:8
Christ will be hated without a cause	69:4	John 15:25
Zeal for God's Temple will consume Christ	69:9	John 2:17
Christ will be given vinegar and gall	69:21	Matt. 27:34; John 19:28-30
Christ's betrayer will be desolate	69:25	Acts 1:20
Christ will speak in parables	78:2	Matt. 13:35
Christ will be worshiped by angels	97:7	Heb. 1:6
Christ is Creator of all	102:25-27	Heb. 1:10-12
Christ's betrayer will be replaced by another	109:8	Acts 1:20
Christ's enemies will bow down to Him	110:1	Matt. 22:44; Mark 12:36; Luke 20:42-43; 22:69; Acts 2:34-35; Heb. 1:13
Christ will be a priest like Melchizedek	110:4	Heb. 5:6; 6:20; 7:17
Christ will be the chief cornerstone	118:22-23	Matt. 21:42; Acts 4:11
Christ will come in the name of the Lord	118:25-26	Matt. 21:9
Christ will assume David's throne	132:11	Acts 2:30

MESSIANIC PREACHING

One great example of preaching Christ from the book of Psalms is that of the apostle Peter on the Day of Pentecost (Acts 2:14-36).

That day, Peter boldly preached the person and work of Christ to the thousands who had gathered. Central to his sermon that won 3,000 souls was his proclamation of Christ, specifically from the Psalms. After quoting the prophet Joel, Peter stood to preach Christ and Him crucified and the book of Psalms was in his mouth. The first sermon in the history of the church was a Christ-exalting sermon from the Psalms:

After declaring that Christ is the one delivered over by the predetermined plan and foreknowledge of God, Peter first expounded Psalm 16:8-11. Then, the apostle proclaimed Psalm 132:11, in which God had promised with an oath that one of his descendants would sit on his throne. Next, Peter reinforced the absolute certainty of the resurrection of Christ by return-ing to Psalm 16:10 and quoting it yet again. Finally, Peter boldly announced the triumphant exaltation of Christ at the right hand of God the Father by citing Psalm 110:1.

So it is with every preacher of the Psalms. The heart of his preaching is always the person and work of the Lord Jesus Christ. Christ is the fulfillment and ultimate realization of the Psalter, the greater Son of David. Prior to His ascension, in His post-resurrection appearances, Jesus showed Himself to be the fulfillment of the entire Old Testament, the substance of all Messianic prophecies and the perfect accomplishment of the sacrificial system. It is with this Christ-centred realization in mind that the expositor must approach the Psalms if he is to expound the Word accurately.

SPIRIT-FILLED DELIVERY

Fourth, expository preaching of the Psalms is Spirit-empowered preaching. The Holy Spirit must enlighten the expositor's mind, enflame his heart and empower his delivery. Rightly did John Knox state: 'True preaching from start to finish is the work of the Spirit.'[16] The same Spirit who authored each psalm must empower the preacher to proclaim them. In authentic preaching, God gives the men He has called supernatural power, energizing their minds and enlivening their souls. The Holy Spirit must enable every aspect of expository preaching, from its preparation to its delivery. If not, the sermon will fall flat.

ILLUMINATING THE PREACHER'S STUDY

In preaching the Psalms, the Holy Spirit must enlighten the study of the preacher, who must be granted spiritual insight into the proper meaning of the biblical text. He needs spiritual illumination in order to understand the spiritual message of the Bible. On the road to Emmaus, Jesus opened the spiritual eyes of the two disciples to understand how He had to suffer and then enter into glory (Luke 24:26, 32). In like manner, the Spirit must enlighten our ability to discern the teaching of Scripture. Spurgeon quipped:

> None but the Holy Spirit can give a man the key to the Treasury of David... May the enlightening Spirit rest upon all students of the Psalms, and grant them to see far more deeply into the hidden meaning of these sacred hymns than we have been enabled to do.[17]

This must be the Spirit-enlightened, eye-opening experience of every expositor.

To this end, the psalmist prayed, 'Open my eyes, that I may behold wonderful things from Your law' (119:18). This opening of one's eyes has to do with removing a veil, or covering. This does not mean that the Word is unclear. To be sure, there is the perspicuity of the Scripture — that is to say, the Word is lucid and clear. There is nothing obscure within the Word of God. Its essential message is blatantly clear. Rather, the psalmist means that whatever is covered is in the *reader* of Scripture, not the Scripture itself. Therefore, there is the need for a covering to be removed — that is, from the eyes of the expositor. When it is removed, he can see the 'wonderful things' in the Word. In the study of the Psalms, the Spirit must enlighten the mind of the expositor, giving penetrating insight into the truths.

EMPOWERING ONE'S VOICE

Moreover, the Spirit must enable the expositor to preach 'in power and in the Holy Spirit and with full conviction' (1 Thess. 1:5). As he has the Psalms open before him, he must say with David: '… do not take your Holy Spirit from me… Then I will teach transgressors Your ways, and sinners will be converted to You' (51:11, 13).

So it must be with every preacher of the Psalms. He must have the power of the Holy Spirit as he proclaims the sacred hymn book, if sinners are to be converted to God. As previously stated, this was Peter's experience on the Day of Pentecost as he preached the Psalms. The apostle was filled with the Holy Spirit and, as a result, 3,000 souls were saved. The same Holy Spirit must empower the preaching of the Psalms today, and when He does, souls will be converted to Christ. They will be made willing in the day of His power (110:3).

WELL-DEVELOPED SERMON

Fifth, expository preaching of the Psalms is logically ordered in thought and well structured in presentation. Such preaching is carefully organized around a central theme with main headings, which must arise from the text. Biblical preaching necessitates a coherent sequence of cogent thought that is highly rational in its communication and well organized in its development. True preaching incorporates biblical exegesis and sound doctrine into a well-thought-out sermon that includes an introduction, smooth transitions, outline, illustrations, application and a compelling conclusion. In the art of expository preaching, all these parts are to be skillfully woven together into a cohesive whole.

Speaking with Orderly Thought

This orderliness will be true in preaching the Psalms. With incomparable genius, God has ordered the structured flow of each inspired song in the Psalter. Each of these divinely inspired worship songs has a built-in structure with sequential thought and careful reasoning. If the expositor preaches verse by verse, stanza by stanza, through an entire psalm, he will deliver an organized sermons. Any preacher who preaches through an entire psalm, as God authored it, supplementing it with a well-planned introduction, application and conclusion, will deliver a well-structured sermon.

For example, Psalm 1 has a coherent unit of thought that is easily identifiable. This first stanza of the psalm (vv. 1-3) contains a central theme and a noticeable progression of thought. If the expositor preaches on this first psalm, line by line, the sermon will, by necessity, be well structured. Then, the second stanza (vv. 4-6) contains a sharp contrast with the first stanza. By preaching this psalm consecutively, verse by verse, the preacher automatically organizes his thoughts and delivers them in an orderly manner.

However, expository preaching is not a mere rambling commentary on the Bible. It is not a running explanation that lacks a central theme or logical development. Neither is it a loose collection of unrelated remarks, disconnected thoughts and offhand comments that are devoid of logical order. Instead, expository preaching presents the main divisions of thought in a clearly structured way and progresses by following a noticeable development of thought.

LIFE-CHANGING MESSAGE

Sixth, expository preaching of the Psalms is preaching that is heart-searching and life-changing. No book of the Bible is as practically connected to daily Christian living as the Psalms. Few books are as evangelistic. John Calvin called the Psalms 'an anatomy of all parts of the soul'.[18] John MacArthur notes, 'The Psalms genuinely reflect real life' and 'cover the full breadth of human experience'.[19] He adds, 'There is a psalm for almost every kind of day'.[20] That is to say, the book of Psalms is real to life. Gordon Fee and Douglas Stuart explain: 'Because the Bible is God's Word, it has eternal relevance; it speaks to all humankind, in every age and in every culture'.[21] Represented in this book are both the exhilarating highs and the depressing lows of life.

THE MANY-SIDED EFFECTS

The Psalter produces a multiple effect when it is preached. This is to say, it encompasses this broad spectrum of life. It addresses both the spiritual highs and emotional lows of life. To this very point, Charles Haddon Spurgeon remarked, 'Whenever you look into David's Psalms, you will somewhere or other see yourself. You never get into a corner, but you find David in that corner. I think that I was never so low that I could not find that David was lower; and I never climbed so high that I could not find that David was up above me'.[22] Consider the effects of preaching the Psalms.

1. Evangelizing souls

From the opening psalm, the Psalms contrast the two roads of life — one leading to life, the other to destruction. In the second psalm, the psalmist calls sinners to show discernment and trust God's Son. Preaching the Psalms makes for strong evangelistic preaching, calling for a decisive commitment on the part of the listener. It offers salvation and destruction, heaven and hell, blessing and cursing, mercy and misery. The expositor positions himself at a fork in the road, calling all men to decide which way they will go.

2. Igniting worship

Preaching the Psalms ignites praise for God in the hearts of believers. This is the highest purpose for which God has redeemed lost sinners. Each psalm was written to lead the hearts of believers to magnify the name of the Lord. When it is preached to responsive hearts, fervent praise is enflamed for God.

3. Cleansing lives

Every psalm is uniquely suited to bring conviction of sin, leading to true repentance. The exposition of these psalms searches
out, convicts, and cleanses the heart of sin.

4. Fortifying hearts

Preaching the Psalms infuses spiritual fortitude into the hearts
of believers. Whenever they face opposition for the sake of righteousness, these transcendent truths bring great strength to
receptive hearts. Through the expounding of this book, believers
are encouraged to press on in the face of mounting persecution.
The book of Psalms brings great consolation to troubled hearts.

THE GENIUS OF EXPOSITORY PREACHING

In summary, expository preaching is the form of preaching that
explains and expounds a passage of Scripture, making known to
the listener the true meaning of its contents, while showing the
practical relevance of its truths for today. Along this line, J. I.
Packer writes, 'The true idea of preaching is that the preacher
should become a mouthpiece for his text, opening it up and applying it as a word from God to his hearers, talking only in order
that the text itself may speak and be heard.'[23] That is to say, the
preacher must make each point from his text in such a manner
that the hearers may discern what God teaches them in His Word.

May the Lord give to His church such expositors in this day.

3

ACQUIRE THE TOOLS

---

*Acquire the books needed to study
and preach the Psalms effectively*

Expository preaching of the Psalms is, admittedly, hard work, requiring strenuous laboring in digging into the biblical text. Such study demands in-depth learning and penetrating insight into the passage. This approach to preaching calls for 'blood, sweat, toil and tears' from all who would enter the pulpit. Truth be known, the biblical preaching of the Psalms requires both perspiration and illumination, both human effort and divine insight. The rigorous study of a psalm demands that meticulous attention be given to understanding many details, including the original languages, historical background, cultural setting, geographical setting, and much more. In order to explore any given psalm, the appropriate study tools are absolutely necessary if one is to grasp its meaning.

In preaching the Psalms, this task is very challenging, largely on account of the fact that this is the largest and most diverse book in the entire Bible. This collection of ancient worship songs covers the widest period of time of any book in the Bible and a full range of subjects, including the creation of the world, the catastrophic flood, the birth of the nation of Israel, its exodus from Egypt, its wilderness wanderings, its possession of the land, its Babylonian exile and its return to the promised land. The vast amount of information that the expositor must master in order to preach the book of Psalms is a sizeable challenge, requiring a wide knowledge of cultural, historical, linguistic, religious and geographic issues, and more besides. To be sure, this is a monumental adventure of great proportions.

HELPFUL AIDS TO STUDY

In order to interpret the Psalms properly, a well-developed library is essential for any preacher. On this point, Charles Spurgeon asserts, 'In order to be able to expound the Scriptures, and as an aid to your pulpit studies, you will need to be familiar with the commentators: a glorious army, let me tell you, whose acquaintance will be your delight and profit.'[1] This is to say, a wealth of information must be accessed if the preacher is to expound the proper meaning of each psalm. If he is to preach the Psalms skillfully, he must accumulate a 'war chest' of books and resources to consult. While many feel that commentaries are a crutch to be avoided, they are, in reality, an absolute necessity to assist any preacher in rightly handling God's Word.

Every expositor should accumulate a strong library, each book making a unique contribution. Therefore, the following general categories of books are needed in the expositor's study.

REFERENCE AND STUDY BIBLES

As a matter of first importance, the expositor of the Psalms will want several good translations of the Bible from which to study the Psalms, and certainly one trusted Bible translation from which to preach. These Bibles should include the following:

REFERENCE BIBLES

The preacher should be able to consult several English translations of the Bible to supplement his study. These should be faithful to the original Hebrew text in which the Psalms were written and should be written in understandable language.

New American Standard Bible (Lockman Foundation)
New King James Version (Thomas Nelson)
English Standard Version (Crossway Publishing)
King James (Authorized) Version (various publishers)
Holman Christian Standard Bible (Holman Publishing)

STUDY BIBLES

In addition, the expositor will want to collect several study Bibles. These reference Bibles contain helpful footnotes at the bottom of each page of the Psalms, as well as an introduction to the book of Psalms itself. They contain a brief summary of each individual psalm and helpful charts. These teaching aids will be helpful in giving the 'big picture' of each psalm to the preacher.

MacArthur Study Bible (Word Publishing)
Ryrie Study Bible (Moody Publishing)
NASB Study Bible (Zondervan Publishing)
The Reformation Study Bible (Thomas Nelson)
The Nelson Study Bible (Thomas Nelson)
Holman Christian Standard Study Bible (Holman
    Publishing)

OLD TESTAMENT INTRODUCTIONS

Further, the well-equipped expositor will want to have a collection of books that provides a general introduction to the Psalms and helps identify the form of individual psalms. These resources are absolutely indispensable and must be carefully read by the preacher who would be true to the Word.

OLD TESTAMENT SURVEYS

Especially insightful are the Old Testament introduction books, which provide the preacher with a macro-look orientation to the Psalms. Here the many unique features of the Psalms and Hebrew poetry are explained. All expositors will need assistance in understanding the literary form, identity of the author, historical background and poetic types of the Psalms.

> C. Hassell Bullock, *An Introduction to the Old Testament* (Moody Publishing)
> Gleason Archer, *A Survey of Old Testament Introduction* (Moody Publishing)
> Irving Jensen, *Jensen's Survey of the Old Testament* (Moody Publishing)
> C. Hassell Bullock, *An Introduction to the Old Testament Poetic Books* (Moody Publishing)
> Andrew E. Hill and John H. Walton, *A Survey of the Old Testament* (Grand Rapids, MI: Zondervan, 2000)
> Mark Dever, *Promises Made: The Message of the Old Testament* (Wheaton, IL: Crossway Books, 2006)

INTRODUCTIONS TO THE PSALMS

Other books will give the preacher an introduction exclusive to the Psalms. These works reveal a more in-depth look at the special intricacies of the Psalms. Critically important to the expositor's library are those books which provide a general introduction to the forms of Hebrew poetry and the peculiarities that accompany its figures of speech.

> Richard P. Belcher, Jr., *The Messiah and the Psalms* (Mentor)
> C. Hassell Bullock, *Encountering the Book of Psalms* (Baker)
> Tremper Longman, III, *How to Read the Psalms* (InterVarsity)
> C. S. Lewis, Harcourt & Brace, *Reflections on the Psalms* (Word)
> William Binne, *A Pathway Into the Psalter* (Solid Ground)
> Geoffrey Grogan, *Prayer, Praise and Prophecy* (Mentor)
> W. Graham Scroggie, *A Guide to the Psalms* (Kregel)
> Jamieson, Fausset, Brown, *A Commentary on the Old and New Testaments* (Hendrickson)

PSALMS COMMENTARIES

Moreover, a preacher of the Psalms needs a variety of commentaries that help excavate the meaning and message of the biblical text. These works, in varying degrees, will provide helpful overviews of each psalm. Some commentaries provide a detailed treatment of the psalm. These technical works offer a critical attention to the Hebrew text, word studies, syntax, ancient Eastern background, critical form, and the like. Other commentaries treat each psalm in a verse-by-verse, or paragraph-by-paragraph manner. In so doing, they call attention to concise summaries, key Hebrew words, historical background, and cross references that will be of considerable help for the expositor. Still other commentaries will even be helpful in packaging the sermon itself.

Exegetical Commentaries

First, basic commentaries on the Psalms need to be sought

which contain a detailed exegetical treatment of the Psalms. These technical works provide a critical attention to the Hebrew text, word studies, syntax, ancient Eastern background, critical form, and the like. They call attention to concise summaries, key Hebrew words, historical background, cross references, etc.

> Peter C. Craige, Marvin E. Tate, Leslie C. Allen, *Word Biblical Commentary,* volumes 19, 20, 21 (Word)
>
> Willem VanGemeren, *The Bible Expositor's Commentary, volume 5: Psalms* (Zondervan)
>
> Franz Delitzsch, *Keil–Delitzsch Commentary on the Old Testament,* volume 5 (Eerdmans)
>
> John Calvin, *Calvin's Commentaries,* volumes 4-6 (Baker)
>
> Robert Davidson, *The Vitality of Worship* (Eerdmans)
>
> Allan Harman, *Psalms* (Mentor)
>
> J. J. Stewart Perowne, *The Book of Psalms* (Zondervan)
>
> Merrill Unger, *Unger's Commentary on the Old Testament: Psalms* (Moody)
>
> Derek Kidner, *Psalms* (InterVarsity, 2 volumes)
>
> David Dickson, *Psalms,* Geneva Series of Commentaries (Banner of Truth)
>
> H. C. Leupold, *Exposition on the Psalms* (Baker)
>
> G. A. F. Knight, *Psalms* (Westminster, 2 volumes)
>
> Michael Wilcock, *The Message of Psalms 1-72* (InterVarsity)
>
> Michael Wilcock, *The Message of Psalms 73-150* (InterVarsity)
>
> Samuel Terrien, *The Psalms* (Eerdmans)
>
> Matthew Henry, *Matthew Henry's Commentary,* volume III (Revell)
>
> Albert Barnes, *Psalms* (Baker)
>
> John Gill, *Exposition of the Old & New Testaments,* volumes 3 and 4 (The Baptist Standard Bearer)

EXPOSITIONAL COMMENTARIES

Further, the preacher of the Psalms should also gather expository commentaries that contain the preaching on the Psalms by other gifted men. These resources are valuable in presenting different preaching styles in expounding the Psalms.

In addition, the expositor should acquire other commentaries of the Psalms which are devotional in their treatment. The contribution of these works is that they can provide pointed quotations, practical applications, colorful illustrations and witty insights into the text.

Finally, the preacher may also want to purchase a few books which focus upon one individual psalm, such as Psalm 23 or Psalm 119. These books provide helpful insight into how the preacher can amplify one psalm into a series of messages. These resources are helpful in a detailed teaching of these psalms.

James Montgomery Boice, *Psalms* (Baker, 3 volumes)
H. A. Ironside, *Psalms* (Zoizeaux)
Alexander Maclaren, *Expositions of Holy Scripture*, volume 4 (Baker)
Allan P. Ross, *Bible Knowledge Commentary: Psalms* (Victor)
Charles Swindoll, *Daily Grind* (Word, 2 volumes)
John Phillips, *Exploring the Psalms* (Loizeaux, 2 volumes)
Calvin Beisner, *Psalms of Promise* (NavPress)
John Stott, *Favorite Psalms, Selected and Expounded* (Moody)
Warren Wiersbe, *Meet Yourself in the Psalms* (Victor)
Ray Stedman, *Psalms of Faith* (Regal)
Ronald Allen, *And I Will Praise Him* (Nelson)
Gerald H. Wilson, *The NIV Application Commentary: Psalms* (Zondervan, 2 volumes)
Charles H. Spurgeon, *Treasury of David* (Baker)
J. M. Flanigan, *What the Bible Teaches: Psalms* (John Ritchie Ltd.)
Steven J. Lawson, *Holman Old Testament Commentary: Psalms 1-75* (Broadman & Holman)
Steven J. Lawson, *Holman Old Testament Commentary: Psalms 76-150* (Broadman & Holman)

HEBREW TOOLS

In addition, the expositor of the Psalms needs basic language tools to help him interact with Hebrew. Depending upon his ability with the original language, he will want a Hebrew Bible and should begin building a Hebrew-language section by gathering reference books which provide detailed insight into the etymology and meaning of Hebrew words used in the Psalms. Reference works such as Hebrew lexicons and grammars are indispensable for uncovering the meaning of words and grammatical constructions in the biblical text. Hebrew dictionaries reveal a word's meaning in the original language, and a lexicon will trace its multiple uses in various contexts. After determining basic definitions, it is important to discover the range of the word's usage in its context through the Old Testament Scripture. Since Hebrew verbs frequently carry exegetical significance, the preacher needs guides to parsing and syntax to help him determine the function and force of key verbs. He should learn enough Hebrew for precision, credibility, and confidence in his preaching.

Hebrew Dictionaries

Begin adding a Hebrew-language section to your library by gathering references which provide explanations into, and definitions of, the etymology and meaning of Hebrew words used in the Old Testament.

> J. W. VanGemeren, *New International Dictionary of Old Testament Theology & Exegesis* (Zondervan, 5 volumes)
> John J. Owen, *Analytical Key to the Old Testament*, volume 3 (Baker)
> Botterweck and Ringgren, *Theological Dictionary of the Old Testament* (Eerdmans, 9 volumes)
> W. E. Vine, *Vine's Complete Expository Dictionary of Old and New Testament Words* (Thomas Nelson)
> Lawrence Richards, *Expository Dictionary of Bible Words* (Zondervan)

Hebrew Concordances and Lexicons

After determining basic Hebrew definitions by using Hebrew dictionaries, it is important to discover the range of the word's usage in its context throughout Old Testament Scripture. Knowing where and how a particular word is used elsewhere, in the Psalms in particular and the Old Testament in general, can be very helpful for understanding the use of a word in a particular passage in the Psalms.

Robert Young, *Analytical Concordance to the Bible* (Eerdmans)

Benjamin Davidson, *The Analytical Hebrew and Chaldean Lexicon* (Hendrickson)

Brown, Driver, Briggs, *Hebrew Lexicon* (Moody)

William Holladay, *A Concise Hebrew and Aramaic Lexicon of the Old Testament* (Eerdmans)

Hebrew Grammars

Since meaning is conveyed not only by words but through grammar itself, Hebrew grammars will provide insight into the importance and significance of grammatical structures in the Hebrew language.

Jay Green, *The Interlinear Hebrew/Greek English Bible*, volume 3 (Assoc. Pub.)

E. W. Bullinger, *Figures of Speech Used in the Bible* (Baker)

Leland Ryken, *Words of Delight* (Baker)

Othmar Keel, *The Symbolism of the Biblical World* (Eisenbrauns)

Wilfred Watson, *Classical Hebrew Poetry* (Sheffield Academic Press)

R. B. Girdlestone, *Synonyms of the Old Testament* (Hendrickson)

HISTORICAL TOOLS

Other books are needed to understand the ancient world in which the psalmist lived. These study tools deal with various aspects of historical background, including customs, culture, politics, religion, literature and geography.

BIBLICAL BACKGROUND

Invaluable are books dealing with the biblical background and customs of the ancient world. These sources provide much-needed insight into the ancient Eastern world of the Hebrew culture and explain references and allusions to Old Testament times.

> William L. Coleman, *Today's Handbook of Bible Times and Customs* (Bethany)
> Madeline and J. Lane Miller, *Harper's Encyclopedia of Bible Life*, revised edition (Harper and Row)
> Ralph Gower & Fred Wight, *The New Manners and Customs of Bible Times,* revised edition (Moody)
> J. A. Thompson, *Handbook of Life in Bible Times* (InterVarsity Press)
> Alfred Edersheim, *Bible History* (Hendrickson)
> Charles F. Pfeiffer, *Old Testament History* (Baker)
> Leon Wood, *A Survey of Israel's History* (Zondervan)
> Jack P. Lewis, *Historical Backgrounds of Bible History* (Baker)
> Walter Kaiser, *A History of Israel* (Broadman & Holman)
> Alfred Hoerth, Gerald Mattingly and Edwin Yamauchi, *Peoples of the Old Testament World* (Baker)
> John Walton, *Chronological and Background Charts of the Old Testament* (Zondervan)

MAPS AND ATLASES

Also, a book of maps which surveys the geography of the ancient world of the Bible will prove necessary. These works give an overview of the geography of the ancient world in the Middle East.

J. I. Packer, Merrill Tenney, William White, eds.,
   The Bible Almanac (Thomas Nelson)
Harry Thomas Frank, *Atlas of the Bible Lands* (Holman)
Thomas Brisco, *Bible Atlas* (Holman)

SERMON RESOURCES

Finally, the expositor will want to purchase books that assist in polishing the sermon. Resources that contain illustrations, quotations and outlines are critically important in helping the sermon manuscript move from exegesis to exposition.

ILLUSTRATION BOOKS

A faithful exposition of any psalm needs illustrations that breathe life into the delivery and help people see the truth. Illustrations also help to make the sermon memorable and inspiring.

Paul Lee Tan, *Encyclopedia of 15,000 Illustrations*
   (Assurance)
Michael P. Green, *Illustrations for Biblical Preaching*
   (Baker)
Kent Hughes (comp.), *1001 Great Stories and Quotes*
   (Tyndale)
Charles Swindoll, *The Tale of the Tardy Oxcart* (Word)
Charles Swindoll, *1,501 Other Stories* (Word)
Clifton Fadiman, *The Little Brown Book of Anecdotes*
   (Hachette Digital, Inc.)

QUOTATION BOOKS

In addition, the preacher will find it helpful to punctuate his sermon with concise, provocative quotes. Sometimes proving to be a great sermon-starter, a quotation book is the friend of the expositor.

Roy Zuck, *The Speaker's Quote Book* (Victor)
Martin H. Manser, *The Westminster Collection of Christian Quotations* (Westminster John Knox Press)
Mark Water, *The New Encyclopedia of Christian Quotations* (Baker)
John Blanchard, *Gathered Gold* (Evangelical Press)
John Blanchard, *More Gathered Gold* (Evangelical Press)
I. D. E. Thomas, *The Golden Treasury of Puritan Quotations* (Moody)
Tom Carter, *2,200 Quotations from the Writings of Charles H. Spurgeon* (Baker)

THE NECESSARY TOOLS

The focus of this chapter has been to establish the kinds of resources that are essential for the careful exposition of the Psalms. The risen Christ has given gifted men to the church (Eph. 4:7-11) to help others understand the meaning and message of the Psalms. It is incumbent upon every expositor to avail himself of these invaluable resources. To be sure, no man is an island unto himself. Every believer — the preacher included — is vitally connected with and mutually dependent upon the larger body of Christ. Thus, each expositor needs the supporting ministry of others around him in order to succeed in his preaching ministry. He needs the writings of other teachers in the church, whose studies have been published for the greater good of others.

May every expositor of the Psalms be a diligent student of the Scriptures and a faithful reader of those books that help him understand what God is saying in the Psalms. Let every preacher of this ancient hymn book be steadfast in his study of these many tools.

--- Unit II ---

THE
EXPLORATION PHASE

---------------[4]---------------

OVERVIEW
THE PSALMS

---

*Become acquainted with an overview
of the literary distinctives of the Psalms*

Whenever the expositor faithfully expounds the
Psalms, the spiritual power of God is unleashed in
the preacher and the congregation. This divinely-
inspired 'hymnal' of the ancient Temple of Israel ignites human
hearts with a holy passion for God. As perhaps no other book in
the Bible, preaching the Psalms uniquely connects people with
God at the deepest level. This towering book gives a majestic
revelation of the awesome, holy character of God. Throughout
the Psalter, God is vividly displayed as sovereignly ruling over,

yet being intimately involved in, the lives of his people.

Given this perspective, James Montgomery Boice maintains:

> There is no more wonderful portion of Scripture than the
> Psalms. They have been a blessing to God's people through
> many generations, first in the Old Testament period when
> they were sung by the people of Israel in their worship at
> the temple in Jerusalem and now in the New Testament
> period when they are recited, sung, memorized, and
> cherished by Christians.[1]

Boice is right. This collection of sacred songs unveils a high view
of God on every page. The perfect character of God is put on
display in breathtaking fashion, as the psalmist is ever pointing his readers upward to God. Here they are led to behold and
adore his infinite glory.

COMFORTING THE AFFLICTED

At the same time, perhaps no inspired book of sacred Scripture
comforts hurting hearts like the Psalms. Boice further notes:

> I have always thought of the psalms as the deepest and most
> spiritual portion of the Word of God ... the psalms touch
> deeply on the hurts, joys, and spiritual aspirations of God's
> people ... they never lose their grasp on God or their faith
> in Him as the great, sovereign, wise, and loving God He is.[2]

Here, in each worship song, is found a healing balm for every
broken spirit. Here is heart-lifting encouragement for every
downcast soul.

RENEWING THE SOUL

Preaching the Psalms restores and renews the crushed hearts of

God's people. There is nothing philosophically abstract or distantly theoretical here. No ivory-tower thinking emerges from these life-giving pages that is disconnected from real life. On the contrary, this worship book is vitally relevant to daily life. Contained in it are the highs and lows of real human experiences, with their victories and defeats, their mountain-top highs and valley lows. From the pinnacle of praise to the pit of despair, this book captures the full range of human emotions. No wonder it is a favourite of God's people everywhere.

MAGNIFYING THE LORD

But, most of all, the psalms led God's ancient people in worshiping him. Should it surprise us that preaching the Psalms should inspire praise for God in the hearts of his people? The exposition of Psalms leads God's people to the adoration of him who is worthy of all praise. This is every believer's ultimate priority, and the book of Psalms uniquely helps fulfill it. When a psalm is genuinely exposited, the psalmist's spiritual heartbeat becomes contagious and spreads from the text to the study, to the pulpit and then to the pew.

In preparing to preach the Psalms, the expositor will first want to read some general introductions to the Psalms. Before he can accurately interpret a psalm, the preacher must have a basic orientation to the historical background, literary style and different classifications of this book as a whole. This requires a familiarity with the unique features of the Psalms, including its message, structure, literature and the ancient world in which it was written. Every preacher of the Psalms must grasp the macro-perspective of this book before he can rightly understand and proclaim an individual psalm. Along this line, the preacher will want to acquaint himself with the following aspects of the Psalms.

DESCRIPTIVE TITLE

The word 'psalms' has many possible meanings, whether it is

taken from the Hebrew or Greek language, or from the super-scriptions. Despite the variety of meanings, each essentially describes the book as a hymn book of praise, designed to lead the people of God in their worship of him.

BOOK OF PRAISES

At first, this praise book now known as the Psalms was unnamed. This was because of the wide variety of these songs. Eventually, the ancient Hebrews called this collection of psalms 'The Book of Praises,' or simply 'Praises'. This original working title reflected its main purpose, which was assisting believers in the proper praises to be given to God. Later, the Septuagint (*LXX*), the Greek translation of the Old Testament during the second-century BC, gave this collection the title 'the book of Psalms'. This is, in fact, what Jesus called the book in his day (Luke 20:42), as well as what the apostles called it (Acts 1:20).

MUSICAL ACCOMPANIMENT

The word 'psalms' comes from a Greek word, which means 'the plucking of strings'. As these songs were initially sung, a stringed instrument, such as a harp or lyre, often accompanied a singer as he praised God. As the title indicates, the Psalms are a collection of worship songs sung with musical accompaniment.

JUBILANT SOUND

The Hebrew title for the book of Psalms is *tehillim*, a Hebrew word meaning 'to make a jubilant sound,' or 'praises'. Thus, the collecting of these 150 psalms into one book, the Psalter, served as the first hymn book for God's people in order to assist them in making a joyful noise in worshiping him.

MULTIPLE AUTHORS

Different individual psalms identify their various authors: Moses (1), David (73), Solomon (2), the sons of Korah (10), Heman (1), Ethan (1), Asaph (12), Haggai (1), Zechariah (1), and Ezra (1). There are also anonymous authors for the remaining forty-seven psalms. The number of the latter could in fact be as low as thirty-four. Nevertheless, the book of Psalms is commonly spoken of as David's writings because he wrote the largest number of individual psalms. Some seventy-five psalms were composed by, or about, David. He is the author, or object of reference, of half the psalms and was the individual solely responsible for arranging the Temple service of song (1 Chr. 25).

A COLLECTION OF WRITERS

Most other books in the Bible were written by one man. A few claim multiple authors. Proverbs is one such example, with both Solomon and Hezekiah making contributions to its wisdom sayings. However, Psalms is a rare book in the Bible in that was written by several men. Thus, it is a joint effort of many authors, who wrote from many diverse experiences of life.

1. David
This noted man of God was the second king of Israel and the 'sweet psalmist of Israel' (2 Sam. 23:1). Known as a man after God's own heart, he became the chief author of exactly half of the Psalms (3-9; 11-32; 34-41; 51-65; 68-70; 86; 101; 103; 108-110; 122; 124; 131; 133; 138-145). Psalm 2 is identified by Acts 4:25 as being written by David. Also, Psalm 95 is credited to David by the author of Hebrews (Heb. 4:7). Psalms 9 and 10 were joined together as one psalm in the Septuagint, indicating Davidic authorship for both.

2. Asaph
A Levitical priest whom David made the worship leader of ancient Israel (1 Chr. 16:4-5), Asaph is credited with writing twelve psalms (50; 73-83). He was a leading singer when the ark

was brought to Jerusalem from its long exile (1 Chr. 15:17-19).

3. The Sons of Korah

These men were a guild of singers and composers of music. The sons of Korah are credited with writing ten psalms (Pss. 42; 44-49; 84–85; 87). Some scholars suggest that these superscriptions could indicate that the Korahites were Levitical performers, rather than the authors, of these particular psalms. In such cases, the title would read, 'For the sons of Korah.'

4. Solomon

David's son Solomon, the third king of Israel, accounted for two psalms (Pss. 72; 127); he was the one who built the Temple for the worship of God in which these psalms would be sung. It is also possible, as some Bible commentators suggest, that the superscription of Psalm 72 indicates that this song was dedicated to Solomon at the beginning of his reign.

5. Moses

This prophet of God was a mighty leader of the Israelite people during their exodus out of Egypt. Moses was the author of the Pentateuch. He also wrote one psalm during the time of the wilderness wanderings (Ps. 90).

6. Heman

A wise man, musician and Ezrahite, Heman was a son of Korah and the founder of the Korahite choir (2 Chr. 5:12; 35:15). This worship leader wrote one psalm (Ps. 88).

7. Ethan

A wise man and an Ezrahite, Ethan was probably a Levitical singer (1 Chr. 6:42; 15:17, 19) and the author of one psalm (Ps. 89).

8. Anonymous

Other authors account for the remaining forty-eight Psalms. Some think that Ezra, post-exilic scribe and priest of Israel, may have been the author of some of these anonymous songs.

EXTENDED PERIOD

Because many different authors wrote the Psalms, the writing of these sacred songs occurred at different times. In all, this spanned a period of some 900 to 1,000 years. The earliest psalm, Psalm 90, was composed by Moses during Israel's forty years of wilderness wanderings (1445–1405 BC) — probably towards the end of this time of severe testing, perhaps around 1410 BC. The last psalm composed, Psalm 126, is thought to have been recorded after the time of Israel's Babylonian exile, during their return to the land of Judah, around 500 BC, or even earlier, about 430 BC, if Psalm 126 was written by Ezra.

A THOUSAND-YEAR PROJECT

Very little is known about the facts of the process of collecting and compiling the Psalter. Since David composed nearly half of the psalms, it seems reasonable to suggest that the vast majority of them were written during the time of his reign (1010–970 BC) and prior to the time of the divided monarchy (931 BC). Those which were obviously written later may possibly have been collected and arranged by Hezekiah's men (eighth century BC) and Ezra's scribal school (fifth century BC). For this reason, dating of the Psalter is open-ended — as early as Moses (1410 BC) and as late as Ezra (430 BC).

1. The Earliest Psalm
The first psalm to be written, Psalm 90, was penned by Moses during Israel's forty years of wilderness wanderings (1445–1405 BC), probably towards the end of this time of severe testing, perhaps around 1410 BC.

2. The Vast Majority
The vast majority of the psalms were written during the kingly reigns of David (1020–970 BC) and Solomon (970–931 BC), around approximately 1000 BC.

3. The last psalm

The last psalm composed, Psalm 126, was probably recorded after Israel's Babylonian exile, perhaps during the time of their return to the land of Judah around 500 BC, or possibly as late as 430 BC, if written by Ezra.

FIVE BOOKS

Also, the preacher must observe that the entire collection of 150 psalms — also called the Psalter — was assembled together into one book in five progressive stages over an extended period of time. Ancient scribes originally grouped the psalms into a series of five smaller books, in which the next book augmented the previous one. Psalm 72:20 makes this clear when it states, 'The prayers of David the son of Jesse are ended.' This verse once marked the end of an earlier, smaller edition of the Psalms. Later books would be supplemented with the remaining psalms. These five books are easily recognizable, as each section concludes with a climactic doxology (Pss. 41:13; 72:18-19; 89:52; 106:48; 150:6).

FIVE BOOKS IN ONE

The book of Psalms is divided into five books. Each of the first three closes with a double 'Amen'; the fourth ends with an 'Amen' and a 'Hallelujah,' and the last book closes the entire collection with a 'Hallelujah'. The book of Psalms grew over the years as the Holy Spirit directed different writers and editors to compose and compile additional worship songs.

These five books within the Psalms are as follows: Psalms 1 –41; 42-72; 73-89; 90-106; 107-150. Psalms 1 and 2 were strategically placed to form the entryway into the sanctuary of the Psalms, and the last five psalms, Psalms 146-150, conclude the book with a long doxology. Although the organization of the Psalter is not inspired, some maintain that these five books of the Psalms correspond to the first five books of the Bible, Genesis through Deuteronomy. Thus, some call the book of Psalms 'The Pentateuch of David' because it mirrors the books of the Law, known as the Pentateuch of Moses. These book divisions are as follows:

BOOK I: PSALMS 1-41

The first forty-one psalms form Book I and were probably gathered together during the early days of the Jewish monarchy by David or Solomon. The entire content of Book I is, for the most part, assigned to David, given that Psalm 1 is anonymous, Psalm 2 is later attributed to David (Acts 4:25); Psalms 9 and 10 were probably one psalm originally, and Psalm 33 is attributed to David in the Septuagint. Special attention must be given to the placing of the first two psalms in the lead position of the Psalms. They were not written first — that distinction belongs to Psalm 90. Rather they were intentionally placed here and stand together as one unit, acting as two doorkeepers for all who enter this temple of truth, the Psalter. These twin psalms speak to all who approach this book, requiring that they take refuge in the Lord.

Because Book I highlights God's power in creation (Pss. 8; 19) and is dominated by the theme of sin and redemption, it is easy to see how it correlates with the book of Genesis. In other words, the psalms of this first book seem to have the character of the book of Genesis in that they focus much upon man. Here is man as God intended him to be, but also man as he actually is. Here is the godly man (Ps. 1) and the ungodly man (Ps. 2). In Psalm 8, we have the first man, exercising dominion over God's creation, with fulfillment in the Second Man, Jesus Christ. Book I concludes with the doxology, a benediction and a double 'Amen and Amen':

> Blessed be the LORD, the God of Israel,
> From everlasting to everlasting.
> Amen and Amen   (41:13).

BOOK II: PSALMS 42-72

These next thirty-one psalms, Psalms 42-72, were subsequently collected some 300 years later during the reign of Hezekiah (*c.* 715–686 BC), Judah's thirteenth king. The 'men of Hezekiah,' a Bible committee that collected Solomon's proverbs (Prov. 25:1), probably organized these psalms and added them to Book I (3-41). This is certainly consistent with Hezekiah's efforts to bring revival to Judah (2 Chr. 29:30; 32:36), as he elevated the forgotten wisdom of David and Solomon (2 Chr. 29:31; 30:26). Or it may be that these psalms were collected in the reign of King Josiah (640–609 BC).

It has been observed that this second book focuses upon Israel's ruin and redemption. Thus, it can be said to relate to the book of Exodus, which documents Israel's redemption from Egyptian tyranny. This second book concludes with Psalm 72, where the glory of the Davidic king fills the land, much like the ending of Exodus, when the glory of God filled the tabernacle. Ultimately, it looks ahead to the glory of the Messiah filling the earth. Book II concludes with the following doxology:

> And blessed be His glorious name forever;
> And may the whole earth be filled with His glory.
> Amen and Amen.
> The prayers of David son of Jesse are ended   (72:19-20).

BOOK III: PSALMS 73-89

The next seventeen psalms, Psalms 73-89, were compiled into Book III. This gathering probably occurred during the same era as Book II, carried out by the men of Hezekiah, or by Josiah. This third book begins with eleven consecutive psalms written by Asaph (73-83) and includes one written by David (86).

This third book is compared to the book of Leviticus because of its focus upon the sanctuary (see Ps. 73). Further, there are numerous references to God's holiness, as stressed in Leviticus, and to the necessity of personal holiness among his people. This third section concludes with the doxology:

> Blessed be the LORD forever!
> Amen and Amen (89:52).

BOOK IV: PSALMS 90-106

This fourth cluster of seventeen psalms, Psalms 90-106, was correlated almost 300 years later, probably during the post-exilic days after Israel had returned to her land under Ezra (458 BC) and Nehemiah (445 BC). This fourth book focuses upon Israel's relapse and recovery in the wilderness, echoing the theme of Numbers. Appropriately, Book IV begins with Psalm 90, the only psalm in the Psalter written by Moses during Israel's forty years of wilderness wanderings. This severe time of testing, recorded in Numbers, parallels Israel's humbling experience in her wilderness years of Babylonian captivity.

Thus, Book IV relates perfectly with Numbers, as it contains references to the wilderness (95:8) and longings for the promised land (105:8-11). Moreover, it documents Israel's relationship to the surrounding nations. Further, it contains the recurring theme of God's kingdom dominating the kingdoms of the nations. This fourth book concludes with a similar doxology:

> Blessed be the LORD, the God of Israel,
> From everlasting even to everlasting.
> Let all the people say, 'Amen'
> Praise the LORD! (106:48).

BOOK V: PSALMS 107-150

These last forty-four psalms constitute Book V and, like Book IV, were most probably collected and added to the Psalter during the post-exilic days of Ezra, almost 600 years after Book I was collated. In the heart of this fifth book is a dominant focus upon the sufficiency of God's Word (Ps. 119), where in almost every verse there is a reference to its perfections.

This emphasis closely parallels the book of Deuteronomy, which is a second giving of the law. In addition, the five concluding psalms call for the universal praise due to the Lord's name (146–150), much like the book of Deuteronomy with its re-emphasis upon the Law. Upon further investigation, the close comparisons between this fifth book and the book of Deuteronomy become clear. This section completes the parallel between Psalms and the Pentateuch. Book V concludes with the passionate doxology which also climaxes the entire Psalter with a dramatic crescendo:

> Let everything that has breath praise the LORD.
> Praise the LORD!   (150:6).

Seeing these five individual books within the Psalms is critically important to understanding the message of this book. They make the Psalms known as 'The Pentateuch of David'. Consideration must be given not only to when each psalm was written, but also to when it was compiled. One must understand the circumstances of the nation of Israel, as best it can be discerned, at the time when the psalm was compiled. The first and last psalms of each of the five books are strategically placed there.

UNIQUE FEATURES

The book of Psalms is, unquestionably, the most unusual and unique book in the entire Bible. Many interesting features cause it to stand out as a book that is one of a kind. There is no other book like it in the Scripture.

FROM SMALLEST TO LARGEST

Uniquely, the Psalms span the entire spectrum of literary

structure. Whether in terms of the size of the book itself, the period of time over which the book was compiled, or the length of both its largest and smallest chapters, the Psalter boasts both extremes. In addition, this ancient hymn book contains the verse at the very centre of the Bible. For these reasons, the book of Psalms is truly one of a kind.

The Longest Project

As has already been noted, the book of Psalms was a long-term writing project — the longest in the Bible — that required approximately 900 to 1,000 years to compose. At the same time, the compilation of the Psalms was a lengthy project, an effort that spanned many centuries. The formation of the Psalter probably began in the early days of Solomon's Temple, or possibly even in the time of David. Later, post-exilic Temple personnel put the last stage of this compilation into its final form, probably in the third century BC. That is a total of almost 700 years to compile the book of Psalms.

The Largest Book

The book of Psalms is easily the largest book in the Bible, containing 150 psalms. If each psalm is considered as a chapter, the Psalms, with 150 literary units, contains the most chapters of any book in the Bible. The next closest is the book of Isaiah, which contains less than half that number, with sixty-six chapters.

The Longest Chapter

Psalm 119 is the longest chapter in the Bible, a unit of 176 verses. This one psalm contains more verses than thirty other entire books in the Bible — Ruth, Esther, Song of Solomon, Lamentations, Joel, Amos, Obadiah, Jonah, Micah, Nahum, Habakkuk, Zephaniah, Haggai, Malachi, Galatians, Ephesians,

Colossians, Philemon, 1 and 2 Thessalonians, 1 and 2 Timothy, Titus, James, 1 and 2 Peter, 1, 2, and 3 John, and Jude.

THE SHORTEST CHAPTER

On the other hand, Psalm 117 is the shortest chapter in the Bible, containing a mere two verses. Psalm 117 is also, interestingly enough, the middle chapter of the English Bible, the very centre of 1,189 chapters found from Genesis through Revelation.

THE CENTRAL VERSE

Also, Psalm 118:8 is the verse at the absolute centre of the 31,173 verses and 1,189 chapters that make up the whole of Scripture.

THE MOST AUTHORS

More authors contributed to Psalms than to any other book in the Bible. The Psalter is a library unto itself, a magnificent literary collection, claiming a multiple authorship of many men. Among them, as already noted, are David, Asaph, the sons of Korah, Solomon, Moses, Heman, Ethan, and more.

THE MOST QUOTED

New Testament writers quote the book of Psalms more than any other Old Testament book. Of the 360 Old Testament quotations or allusions in the New Testament, 112 are from the Psalms. In addition, 97 of the 150 psalms — that is, almost two-thirds — are quoted in twenty-three of the twenty-seven New Testament books. No other book of the Bible is so interwoven into the fabric of the whole of Scripture.

THE MOST PROPHECIES

The book of Psalms contains more Messianic prophecies about the coming of the Lord Jesus Christ than any other Old Testament book. The psalms reveal him as the Son of God (2) and the Son of Man (8), in his perfect obedience (40:6-8), despicable betrayal (41:9), violent crucifixion (22), triumphant resurrection (16), victorious ascension (68:18), and royal enthronement (110). He is the chief cornerstone for those who believe, but a stumbling stone for those who refuse to do so (118:22-23).

THE BIG PICTURE

This chapter has emphasized that the expositor must see the larger picture of the Psalms as a whole before he can skillfully preach any one psalm. Gaining a general overview of the entire Psalter is a necessary prerequisite before the message of each individual psalm can be most fully obtained and rightly expounded. In other words, one must fly over the forest before attempting to climb any one particular tree. Understanding the authors, genres, features and divisions of the Psalms will assist any expositor in seeing its specific nuances as he comes to preach this divinely inspired book.

Every expositor of the Psalms should secure this enlarged perspective of this book as he begins the journey of preaching its many riches. Let every preacher of this inspired hymnal gain this wide-angle focus of the entire Psalter. Only then will he be able to narrow his focus to an individual psalm.

SELECT THE APPROACH

*Prayerfully decide which psalm
or series of psalms is to be preached*

As the expositor prepares to preach the Psalms, a strategic decision must be made regarding which individual psalm, or series of psalms, is to be preached. Preferably, he will choose a series that allows him to expound many psalms. Or perhaps, in a more in-depth fashion, he may want to bring several messages from one psalm. Whatever approach is adopted, one of the most important decisions the expositor will make is determining which psalm to preach and, in connection with this, how many other psalms are to be addressed.

Sinclair Ferguson notes the importance in preaching of selecting the right text or series when he writes:

> Unless the preacher is committed to a series that lasts for
> years, exposition still requires selection. It takes place less
> frequently when entire books are to be expounded… The
> choice of book [text] to be expounded systematically is of
> immense importance to the preacher and in a profound
> sense to the whole ethos of the congregation's life. A series
> that 'fails' may have far more disastrous consequences
> for the congregation than one sermon that fails! A right
> choice is therefore a matter of singular importance.[1]

Ferguson here underscores the vital importance of making the
right choice of a text in preaching.

THE UNIQUE CHALLENGE

Perhaps more so than for any other book in the Bible, this selection process of a text from the Psalms is especially challenging.
The reason I say this is simple. There are so many more options
open to the expositor who preaches the psalm than in any other
Bible book. The sheer size of the Psalter makes this so. Unless
one decides to preach all 150 psalms, critical decisions must be
made regarding which psalms to preach on. This begins with
knowing what the options are.

How should the choice be made? How can the expositor make
the right selection? What are the various options available to
him? What are the contributing factors in making such a decision? This chapter will investigate what the different strategies
are that can be adopted in preaching the Psalms and how the
choice should be made.

VARIOUS APPROACHES

In order to know what approach to take, the preacher of the

Psalms must know the various possibilities at his disposal. Any of the following basic approaches are viable for him. He may preach: (1) random psalms; (2) consecutive psalms; (3) similar psalms; (4) blocks of psalms; (5) one psalm; or (6) every psalm.

SELECTED PSALMS

First, the preacher may choose to address individual psalms from seemingly random places in the Psalter. This approach will give the congregation a sampling of the various types of psalms. Such an approach may have a haphazard feel about it, but a definite reason exists in the mind of the preacher. Some psalms seem to tower over others and beg to be preached. The expositor may prioritize these key psalms and preach them in a representative way (1; 2; 8; 15; 19; 22; 23; 24; 25; 30; 32; 34; 40; 42; 46; 51; 53; 63; 71; 72, etc.). For example, this was the approach adopted by Charles Swindoll,[2] Warren Wiersbe,[3] Ray Stedman,[4] Ronald Allen,[5] and Calvin Beisner.[6] These are expositors whose sermons on the Psalms are in print, and who have preached on a series of psalms at random.

CLUSTERED PSALMS

Second, the expositor may choose to preach groupings of psalms which cluster together within the Psalter. These noticeable blocks of psalms, which were compiled and arranged in consecutive order, are connected by a similar experience or theme. For example, one could preach a short series on the following psalms:

Psalms 3-7	Trials of the godly
Psalms 9-15	The godly and the wicked
Psalms 42-49	Tribulation and triumph
Psalms 73-83	Psalms of Asaph concerning worship
Psalm 93-99	Enthronement psalms
Psalms 120-134	Psalms of ascent
Psalms 146-150	Psalms of hallelujah

SIMILAR PSALMS

Third, the psalms are distinguished by various classifications, or styles. This will be addressed later, in Chapter 7. For our purposes here, it should be noted that a preaching series could be based upon similar kinds of psalms:

1. The *royal* psalms, which anticipate Christ as King (2; 18; 20; 21; 45; 72; 89; 101; 110; 144);

2. The *penitential* psalms, which convey deep contrition and repentance for sin, coupled with God's grace and forgiveness which restores the sinner (6; 25; 30; 32; 38; 39; 40; 51; 102; 130);

3. The *hallelujah* psalms, which repeatedly employ the term 'hallelujah,' expressing soul-enraptured praise to God (111-113; 115-117; 146-150); or

4. The *imprecatory* psalms, which implore God's vindication of persecuted saints and His just punishment of the godless persecutors.

Choosing any one of these classifications would surely produce a powerful and highly practical preaching series that would significantly enrich God's people.

CONSECUTIVE PSALMS

Fourth, an expositor could choose to preach consecutively through major blocks of psalms in sequential order, regardless of their literary type. For example, he could preach ten sermons on Psalms 1–10, and then break off to preach another series on a different book in the Bible. He could later return to preach ten more sermons on Psalms 11–20, and so on. He could eventually work his way through the entire Psalter in fifteen installments. While it might be imposing too much on both the preacher and the congregation to preach through all 150 psalms consecutively, it might be an attainable goal to cover ten psalms at a time over an expanded period.

ONE PSALM

Fifth, one could preach a multiple-sermon series from one psalm. Many of the psalms can be opened up to accommodate an entire preaching series — an *excellent* series, at that. Some of these individual psalms that could support a series of sermons are Psalms 23; 32; 51; 119 and 139, to name just a few. Many noted expositors have preached lengthy series through individual psalms. These include Martyn Lloyd-Jones, on Psalm 42,[7] and F. B. Meyer on Psalm 23.[8] Other expositors have preached a lengthy series through Psalm 119, modelled by Charles Bridges,[9] Thomas Manton,[10] John Calvin,[11] James Montgomery Boice,[12] and Jay Adams.[13]

EVERY PSALM

Sixth, the expositor could choose to preach consecutively through the entire Psalter. Such a strategy would require several years to fulfill. Certainly, there are key considerations in this approach, such as the ability of the preacher and the maturity of the congregation. James Montgomery Boice preached the entire book of Psalms, psalm by psalm, at Tenth Presbyterian, Philadelphia, and John MacArthur taught the first seventy-five psalms early in his pastoral ministry at Grace Community Church, Los Angeles.

INTENTIONAL CHOICE

After weighing up these various approaches to preaching the Psalms, the expositor must choose which approach will be best for his ministry — most specifically, for those who sit under his preaching. Several factors need to be considered in regard to determining the right selection of psalms, among them the following:

SPIRITUAL DIRECTION

Above all, the one who would preach the Psalms should earnestly pray, seeking God's leadership in this matter. God alone knows the true needs of any congregation and the most appropriate means of ministering to those needs. Without question, God desires to lead His servant in *what* he preaches to His people. He places into the mind and heart of His servant what he desires Him to proclaim.

BALANCED FOCUS

Every preacher will want to present a balanced diet of spiritual food to his congregation. This includes a wide variety of biblical truths, expressed in different tones and contrasting moods. He will want to consider the right distribution between the Old and New Testament. If the congregation has received a steady diet of New Testament books, a longer series from the Psalms may be well in order.

CONGREGATIONAL MATURITY

Whether a congregation has already cultivated an appetite for expository preaching will affect how long the series should be. A congregation that is new to expositional preaching may not be ready to hear *all* 150 psalms preached in consecutive order. A shorter series may be more reasonable. At the same time, a church that has sat under a steady diet of biblical preaching may be ready and eager for a protracted series on the Psalms.

INDIVIDUAL NEEDS

Careful consideration must be given by the preacher to a congregation's spiritual needs. What are the pressing issues they are facing? What hurting hearts need encouraging? What low views of God need to be elevated? What areas of sin need exposing? What haughty hearts need lowering? Sinclair Ferguson writes:

> Our preaching is not to be 'need-determined,' but it must be 'people-oriented'. The preacher operates with two horizons; (1) the text of Scripture and (2) the people of God and their environment in the world. He ought not normally to make his selection without consciously bringing these two horizons together.[14]

This refers not to the felt needs of the people, which are superficial, but to those *real* needs which are mainly unfelt until brought to the surface by the preaching of the Word.

PERSONAL GIFTEDNESS

The number of psalms to be preached and the length of the series may depend, in large part, upon the personal maturity, ability and discipline of the preacher. Quite honestly, it will require an effective preacher to hold the attention of a congregation for a long series. The preacher must honestly review his own ability and assess whether he can maintain the attention of his congregation.

A FINAL THOUGHT

As discussed in this chapter, this is the selection process through which every expositor must travel. By contrast, such a process is not required if one is simply preaching through, say, Ephesians or Philippians. These epistles are small enough in size to be easily manageable in a preaching series, since they are only six and four chapters long respectively.

But the book of Psalms, consisting 150 individual worship songs, poses a major challenge to all expositors, regardless of the abilities and maturity of the expositor. Thus, the preacher, by necessity, has to make certain determinative decisions. Will he preach only some of them? If so, which ones? Or will he preach all 150 psalms? These are the real concerns facing every preacher of the Psalms.

A Word to the Wise

As a word of wisdom and caution, Ferguson again offers this final thought concerning the preacher's conviction and determination of how to preach the psalms. He remarks:

> Under all ordinary circumstances an expository series should not be unduly prolonged. In this matter, men's tastes and gifts differ very considerably. There are men who have such ability as preachers and find themselves in such circumstances that long series of exposition may be justified. But such men and circumstances are rare. It ought to be remembered in this context that the great series of sermons preached by Chrysostom, Luther, and Calvin, and others, generally included several sermons preached each weekday, so that the entire series was not prolonged to many years. People need breadth and variety in their spiritual diet.[15]

The factors to be taken into consideration in making a preaching decision, as it relates to the Psalms, have been addressed in this chapter. May the Lord guide each preacher in the choices he makes in expositing this towering book, the Psalms.

UNDERSTAND
THE TYPES (I)

Know the main literary types of the Psalms

Having selected the psalm, the expositor should next give attention to the classification of the psalm to be preached. In the world of music, there are different types of musical songs — classical, popular, opera, ballad, country-and-western, bluegrass, rock, folk, Christian. In like manner, there are various kinds of praise songs in the Psalms. Each classification has its own feel and flow to it, one that distinguishes it from another kind. It is helpful, even necessary, to discern the literary classification if the preacher is to rightly approach the text and correctly handle the Psalms.

Interpreters have identified as many as ten different kinds of psalms. Understanding these genres greatly helps interpretation. Among the various types of psalms, the following are considered to be the basic categories: individual lament, community lament, individual thanksgiving, community thanksgiving, general praise, descriptive praise, enthronement, pilgrimage, royal, imprecatory, wisdom, or didactic psalms.

RECOGNIZING THE CLASSIFICATIONS

To this point, James Montgomery Boice notes, 'There are various types of psalms — the scholars call them genres — and … it is often helpful to remember the type one is dealing with in a specific psalm.'[1] The more familiar the expositor becomes with the Psalms, the more easily he will recognize these classifications.

Each genre of psalm has its own distinctive pattern and personality. Each classification progresses from one level of thought to the next in predictable fashion. As one becomes acquainted with the basic arrangements of each class of Psalms,[2] he is better able to interact with the unique features of each type. What are distinguishing characteristics that allow a psalm to be assigned to a literary group?

In this chapter, we will begin considering the various types of psalms that are contained in the Psalter. This list is so extensive that it will continue into the next chapter. Presently, we want to consider the major types of psalms that are most commonly used. This begins with the category known as:

LAMENT

In the Psalter, the largest group of psalms is the Lament psalms. There are more than sixty lament psalms, including both individual and corporate laments. In the lament, the psalmist opens his heart honestly to God, a heart often filled with sadness, fear, or even anger. These highly emotionally-charged songs record the psalmist's desperation for God's deliverance in the midst of his personal sufferings. Here is the psalmist's heart cry to God to be rescued in the day of extreme trouble and pain (3-7; 12-13; 22; 25-28; 35; 38-40; 42-44; 51; 54-57; 59-61; 63-64; 69-71; 74; 79-83; 85-86; 88; 90; 102; 109; 120; 123; 130; 140-143). With most psalms, the lament eventually turns to the Lord with confidence.

INDIVIDUAL LAMENT: THE PERSECUTED

These individual lament psalms arise out of personal circumstances when the psalmist's enemies have persecuted him (3-5; 7; 11; 17; 23; 27; 57; 63). They are seeking to do him great harm. These are prayers for help in times of excruciating distress. They follow a predictable flow of thought, which, using Psalms 3 as an example, usually runs as follows:

1. Problem Stated

These individual lament psalms usually begin with an introductory cry to God. In his distress, the psalmist turns to God and pours out his heart. This beginning address to God is an expression of the psalmist's complaint against his enemies (3:1-2; 4:2; 5:9-10; 7:6, 14-16; 11:1b-3; 17:7-12; 23:5; 27:2-3, 6, 12; 57:4, 6; 63:9-10):

> O LORD, how my adversaries have increased;
> Many are rising up against me.
> Many are saying of my soul,
> 'There is no deliverance for him in God'   (3:1-2).

2. God Trusted

Having stated his problem to God, the psalmist then expresses his unwavering confidence in God. He turns from his complaint and declares his full trust in God. In the midst of his suffering, the psalmist chooses to rest securely in God's protection and deliverance (3:3-6; 4:3b, 8; 5:3-7; 7:1, 9-11; 11:1a, 4-7; 17:6-8, 14b-15; 23:1-6; 27:1-3, 5, 13-14; 57:1-3, 10; 63:3-5). Psalm 3 unfolds in this manner:

But You, O LORD, are a shield about me,
My glory, and the One who lifts my head.
I was crying to the LORD with my voice, and He
   answered me from His holy mountain.
I lay down and slept;
I awoke, for the LORD sustains me.
I will not be afraid of ten thousands of people who have
   set themselves against me round about   (3:4-6).

3. God Petitioned

With confidence in God, the psalmist requests that He intervene on his behalf and rescue him. The psalm records the psalmist petitioning God for divine intervention and deliverance (3:7-8; 4:1, 6b; 5:1-3, 8, 10-11; 7:1-9; 17:1-2, 6-9, 13-14a; 27:4, 7-12; 57:1). Psalm 3 concludes this way:

Arise, O LORD; save me, O my God!
For You have smitten all my enemies on the cheek;
You have shattered the teeth of the wicked   (3:7).

4. God Praised

This individual lament psalm concludes with an exhilarating expression of praise for God, who is his deliverance.

Salvation belongs to the LORD;
Your blessing be upon Your people!   (3:8).

INDIVIDUAL LAMENT: THE SICK

In this classification of psalms, the psalmist finds himself plagued with a physical illness. The result is an intense time of spiritual anguish and, hence, his lament. He complains against God's discipline who uses his enemies as the rod of His divine correction. But the psalmist trusts God, petitioning Him to remove his sickness and suffering. He believes that in due time, deliverance will come from God (6; 13; 22; 30-32; 35; 38; 39; 41; 51; 69; 71; 88; 91; 102; 103; 130).

1. Problem Stated

These psalms, for the most part, begin with the psalmist identifying what is the trial that he is undergoing. It may be a time of physical suffering, resulting in emotional anguish perhaps due to sin (6:1; 13:1-2; 22:14-15, 17-18; 30:1-3, 8-9; 31:7, 9b-10; 32:3, 5-6; 35:1, 3, 20-21; 30:7, 11, 17-18; 39:2-3, 13; 41:3-5; 51:1-14; 69:2-3, 5, 19; 71:9, 19-21; 88:3-5; 91:3-7; 102:2-11, 13-17; 103:3-4, 10; 130:3-4). In like manner, Psalm 6 begins with the problem stated:

> O LORD, do not rebuke me in Your anger,
> nor chasten me in Your wrath   (6:1).

2. God Trusted

Then, in the midst of his heavy emotional lament, the psalmist calls out to God and puts his trust in Him, who is ever faithful to deliver (6:4, 10; 13:5-6; 22:3-5, 9-10, 24, 26-31; 30:2, 5, 6a, 10; 31:1a, 6, 9a, 14-20, 21-24; 32:1-2, 5, 10; 35:4-10, 24; 39:4-6, 7-8; 51:1-12, 17; 69:13-18, 33; 71:1, 6, 7b-8, 14-21; 91:1-13; 102:1-2, 12-22, 25-28; 103:7-18; 130:3-8). Psalm 6 progresses to this trust expressed:

> Be gracious to me, O LORD, for I am pining away;
> Heal me, O LORD, for my bones are dismayed.
> And my soul is greatly dismayed;
> But You, O LORD — how long?
> Return, O LORD, rescue my soul;
> Save me because of Your lovingkindness…
> All my enemies will be ashamed and greatly dismayed;
> They shall turn back, they will suddenly be ashamed
>   (6:2-4, 10).

3. Perplexity Expressed

After expressing his lament to God, the psalmist complains against God. These outbursts acknowledge how painful His divine discipline is. This is often expressed by the familiar refrain, 'How long?' (6:5; 13:1; 22:1-2, 15c; 30:5a, 7; 32:4; 35:13c-14; 38:2-3; 39:9-11; 71:20; 88:6-9, 14-18; 102:9-11, 23). In Psalm 6, this perplexity is expressed by David:

For there is no mention of You in death;
in Sheol who will give You thanks?   (6:5).

4. Sorrow Expressed

Next, the psalmist turns his complaint against his enemies, whom God is using to chasten him (6:7, 10; 13:2b, 4; 22:7-8, 12-13, 16; 30:1c; 31:1b, 11-13, 18; 35:1, 3-8, 11-17; 38:11, 12, 19-20; 41:5-9; 69:4-5, 14, 18-19, 21; 71:10-11; 91:8; 102:8). Psalm 6 demonstrates this conclusion:

My eye has wasted away with grief;
it has become old because of all my adversaries…
All my enemies will be ashamed and greatly dismayed;
they shall turn back, they will suddenly be ashamed
                    (6:7, 10).

COMMUNITY LAMENT

Within the lament psalms, there are also community laments of the people. These expressions of sorrow follow the same pattern as the laments of individuals. In these, a national crisis alarms the psalmist, who approaches God on behalf of the people. The plural pronouns most often mark these community laments as being corporate in nature (44; 60; 74; 77; 79; 80; 83; 85; 90; 94; 123; 126; 137). In most cases, the national lament psalm is shorter than the individual lament. Psalm 79 will serve as our example below:

1. Problem Stated

In these community laments, the psalmist speaks on behalf of the nation, stating the problem to God. In these, there is often expressed their devastating defeat in war (44:9-16; 60:1-3, 10; 74:1, 3-8; 77:1-2, 5-9; 79:1-4; 80:13-17; 83:2-8; 85:4-7; 90:7-10; 94:4-7; 123:3-4; 126:1-2a; 137:1-4). Psalm 79 begins with the problem stated:

O God, the nations have invaded Your inheritance;
they have defiled Your holy temple;

they have laid Jerusalem in ruins.
They have given the dead bodies of Your servants for
    food to the birds of the heavens,
the flesh of Your godly ones to the beasts of the earth.
They have poured out their blood like water round about
    Jerusalem;
and there was no one to bury them.
We have become a reproach to our neighbors,
a scoffing and derision to those around us   (79:1-4).

2. Perplexity Expressed

Here, the psalmist turns to God in solemn consternation and expresses soberly, 'How long, O Lord? Will You be angry forever?' (44:9-14, 23-24; 60:1-3, 10; 74:1, 10-11; 77:7-9; 79:5-6, 12-13; 80:4-17; 85:4-7; 90:7-10). Psalm 79, for example, next records the perplexity expressed:

How long, O LORD? Will You be angry forever?
Will Your jealousy burn like fire   (79:5)?

3. God Petitioned

Having voiced his complaint against God, the psalmist petitions God for deliverance from His heavy hand against them. He requests that their enemies no longer succeed in their malicious threats and attacks (44:23-26; 60:5, 11; 74:2-3, 18-23; 79:6-12; 80:1-3, 7, 14-15, 19; 83:1-3, 9-18; 85:4, 6; 90:12-17; 94:1-3; 123:3-4; 126:4; 137:7). Such a petition to God is recorded in Psalm 79:

Pour out Your wrath upon the nations which do not know
    You,
and upon the kingdoms which do not call upon Your
    name.
For they have devoured Jacob and laid waste his habitation.
Do not remember the iniquities of our forefathers against
    us;
let Your compassion come quickly to meet us, for we are
    brought very low.

Help us, O God of our salvation, for the glory of Your
    name;
And deliver us and forgive our sins for Your name's sake.
Why should the nations say, 'Where is their God?'
Let there be known among the nations in our sight,
Vengeance for the blood of Your servants which has
    been shed.
Let the groaning of the prisoner come before You;
According to the greatness of Your power preserve those
    who are doomed to die.
And return to our neighbors sevenfold into their bosom
The reproach with which they have reproached You,
    O LORD   (79:6-12).

4. Praise Vowed

These community laments often conclude with a vow to praise
God. The psalmist purposes that he declare God's greatness
because He will surely deliver them from the effects of their
enemies. Implicit in this vow is a declaration of their trust in
God (44:1-8; 60:4, 12; 74:12-17; 77:10-20; 79:13; 80:1-2a, 3, 7,
19; 83:18; 85:1-3, 8-13; 90:1-2; 94:9-14, 18-19, 22-23; 123:2).
Psalm 79 concludes with the following vow of praise:

So we Your people and the sheep of Your pasture will
    give thanks to You forever;
to all generations we will tell of Your praise   (79:13).

THANKSGIVING

The next prominent classification is the thanksgiving psalms. In
these worship songs, the psalmist expresses a profound awareness of God's bountiful blessings. These psalms are often voiced
when the Lord answers prayer, as they record gratitude to God
for His abundant mercies. Some are individual thanksgiving
psalms, others are national. These psalms, sometimes called
psalms of declarative praise, express joy to the Lord because
of His goodness, faithfulness, and protection. There are ten

individual psalms of thanksgiving (18; 30; 32; 34; 40; 66; 92; 116; 118; 138) and six community (corporate) psalms of thanksgiving (65; 67; 75; 107; 124; 136) in the Psalter.

INDIVIDUAL THANKSGIVING

The psalmist expresses himself with heartfelt gratitude to God, expressing thanks for divine blessings bestowed upon him personally (18, 30, 31, 32, 40, 66, 92, 116, 118, 120). These psalms follow a slightly different arrangement and include five key elements.

1. Gratitude Declared

Most often, these individual thanksgiving psalms begin with a burst of excitement. At the beginning, the psalmist declares what good thing the Lord has done (18:1-3, 6; 30:1; 32:1-2; 40:1; 66:17; 116:1-2; 118:1-4; 120:1). This is how the psalmist begins Psalm 32:

> How blessed is he whose transgression is forgiven,
> Whose sin is covered!
> How blessed is the man to whom the LORD does not
>   impute iniquity,
> And in whose spirit there is no deceit   (32:1-2)!

2. Problem Stated

Next, the psalmist will provide the background to understand what his problem is. It was out of this difficulty that God must act (18:3-5, 7-19, 47-48; 30:2-3, 6-9, 11-12a; 31:8-13, 21-22; 32:3-4; 40:2-3, 12, 14; 66:5-12, 14 16-19; 92:9-11; 116:3, 8-9; 118:5, 7, 10-13, 18; 120:1-3, 6, 7). Psalm 32 demonstrates how the psalm advances to the problem stated:

> When I kept silent about my sin,
> my body wasted away through my groaning all day long.
> For day and night Your hand was heavy upon me;
> my vitality was drained away as with the fever heat of
>   summer   (32:3-4).

3. Deliverance Confessed

Having stated the problem, the psalmist acknowledges the reality of God's deliverance (18:6, 16-24, 43; 30:2-3, 10; 31:7-8, 19, 21-22; 32:5; 40:2-3, 11; 66:9, 19, 20; 92:2, 11; 116:1-2, 5-8, 12, 16; 118:1, 5, 13, 18, 21, 23, 29). Most often, he explained that he cried out to the Lord, who heard and rescued him. Psalm 32 progresses to this next step:

> I acknowledged my sin to You,
> And my iniquity I did not hide;
> I said, 'I will confess my transgressions to the LORD,
> And You forgave the guilt of my sin'   (32:5).

4. Wisdom Shared

The psalmist often reflected upon his deliverance and passed along a life lesson to those who heard him (48:25-26; 32:8-10; 66:20; 118:25-29). Psalm 32 represents this when it states:

> I will instruct you and teach you in the way which you
>   should go;
> I will counsel you with My eye upon you.
> Do not be as the horse or as the mule which have
>   no understanding,
> Whose trappings include bit and bridle to hold
>   them in check,
> Otherwise, they will not come near to you.
> Many are the sorrows of the wicked,
> But he who trusts in the LORD, lovingkindness
>   shall surround him   (32:8-10).

5. Praise Invited

With a concluding note, the psalmist vowed to praise God. He also invited others to join with him in praising God (18:46-49; 30:4-5, 12; 31:21-23; 32:11; 66:1-9, 13-15, 20; 92:1-5, 8, 15; 116:13-14; 118:1-4, 17, 19, 21, 26-28). In Psalm 32:11, the psalmist concluded by instructing others to praise God:

> Be glad in the LORD and rejoice, you righteous ones;

and shout for joy, all you who are upright in heart.

COMMUNITY THANKSGIVING

In these psalms, corporate gratitude to God is expressed. There are two defining elements: a national crisis and the relief from the crisis. The communal aspect is indicated by the use of plural pronouns, i.e., 'we,' 'our' (65; 66; 107; 118; 124; 129).

1. Praise Rendered
Five of the six community psalms of thanksgiving begin with an opening declaration of praise. Here is expressed an invitation to give thanks to God (65:1-2; 66:1-2; 107:1-3; 118:1-4; 124:1-2). Psalm 65 starts with this element:

> There will be silence before You, and praise in Zion, O
>   God,
> And to You the vow will be performed.
> O You who hear prayer, to You all men come   (65:1-2).

2. Problem Stated
The psalmist next states the problem which has created the crisis. Whatever is the national distress, usually foreign oppressions, with the prospect of death, what lays at the heart of the problem is the sin of the people (65:3a; 66:10-12; 107:4-5, 10-12, 17-20, 25-27; 118:7, 10-13, 18; 124:2b-3; 129:1-3). Psalm 65 next states:

> Iniquities prevail against me (65:3a).

3. Grace Reported
An initial report is given by the psalmist regarding what God has done for them. Their deliverance is an accomplished fact. This documents their well-founded reason to offer thanks to God (65:3; 66:5-12; 107:4-7, 10-14, 17-20, 23-30; 118:5, 10-13; 124:2b-3a; 129:2-3). Psalm 65 explains:

> As for our transgressions, You forgive them (65:3b).

4. Past Appealed

Next, the psalmist appeals to past history and remembers God's mighty works and power to save (65:3-8; 66:5-12; 107:33-41; 124:8). Psalm 65, for example, reveals this step:

> By awesome deeds You answer us in righteousness,
> O God of our salvation,
> You who are the trust of all the ends of the earth and of
>   the farthest sea;
> Who establishes the mountains by His strength,
> Being girded with might;
> Who stills the roaring of the seas,
> The roaring of their waves,
> And the tumult of the peoples.
> They who dwell in the ends of the earth stand in awe of
>   Your signs;
> You make the dawn and the sunset shout for joy
> (65:5-8).

5. Deliverance Explained

The reason for God's deliverance of His people is found not in their goodness, but in His own grace. God's unconditional love for His own people lays behind His acts of deliverance (65:9-13; 66:20; 107:1, 43; 118:1, 29; 124:1-2, 8; 129:4a). In Psalm 65, we clearly see this next stage:

> You visit the earth and cause it to overflow;
> You greatly enrich it;
> The stream of God is full of water;
> You prepare their grain, for thus You prepare
>   the earth.
> You water its furrows abundantly,
> You settle its ridges,
> You soften it with showers,
> You bless its growth.
> You have crowned the year with Your bounty,
> And Your paths drip with fatness.
> The pastures of the wilderness drip,

And the hills gird themselves with rejoicing.
The meadows are clothed with flocks
    and the valleys are covered with grain   (65:9-13b).

6. Fervent Praise

Finally, these community psalms of thanksgiving contain either
a declaration of praise, a vow of praise, or an invitation to praise
(65:13c; 66:3-4, 20; 107:1-3, 8, 15, 21, 31-32, 43; 118:1-4, 17, 19,
21, 28-29). In like manner, Psalm 65 concludes: 'They shout for
joy, yes, they sing' (65:13c).

PRAISE

The next classification of psalms to be considered is the praise
psalms easily recognized by their exuberant praise for God. This
kind of psalm expresses adoration for God based upon who
He is and His greatness toward His people. Here, God is to be
praised as Creator of the universe (8; 19; 104; 148). Further, He
is to be praised as the protector and provider of His people (66;
100; 111; 114; 149). Also, God is to be praised as the Lord of history (33; 103; 113; 117; 145-147).

PRAISE GOD THE CREATOR

In these psalms, the psalmist praised God for His astounding
work in creation which marked the beginning of world history.
By His act of creation, the world rightly belongs to God and
gives Him unrestricted rights and privileges over the universe,
which He alone made (8; 19a; 33; 104; 136).

1. Praise Declared

In considering God's greatness, the psalmist could not contain
himself in announcing praise to God. God is adored because He
is majestic and worthy to be praised. Thus, Psalm 8 begins with
a burst of praise:

O Lord, our Lord, how majestic is Your name in all the
  earth,
Who have displayed Your splendor above the heavens
                                        (8:1).

2. Praise Explained

The psalmist then gives the specific reasons for his praise of
God. The reason that he magnifies God's name is from nursing babes to heavenly bodies, God is Lord of all. His works in
creation from celestial bodies to mankind elicit praise for God.
The cause of worship is always the greatness of God. Psalm 8
explains the compelling reason for such praise:

From the mouth of infants and nursing babes You have
  established strength
Because of Your adversaries,
To make the enemy and the revengeful cease.
When I consider your heavens, the work of Your fingers,
The moon and the stars, which You have ordained;
What is man that You take thought of him,
And the son of man that You care for him?
Yet You have made him a little lower than God,
And You crown him with glory and majesty!
You make him to rule over the works of Your hands;
You have put all things under his feet,
All sheep and oxen, and also the beasts of the field,
The birds of the heavens and the fish of the sea,
Whatever passes through the paths of the seas   (8:2-8).

3. Praise Repeated

The psalmist concludes with a final exhortation to praise God.
The psalm climaxes as it commenced, with praise offered to
God. This is to be the beginning and end of our existence, as
well.

O Lord, our Lord,
How majestic is Your name in all the earth!   (8:9).

PRAISE GOD THE PROVIDER

Other praise psalms magnify God's name because of the great protection that He provides for His people. God has chosen His own and will never forsake them in this world (66; 100; 111; 114; 149). An excellent representation of this psalm classification is Psalm 100.

1. Praise Declared

These praise psalms begin with a fervent call by the psalmist to all the earth to come and praise God. All men should praise God everywhere. Psalm 100 begins:

> Shout joyfully to the LORD, all the earth.
> Serve the LORD with gladness;
> Come before Him with joyful singing…
> Enter His gates with thanksgiving
> And His courts with praise.
> Give thanks to Him, bless His name   (100:1-2, 4).

2. Praise Explained

In this final section, there comes a full development of the reason for praise. Praise should be given to God, the psalmist says, because He alone is God. He is the Shepherd of His people, who protects them from all harm and provides for their needs. God is good, loving and faithful. Thus, all people should give Him praise. Psalm 100 then explains the reason for the psalmist's praise:

> Know that the LORD Himself is God;
> It is He who has made us, and not we ourselves;
> We are His people and the sheep of His pasture…
> For the LORD is good;
> His lovingkindness is everlasting
> And His faithfulness to all generations   (100:3, 5).

PRAISE GOD THE SOVEREIGN

Further, other praise psalms give glory to God because He is the Sovereign Lord of history (33, 103, 113, 117, 145-147). That God is actively ruling over history should be a cause for great celebration from those who know Him.

1. Praise Declared
In these particular psalms, all men are immediately exhorted to give praise to God. With the accompaniment of instruments, praise is to be offered to God. Thus, Psalm 33 starts:

> Sing for joy in the LORD, O you righteous ones;
> Praise is becoming to the upright.
> Give thanks to the LORD with the lyre;
> Sing praises to Him with a harp of ten strings.
> Sing to Him a new song; play skillfully with a shout of joy.
> For the word of the LORD is upright,
> And all His work is done in faithfulness   (33:1-4).

2. Praise Explained
In the next progression, the psalmist gives reason why God should be so exuberantly praised. It is because He rules over the nations. His eternal purposes cannot be overturned. His divine counsel overrules the counsel of the nations. Thus, we read in these psalms that the compelling reason for praise to God is His absolute supremacy. God is unhindered in His sovereign rule (33:10-17). God is unhindered in His sovereign rule:

> The LORD nullifies the counsel of the nations;
> He frustrates the plans of the peoples.
> The counsel of the LORD stands forever,
> The plans of His heart from generation to generation.
> Blessed is the nation whose God is the LORD,
> The people whom He has chosen for His own
>   inheritance.
> The LORD looks from heaven;

He sees all the sons of men; from His dwelling place He
    looks out
On all the inhabitants of the earth,
He who fashions the hearts of them all,
He who understands all their works.
The king is not saved by a mighty army;
A warrior is not delivered by great strength.
A horse is a false hope for victory;
Nor does it deliver anyone by its great strength
                                                        (33:10-17).

3. Trust Expressed

Finally, the psalmist expresses complete trust in God, who reigns
above. Because God is in control of all things, believers may wait
patiently upon Him. They need not rush ahead recklessly, but
may wait patiently on God. Consequently, these psalms conclude with bold statements of trust, such as this one in Psalm 33:

Behold, the eye of the LORD is on those who fear Him,
On those who hope for His lovingkindness,
To deliver their soul from death
And to keep them alive in famine.
Our soul waits for the LORD;
He is our help and our shield.
For our heart rejoices in Him,
Because we trust in His holy name.
Let your lovingkindness, O LORD, be upon us,
According as we have hoped in You   (33:18-22).

DIDACTIC

Another type of psalm is the highly instructive psalms known as
didactic psalms, which provide practical guidelines to God's will.
These worship songs convey practical direction for daily living in
the pursuit of God's path (1; 36; 37; 49; 73; 112; 127; 128; 133). Here
is how God wants us to live our lives. Often this divine instruction
is expressed in the Torah, or written Law of God (1; 19; 119).

WISDOM TEACHING

In the wisdom psalms, the psalmist teaches a world view that sits in stark contrast the polar opposites of life and death, wisdom and folly, the way of the righteous and the way of the wicked, blessing and destruction (32; 34, 37; 49; 73; 112; 127; 128; 133). This strong contrast between the two paths of life closely reveals the motifs found in the wisdom literature of the book of Proverbs.

1. Wisdom Admonitions

These wisdom psalms are characterized by their many admonitions which challenge the reader to walk circumspectly (32:9; 34:11-14; 37:1, 3, 4, 5, 8; 49:16-19). In Psalm 37, these admonitions to pay heed to divine wisdom begins this psalm:

> Do not fret because of evildoers,
> Be not envious toward wrongdoers…
> Trust in the LORD and do good;
> Dwell in the land an cultivate faithfulness.
> Delight yourself in the LORD…
> Trust also in Him, and He will do it…
> Cease from anger and forsake wrath;
> Do not fret; it leads only to evildoing   (37:1, 3-5, 8).

2. Pithy Proverbs

Further, wisdom psalms contain the use of proverb-like expressions, which are compressed, pithy sayings that contain maxims or adages of life (34:6-8; 37:1-2, 16, 21; 49:20; 127:2, 3; 133:1). Psalm 37 contains these proverbs:

> For they will wither quickly like the grass
> And fade like the green herb   (37:2).

3. Comparative Similes

These wisdom psalms are also known for their use of similes, in which a comparison is made using 'like' or 'as'. Many of these similes are drawn from the animal world and the world of nature, but their use is not restricted exclusively to wisdom psalms (32:9; 37:2, 6, 20, 35; 49:14, 20; 73:20; 127:4; 128:3; 133:2, 3). Many comparative similes are used in Psalm 37:

> For they will wither quickly like the grass
> And fade like the green herb...
> He will bring forth your righteousness as the light
> And your judgment as the noonday...
> But the wicked will perish;
> And the enemies of the LORD will be like the glory of the
>   pastures,
> They vanish — like smoke they vanish away...
> I have seen a wicked, violent man
> Spreading himself like a luxuriant tree in its native soil
>   (37:2, 6, 20, 35).

4. Antithetical Ways

Moreover, the wisdom psalms sharply contrast the two ways of life. They show the wide discrepancy between the wise and the foolish, the righteous and the wicked (34:14-15; 37:7, 9-22, 32-34, 37-38; 73:3-12, 13, 27-28; 127:1-2). Psalm 37 contains many such contrasts between the righteous and the unrighteous:

> Rest in the LORD and wait patiently for Him;
> Do not fret because of him who prospers in his way,
> because of the man who carries out wicked schemes...
> For evildoers will be cut off,
> But those who wait for the LORD, they will inherit the land.
> Yet a little while and the wicked man will be no more;
> And you will look carefully for his place and he will not
>   be there.
> But the humble will inherit the land
> And will delight themselves in abundant prosperity.
> The wicked plots against the righteous
> And gnashes at him with his teeth.
> The Lord laughs at him,
> For He sees his day is coming.
> The wicked have drawn the sword and bent their bow

To cast down the afflicted and the needy,
To slay those who are upright in conduct.
Their sword will enter their own heart,
And their bows will be broken.
Better is the little of the righteous
Than the abundance of many wicked.
For the arms of the wicked will be broken,
But the LORD sustains the righteous.
The LORD knows the days of the blameless,
And their inheritance will be forever.
They will not be ashamed in the time of evil,
And in the days of famine they will have abundance.
But the wicked will perish;
And the enemies of the LORD will be like the glory of the
    pastures,
They vanish — like smoke they vanish away.
The wicked borrows and does not pay back,
But the righteous is gracious and gives.
For those blessed by Him will inherit the land,
But those cursed by Him will be cut off…
The wicked spies upon the righteous
And seeks to kill him.
The LORD will not leave him in his hand
Or let him be condemned when he is judged.
Wait for the LORD and keep His way,
And He will exalt you to inherit the land;
When the wicked are cut off, you will see it…
Mark the blameless man, and behold the upright;
For the man of peace will have a posterity.
But transgressors will be altogether destroyed;
The posterity of the wicked will be cut off
                                    (37:7, 9-22, 32-34, 37-38).

5. Righteous Qualities

These wisdom psalms also detail many of the godly qualities of
the righteous, who walk according to divine wisdom. Their personal integrity and activity is noticeably being conformed to the
law of God (32:11; 37:21, 26, 30-31):

The wicked borrows and does not pay back,
But the righteous is gracious and gives…
All day long he is gracious and lends,
And his descendants are a blessing…
The mouth of the righteous utters wisdom,
And his tongue speaks justice.
The law of his God is in his heart;
His steps do not slip   (37:21, 26, 30-31).

6. Righteous Rewarded

Another feature of the wisdom psalms is they emphasize many of the benefits that come to the righteous. Much good comes from the LORD to those who live according to divine wisdom (34:15, 17, 19; 37:6, 16, 17, 25, 29, 30-31, 39-40).

He will bring forth your righteousness as the light
And your judgment as the noonday…
Better is the little of the righteous
Than the abundance of many wicked.
For the arms of the wicked will be broken,
But the LORD sustains the righteous…
I have been young and now I am old,
Yet I have not seen the righteous forsaken
Or his descendants begging bread…
The righteous will inherit the land
And dwell in it forever.
The mouth of the righteous utters wisdom,
And his tongue speaks justice.
The law of his God is in his heart;
His steps do not slip…
But the salvation of the righteous is
    from the LORD;
He is their strength in time of trouble.
The LORD helps them and delivers them;
He delivers them from the wicked and saves them,
Because they take refuge in Him
                    (37:6, 16-17, 25, 29-31, 39-40).

TORAH TEACHING

Another type of teaching psalm is the Torah psalm, which focuses upon the Law. At the heart of the Pentateuch is the Law, which was given to Israel on Mount Sinai to govern all aspects of Israel's life. Strictly speaking, only three psalms can be designated Torah psalms in a primary way (1; 19; 119). While other psalms address the Torah, the Law is not their primary focus (18; 25; 33; 68; 78; 81; 89; 93; 94; 99; 103; 105; 111; 112; 147; 148). In the proper sense, they are not considered Torah psalms.

1. Blessed Promise

In these Torah psalms, the psalmist begins by pronouncing divine approval on those who follow the way of living as commanded in the Law (1:1; 119:1-2). Such psalms often begin as does Psalm 1, with a pronouncement of blessedness. This is a promise of divine favor, which includes a right standing before God involving happiness, peace, satisfaction, and joy: 'How blessed is the man' (1:1a).

2. Antithetical Ways

As with the wisdom psalms, these Torah psalms contrast the two ways of life. They set in stark contrast the way of the righteous and the way of the wicked. Psalm 1 states these opposites are clearly seen:

> … who does not walk in the counsel of the wicked,
> Nor stand in the path of sinners,
> Nor sit in the seat of scoffers!
> But his delight is in the law of the LORD,
> And in His law he meditates day and night…
> The wicked are not so.
> But they are like chaff which the wind drives away.
> Therefore the wicked will not stand in the judgment,
> Nor sinners in the assembly of the righteous.
> For the LORD knows the way of the righteous,
> But the way of the wicked will perish   (1:1b-2, 4-6).

3. Comparative Similes

These Torah psalms are also known for their use of similes. Often drawn from nature, once again, these comparisons using 'like' and 'as' serve to paint pictures of what the man looks like who delights in God's Law, as well as the one who departs from His Word. Psalm 1 uses two main comparative similes, which illustrate the righteous man and the unrighteous man. The former is like a tree planted by a river, the latter like a bush in the desert:

> He will be like a tree firmly planted by streams of water,
> Which yields its fruit in its season.
> And its leaf does not wither;
> And in whatever he does, he prospers   (1:3).

7

UNDERSTAND
THE TYPES (II)

Know the further literary types of the Psalms

I n the last chapter, we began considering the various literary types of psalms. It is important that every expositor familiarize himself with these different classifications in order to properly understand the psalm's development of thought. This awareness will also help him discern the tone and trajectory that is common to each type of psalm. Each classification has its own unique features that help distinguish it to both the preacher and the listener. Wise is the expositor who becomes familiar with these different types.

No book in the Bible has such a wide diversity of literary types as the book of Psalms. For this reason, it is imperative for the expositor to rightly identify the type of psalm. Yet, how can the preacher begin to discern the kind of psalm that he is intending to preach? What clues should he look for in the psalms? What are the considerations that he should evaluate? Determining these vital clues, in part, unlocks the vast riches that is the treasury of David. The following are general criteria, which are helpful for identifying any given psalm's classification.

DETERMINING THE PSALM'S TYPE

First, consider the *subject matter*. The various types of psalms can be identified by the content of that particular psalm's message, from the didactic teaching of the wisdom psalms, to the Messianic hope of royal psalms, to the personal crisis of the lament psalms, to the divine justice of the imprecatory psalms, to the expressed gratitude of the thanksgiving psalms, to the purposeful worship of the pilgrimage psalms, to the transcendent glory of the enthronement psalms.

Second, note the *authorial tone*. Also, the different types of psalms can be recognized by their mood, ranging from the painful despair of lament psalms to the zealous intensity of imprecatory psalms. A further diversity can be noted from the humble contriteness of thanksgiving psalms to the joyful celebration of pilgrimage psalms. Still further examples of this range are witnessed in the sheer majesty of the enthronement psalms.

Third, discover the *literary structure*. Certain types of psalms take on predictable patterns that are indicators of their classification. For example, the lament psalm will follow a routine form of: address, lament, confession, petition, assurance, praise. Other types of psalms will take on their own repeating patterns.

CONTINUED ANALYSIS OF TYPES

In this chapter, we want to continue to specifically identify the various kinds of literary types in the Psalms and the distinctives of each. Again, it must be recognized that there is some variance and overlap from one classification of psalm to another. The following are yet further classifications of psalm types:

KINGSHIP

Another prominent type of psalm is the kingship psalm. This classification of psalms focuses upon either the earthly king of Israel — the Davidic king — or the heavenly king of the universe — Yahweh. These psalms feature the earthly king, look ahead ultimately to the coming of Christ to reign over the earth (2; 18; 20; 21; 45; 47; 72; 89; 93; 95-99; 101; 110; 132; 144). The stress is upon the sovereignty of God in creation, providence, and salvation.

ROYAL

Royal psalms highlight the reign of the anointed king of Israel and his many conquests over the foreign powers that threatened their national security. These high points in the reign of the monarch are ascribed to God Himself, who has established the Davidic king on Israel's throne to rule with justice and righteousness. Further, these royal psalms look forward to the coming of the Messiah, the greater Davidic King, who will triumph where their earthly kings failed (2; 18; 20; 21; 45; 72; 89; 101; 110; 132; 144). The normal parts of these psalms are as follows:

1. God's Enemies
As the monarch of Israel, the Davidic king faces opposition from many foreign powers. The central focus is upon the king of Israel, God's anointed, the Davidic king. Ultimately, they look ahead to the Lord Jesus Christ. In Psalm 2, the surrounding nations are viewed as rising up in resistance against an earthly king. Prophetically, this looks ahead to the coming of the Messiah and the opposition He will face from earthly powers (Acts 4:25-26; 13:33):

Why are the nations in an uproar
And the peoples devising a vain thing?
The kings of the earth take their stand
And the rulers take counsel together
Against the LORD and against His Anointed, saying,
'Let us tear their fetters apart
And cast away their cords from us!'   (2:1-3).

2. God's Sovereignty

In the face of such opposition, royal psalms testify to the absolute sovereignty of God over the nations. No foreign power can thwart God's supreme authority over all mankind. How futile to resist heaven's King (2:4-6; 18:1-3, 7-15, 45-50; 20:6; 45:6-9; 89:11-14, 17-37; 110:1-2, 4; 132:11-13; 144:3). Psalm 2 continues:

He who sits in the heavens laughs,
The Lord scoffs at them.
Then He will speak to them in His anger
And terrify them in His fury, saying,
'But as for Me, I have installed My King
Upon Zion, My holy mountain'   (2:4-6).

3. God's Victory

Because God is sovereign, possessing all authority in heaven and earth, victory over all foreign powers belongs exclusively to Him. God alone gives victory to Israel's kings. Deliverance is not found in horses and chariots. The success of the king's reign depends upon his relationship with God. This God/king relationship is so close that it is often pictured as a Father/son relationship. Ultimately, Psalm 2 looks ahead to the victory God will give to the Messiah, His own divine Son (2:7-9, 12; 18:16-45; 20:1-9; 21:2-12; 45:5; 72:12-15; 89:38-45; 1210:3, 5-7; 132:13-18):

I will surely tell of the decree of the LORD:
He said to Me, 'You are My Son, today I have begotten
   You.

Ask of Me and I will surely give the nations as Your
  inheritance,
And the very ends of the earth as Your possession.
You shall break them with a rod of iron,
You shall shatter them like earthenware'...
Do homage to the Son,
that He not become angry, and you perish in the way,
For His wrath may soon be kindled.
How blessed are all who take refuge in Him   (2:7-9, 12)!

4. Concluding Appeal

In light of God's irresistible rule, the psalmist urgently counsels all peoples to trust in the LORD. The nations, especially their
rulers, should cease their attempts at autonomy and submit to
the one true God, Yahweh (2:10-12; 18:43-50; 20:1-5, 7-9; 21:1-
13; 45:1-4, 10-17; 72:1-10, 16-20; 89:1-10, 15-16, 46-52; 101:1-8;
132:1-10; 144:1-2, 5-15). Psalm 2 concludes in this manner:

Now therefore, O kings, show discernment;
Take warning, O judges of the earth.
Worship the LORD with reverence
And rejoice with trembling.
Do homage to the Son, that He not become angry, and
  you perish in the way,
For His wrath may soon be kindled.
How blessed are all who take refuge in Him   (2:10-12)!

ENTHRONEMENT

The enthronement psalms are a kind of kingly psalm that is characterized by the repeated expression 'the LORD reigns.' This pithy,
but profound, statement of faith underscores the sovereignty of
God over all creation. An earthly king sat on Israel's throne, but
he merely represented a greater and higher King, Yahweh, who
reigned above. In light of the repeated failures of the Davidic kings,
God's people needed to be reminded that the LORD reigns with
perfect justice over the whole world (47; 93; 95; 96; 97; 98; 99).

1. God's Sovereignty

These enthronement psalms are identified by the familiar refrain 'The LORD reigns.' This statement of faith declares the absolute, unrivalled sovereignty of God over all peoples and places. Despite the failures of earthly kings and the tottering of Israel's security, the LORD reigns (47:8; 93:1; 96:10; 97:1; 99:1). Psalm 93, for example, begins with this bold foundational statement, 'The LORD reigns':

> The LORD reigns, He is clothed with majesty;
> The LORD has clothed and girded Himself with strength
> (93:1a, b).

2. Over Creation

God does not stand apart from His creation, but does constantly rule over all He has made. He is LORD over all the earth, the sole Creator and Controller of the earth and all it contains. All creation and providence is under the omnipotent hand of His theocratic government (93:1c; 95:4-6; 96:1-5, 10-13; 97:6, 9; 98:7-9). To this end, Psalm 93 states:

> Indeed, the world is firmly established, it will
>   not be moved   (93:1c).

3. Over Time

As the One who eternally existed before creation, God has been sovereign from all eternity past. God has not recently assumed the exercise of His supreme authority. His all-powerful throne predates all earthly kingdoms. Psalm 93 declares this pre-existent eternal reign:

> Your throne is established from of old;
> You are from everlasting   (93:2).

4. Over the Nations

From upon His throne on high, God reigns over all the nations. He sovereignly appoints their times in history and their destinies into the future. The LORD uses even foreign oppressors to accomplish His eternal purposes. No one can thwart His sovereign decree (47:2-3, 7-9; 93:3-4; 96:1, 3, 9; 97:1, 5-7; 98:2-9; 99:1-3). Psalm 93 adds:

> The floods have lifted up, O LORD,
> The floods have lifted up their voice,
> The floods lift up their pounding waves.
> More than the sounds of many waters,
> Than the mighty breakers of the sea,
> The LORD on high is mighty   (93:3-4).

5. Over His People

Finally, the psalmist declares that God reigns in absolute holiness over His chosen people. This sovereign rule is mediated by His Word. God's divine testimonies, recorded infallibly in Scripture, produce personal holiness in the lives of His people. The sanctifying power of His Word causes His people to adorn His house with His holy character (47:4; 93:5; 95:6-11; 96:9; 97:12; 98:1, 3; 99:3, 5, 9). Psalm 93 concludes with this emphasis:

> Your testimonies are fully confirmed;
> Holiness befits Your house,
> O LORD, forevermore   (93:5).

IMPRECATORY

Motivated by fiery zeal for God's glory, the imprecatory psalms invoke His wrath and judgment upon His enemies. These psalms cry out for the righteous to be vindicated by God punishing the wicked. In these provocative works are found a plea for the curses of God upon those who rise up against Him. The psalmist calls upon the Lord to punish the wicked and defend him as he carries out God's work in the midst of his persecutors (7; 35; 40; 55; 58-59; 69; 79; 109; 137; 139; 140; 144).

RECOGNIZING THE PURPOSES

Imprecatory psalms serve the following purposes: (1) to demonstrate God's holy hatred of sin and His righteous judgment toward the wicked: 'And men will say, "Surely there is a reward for the righteous; surely there is a God who judges on earth!"' (58:11); (2) to show the authority of God over the wicked, 'Destroy them in wrath, destroy them that they may be no more; That men may know that God rules in Jacob to the ends of the earth' (59:13); (3) to lead the wicked to see the Lord, 'Fill their faces with dishonor, that they may seek Your name, O LORD' (83:16); (4) to cause the righteous to praise God: 'I will give thanks to the LORD according to His righteousness and will sing praise to the name of the LORD Most High' (7:17).

Therefore, out of zeal for God and abhorrence of sin, the psalmist calls on God to punish the wicked and to vindicate the righteous. It must be remembered that all these imprecatory psalms are, except two, offered by David, who serves as king of Israel, the protector of the nation, the commander-in-chief of Israel's armies. It is victory in a just war for which he prays. Also, they are presently being prayed in heaven.

INDIVIDUAL IMPRECATORY

In these 'psalms of anger,' the psalmist asks God to bring divine judgment upon his own enemies. These ungodly foes seek to do him much harm and he asks God to serve justice against them (35; 55; 59; 79; 109).

1. Help Petitioned
As the psalmist is surrounded by enemies, he pleads with God to intervene and defeat them. He asks that God fight on his behalf and devastate his enemies (35:1-3, 19-25; 55:1-3, 16-21; 59:1-4; 59:1-3, 13-15, ; 79:1-5, 8-9; 109:1-5, 26-29). Psalm 35 begins with, and later returns to, this very plea:

Contend, O Lord, with those who contend with me;
Fight against those who fight against me.
Take hold of buckler and shield
And rise up for my help.
Draw also the spear and the battle-axe to meet those
    who pursue me;
Say to my soul, 'I am your salvation'...
Do not let those who are wrongfully my enemies rejoice
    over me;
Nor let those who hate me without cause wink maliciously.
For they do not speak peace,
But they devise deceitful words against those who are
    quiet in the land.
They opened their mouth wide against me;
They said, 'Aha, aha, our eyes have seen it!'
You have seen it, O Lord, do not keep silent;
O Lord, do not be far from me.
Stir up Yourself, and awake to my right
And to my cause, my God and my Lord.
Judge me, O Lord my God, according to Your
    righteousness,
And do not let them rejoice over me.
Do not let them say in their heart, 'Aha, our desire!'
Do not let them say, 'We have swallowed him up!'
                              (35:1-3, 19-25)!

2. Imprecation Expressed

The focal point of these individual imprecatory psalms is the
plea of the psalmist for God to judge his enemies (35:4-8; 55:9-
11; 59:5-8, 12-15; 69:22-28; 79:6-7, 10-12; 109:6-20). Psalm 35
requests that divine judgment fall upon the psalmist's foes:

Let those be ashamed and dishonored who seek my life;
Let those be turned back and humiliated who devise evil
    against me.
Let them be like chaff before the wind,
With the angel of the Lord driving them on.
Let their way be dark and slippery,

With the angel of the LORD pursuing them.
For without cause they hid their net for me;
Without cause they dug a pit for my soul.
Let destruction come upon him unawares,
And let the net which he hid catch himself;
Into that very destruction let him fall   (35:4-8).

3. Praise Vowed

Moreover, the psalmist vows in the midst of his mounting dangers, to praise God, who will hear his cry for help (35:9-10, 18, 27-28). Psalm 35 expresses this confidence:

And my soul shall rejoice in the LORD;
It shall exult in His salvation.
All my bones will say, 'LORD, who is like You,
Who delivers the afflicted from him who is too strong
     for him,
And the afflicted and the needy from him who robs
     him?'...
I will give You thanks in the great congregation;
I will praise You among a mighty throng...
Let them shout for joy and rejoice, who favor my
     vindication;
And let them say continually, 'The LORD be magnified,
Who delights in the prosperity of His servant.'
And my tongue shall declare Your righteousness
And Your praise all day long   (35:9-10, 18, 27-28).

4. Crisis Detailed

Next, the psalmist details the harm done to him by his enemies. Considerable personal injury has been suffered by the psalmist (35:11-16; 55:12-15; 59:3, 6-7, 14-15). Psalm 35 details the personal damages that have been inflicted upon the writer:

Malicious witnesses rise up;
They ask me of things that I do not know.
They repay me evil for good,
To the bereavement of my soul.

But as for me, when they were sick, my clothing was
    sackcloth;
I humbled my soul with fasting,
And my prayer kept returning to my bosom.
I went about as though it were my friend or brother;
I bowed down mourning, as one who sorrows for a mother.
But at my stumbling they rejoiced and gathered them-
    selves together;
The smiters whom I did not know gathered together
    against me,
They slandered me without ceasing.
Like godless jesters at a feast,
They gnashed at me with their teeth   (35:11-16).

COMMUNITY IMPRECATORY

Much like the individual imprecations, there is one psalm, Psalm
137, which is expressed on behalf of the entire believing community. It is a request for divine justice and eventual judgment
to be served on Israel's enemies, the Babylonians. This psalm
was written while God's people languished under Babylonian
captivity. Psalm 137 develops as follows:

1. Distress Spoken
As one deeply distressed, the psalmist speaks for all God's
people during their painful ordeal in Babylonian exile. He pours
out his sorrowful heart to God, as they could no longer sing to
God. Psalm 137 expresses this sorrowful lamentation:

By the rivers of Babylon,
There we sat down and wept,
When we remembered Zion.
Upon the willows in the midst of it
We hung our harps.
For there our captors demanded of us songs,
And our tormentors mirth, saying, 'Sing us one of the
    songs of Zion.'

How can we sing the LORD's song in a foreign land
                                                    (137:1-4)?

2. Praise Vowed

Having stated his distress, the psalmist declares his vow of praise for God. Though the people of God suffer greatly, they will, nevertheless, declare God's greatness with much joy. Psalm 137 states:

> If I forget you, O Jerusalem,
> May my right hand forget her skill.
> May my tongue cling to the roof of my mouth
> If I do not remember you,
> If I do not exalt Jerusalem
> Above my chief joy   (137:5-6).

3. Imprecation Expressed

Finally, the psalmist, representing all God's people in Babylonian captivity, requests that God deal with his enemies, those who oppress God's people, as they have dealt with him and devastate them. Psalm 137 concludes:

> Remember, O Lord, against the sons of Edom
> The day of Jerusalem,
> Who said, 'Raze it, raze it to its very foundation.'
> O daughter of Babylon, you devastated one,
> How blessed will be the one who repays you
> With the recompense with which you have repaid us.
> How blessed will be the one who seizes and
>   dashes your little ones
> Against the rock   (137:7-9).

TRUST

Yet another major classification of psalms is the trust psalms. These worship songs express the psalmist's confidence that God may be trusted in times of difficulty and despair. Though the earth may

sway and circumstances be in upheaval, God's providential care
should be readily acknowledged and resolutely trusted. Those who
have believed in Him should express immovable faith in Him with
the entirety of their lives (11; 16; 23; 27; 62; 63; 91; 121; 125; 131).

INDIVIDUAL TRUST

In these psalms of trust, the psalmist declares his personal trust
in the LORD. In his darkest hours of difficulty, he will intentionally abide in God. In so doing, he calls upon others to do the
same. Along with this individual trust in God is contained a
lament. The lament and the trust are interconnected (4; 16; 23;
27; 62; 73). The psalmist's faith in God is refined by the fiery
trial. Its various parts, by and large, are as follows:

1. Trust Declared
The dominant feature of this type of psalm is a declaration of the
psalmist's trust in God. Strong and firm is his individual faith in
the LORD (4:3, 8; 16:1b, 2, 7b-10; 23:1-3; 27:1a, 2a, 3, 5b-6a, 8, 9b,
10, 13; 62:1-2, 5-7, 11-12; 73:1, 17, 18-20, 23-28). These psalms
begin by expressing this trust in God, and such confidence continues throughout the psalm. Psalm 62 begins by expressing this
trust in God, a theme which continues throughout the psalm:

> My soul waits in silence for God only;
> From Him is my salvation,
> He only is my rock and my salvation,
> My stronghold; I shall not be greatly shaken...
> My soul, wait in silence for God only,
> For my hope is from Him.
> He only is my rock and my salvation,
> My stronghold; I shall not be shaken.
> On God my salvation and my glory rest;
> The rock of my strength, my refuge is in God...
> Once God has spoken;
> Twice I have heard this:
> That power belongs to God;

And lovingkindness is Yours, O Lord,
For You recompense a man according to his work
(62:1-2, 5-7, 11-12).

2. Lament Spoken

With each of these individual psalms of trust, there is mention
of the crisis in which the psalmist finds himself. He describes
the dire circumstances in which he calls out to God with his
trust (4:1, 2; 16:4; 23:4-5; 27:1b, 2-3, 5, 11b, 12; 62:3-4; 73:3-15,
21-22). Psalm 62 laments:

How long will you assail a man,
That you may murder him, all of you,
Like a leaning wall, like a tottering fence?
They have counseled only to thrust him down from his
high position;
They delight in falsehood;
They bless with their mouth,
But inwardly they curse   (62:3-4).

3. Others Invited

Having declared his own trust in God, the psalmist now invites
others to do the same (4:4-5; 27:14; 62:8, 10). He urges all to follow
his example of resting in the Lord. Psalm 62 invites all who hear:

Trust in Him at all times, O people;
Pour out your heart before Him;
God is a refuge for us…
Do not trust in oppression
and do not vainly hope in robbery;
If riches increase, do not set your heart upon them
(62:8, 10).

4. Trust Explained

The basis of this trust in God is built upon a sturdy foundation, the goodness and greatness of God (4:7; 16:5-6, 11; 23:1;
62:11-12a). Psalm 62 concludes by emphatically stating his trust
in God:

Once God has spoken;
Twice I have heard this;
That power belongs to God;
And lovingkindness is Yours, O Lord   (62:11-12a).

COMMUNITY TRUST

These community psalms of trust are very similar to the individual one, except these songs use the plural pronouns 'we' or 'our' (90; 115; 123; 124; 125; 126). In other words, the trust is a community trust, corporately exercised by all the people.

1. Trust Declared
These psalms begin with a firm statement of faith in God, a trust that is unshakable (90:1-2; 115:1, 9b, 10b, 11b; 123:2-3; 124:6; 125:1-2; 126:1-3). All who trust God will be immovable. Psalm 125 begins this way:

Those who trust in the LORD
Are as Mount Zion, which cannot be moved
But abides forever   (125:1).

2. Trust Fortified
The firm foundation for the believers' trust in God is the LORD's immovable character and irrevocable purposes which cannot be shaken (115:12-13; 123:1; 124:8; 125:2). Psalm 125 expresses this trust:

As the mountains surround Jerusalem,
so the LORD surrounds His people
from this time forth and forever   (125:2).

3. Personal Crisis
The underlying need for their trust in God is the encroaching presence of the wicked, which threatens the stability and success of the land (90:3-11; 115:2; 123:3b-4; 124:1-5, 7; 125:3). Psalm 125 states the crisis:

For the scepter of wickedness shall not rest
    upon the land of the righteous,
So that the righteous will not put forth their
    hands to do wrong   (125:3).

4. God Petitioned

Amid the invading crisis, the psalmist petitions God to intervene and do good (90:12-15, 17; 115:14-15; 123:3; 125:4-5;
126:4). He appeals to the Lord to intervene and to uphold God's
people. Psalm 125 concludes this way:

Do good, O LORD, to those who are good
And to those who are upright in their hearts.
But as for those who turn aside to their crooked ways,
The LORD will lead them away with the doers of iniquity.
Peace be upon Israel   (125:4-5).

ACROSTIC

Several of the psalms employ a favorite literary device known
as an alphabetical acrostic. In this form of communication,
the first letter of the first word of a line, verse, or stanza begins
with the next, successive Hebrew consonant in the alphabet and
advances progressively in sequential order through the twenty-
two consonants of the Hebrew letters. This medium, no doubt,
served to assist in memorizing the psalms, especially when
set to music. Likewise, it conveyed the ordered structure of
the psalm and organized thought as recorded by the author. It
also indicated the full breadth of the subject matter addressed,
expressing comprehensive thought, i.e., from A to Z.

Psalms 9 and 10: These psalms contain an irregular
acrostic that runs through their verses.

Psalms 25 and 34: These are the only two psalms which
build with the acrostic of the entire Hebrew alphabet of
all twenty-two letters.

Psalms 111 and 112: Each of these psalms has ten verses with twenty-two lines on which each letter builds.

Psalm 119: This is the most advanced psalm having twenty-two stanzas of eight verses, each stanza beginning with the next letter of the Hebrew alphabet, stressing the perfection of God's Word.

Psalm 145: The psalm has twenty-one verses, omitting the Hebrew letter '*nun*' between verses 13 and 14.

MISCELLANEOUS

There are still other smaller categories of psalms that, according to similarities, allow them to be grouped together in various ways. When classified more specifically as to subject matter and attitude of writing, many different types of psalms begin to emerge, as we have already seen. Still, additional classifications for psalms are distinguishable, including:

Salvation Psalms. These psalms, though few in number, review the history of God's saving works among His people, wherein He rescues them from danger and harm's way. Especially highlighted is God's deliverance of Israel from bondage in Egypt (78; 105; 106; 135; 136).

Zion Psalms. These psalms focus upon the holy city, Jerusalem, the place where the Temple was built and where the Davidic king exercised authority (46; 48; 76; 84; 87; 122).

Pilgrim Psalms. These festive psalms promote a heart for praising God as Israel traveled to Jerusalem to celebrate their three annual feasts (43; 46; 48; 76; 84; 87; 120-134). These all have the heading 'A song of ascents,' referring to Israel's ascent upward to Jerusalem. The contents of these psalms describe the trip to Jerusalem taken by pilgrim worshipers.

THE NEED OF THE HOUR

In this critical hour of church history, pastors must recapture the centrality and pungency of biblical preaching as it once rose to prominence in the Reformation and in other golden eras of the church. The need of the hour is expository preaching that is text-centered, Word-driven, genre-sensitive, and God-exalting. May the Lord of the church raise up a new generation of expositors who are armed with the sword of the Spirit and able to handle the full spectrum of biblical genres. May the plea of Charles Haddon Spurgeon who witnessed the decline of dynamic preaching in his day be heard and answered in this day:

> We want again Luthers, Calvins, Bunyans, Whitefields, men fit to mark eras, whose names breathe terror in our foemen's ears. We have dire need of such. Whence will they come to us? They are the gifts of Jesus Christ to the Church, and will come in due time. He has power to give us back again a golden age of preachers, and when the good old truth is once more preached by men whose lips are touched as with a live coal from off the altar, this shall be the instrument in the hand of the Spirit for bringing about a great and thorough revival of religion in the land. I do not look for any other means of converting men beyond the simple preaching of the gospel and the opening of men's ears to hear it. The moment the Church of God shall despise the pulpit, God will despise her. It has been through the ministry that the Lord has always been pleased to review and bless His Churches.[1]

May this prayer be answered in this hour.

8

CONSIDER
THE TITLE

*Determine the relevance
the title supplies to the psalm*

To this point, the preparatory steps that the expositor must take in order to effectively expound a psalm are being traced. A particular psalm has been selected, and its classification has been determined. Now the expositor is ready to begin to examine the psalm itself. This task starts with noting its superscription, if there is one. Such a descriptive title sits atop many of the psalms. These headings provide helpful information in understanding each psalm.

More than three-fourths of the psalms include a superscription. That is a total of 116 psalms to be exact. While many of the titles, perhaps most, may have been added long after the writing of the psalm, they nevertheless are to be considered helpful. These notations contain valuable information for rightly understanding the psalms' literary and historical context. These psalm titles indicate authorship, literary category, and historical context. These important inscriptions indicate who wrote the psalm and the specific circumstance in which the author found himself.

INTRODUCTORY HEADINGS

There are only thirty-four psalms without an introductory title. These are sometimes called 'orphan' psalms, being without a heading. They are found mainly in Books III through V. These anonymous worship songs tend to come in clusters: Psalms 91; 93-97; 99; 104-107; 111-119; 135-137; 146-150. In Books I and II, only Psalms 1-2; 10; 33; 43; 71 lack titles. Though Psalms 10 and 43 are without titles, they are actually continuations of the preceding psalms. Further, some headings serve as psalm endings and reveal musical instructions — and nothing more. For example, the title on Psalm 55 reads, 'To the choir director; according to Jonath elem rehokim.' These inscriptions assist the worship leader and congregation in understanding and singing these worship songs.

The psalms' titles are to be considered accurate and reliable, though commentators disagree on whether they are inspired. Many support the antiquity and authenticity of the psalm headings.[1] Expositors readily accept the inspiration of the psalm headings and endings outside the Psalter (e.g., 2 Sam. 22:1; Isa. 38:9; Hab. 3:1, 19), therefore one should accept the psalm headings and endings within the Psalter. Thus, expositors should note the following aspects of these opening superscriptions:

BIBLICAL AUTHOR

First, the superscriptions help identify the author of many of the psalms. The psalmists include: (1) David (75 psalms); (2) Asaph (50; 73; 74-83); (3) the sons of Korah (42; 44; 45; 47-49; 84; 85; 87); (4) Solomon (72; 127); (5) Moses (90); (6) Heman (88); (7) Ethan (89); and (8) other anonymous authors. Thus, these titles help to determine many authors of the psalms.

A MATTER OF DEBATE

It should be understood that determining the author of a psalm is a matter of some debate. The controversy centers around the use of the Hebrew preposition *le*, translated as either 'of' or 'for' in the superscription. The question revolves around whether it should be translated 'by,' 'for,' or 'to.' In the latter case, the preposition would indicate that the psalm is dedicated to the one named, not written by him. However, the preposition is best understood in the authorial sense unless there are indications to the contrary.

One such example is the familiar heading 'A psalm of David.' Willem A. VanGemeren notes:

> The difficulty of how to understand the preposition *le* ('for,' 'belonging to,' or 'concerning') is crucial in determining authorship… Essential to the matter of authenticity is the exegetical issue of the meaning of the preposition 'of' in the headings, e.g., A Psalm *of* David. The preposition raises two concerns: the ambiguity of meaning and the ambiguity of use. First, the *meaning* of the preposition *le* is largely determinative. It may be translated in a variety of ways: 'to,' 'of,' 'concerning,' 'associated with,' 'dedicated to.' It is clear that the translation 'of David' is significantly different from the rendering 'concerning David.' Second, the use in the Psalter is equally ambiguous.[2]

THE AUTHORIAL SENSE

When determining a psalm's writer, it is generally agreed that it is best to understand the preposition *le* ('of') as an indication of authorship. C. Hassell Bullock writes, 'I suggest that we understand the term in the authorial sense unless there are indications to the contrary, whether in the superscription or the content of the poem itself. This is the view of Calvin. This preposition is prefixed to the names of David, Solomon, Moses, Asaph, the sons of Korah, and the two Ezrahites. It is difficult to ignore all these associations and deny that any of them are authorial.'[3] The content of Psalm 51, for example, confirms that David wrote Psalm 51, as the heading, 'a psalm of David,' indicates.

HISTORICAL SETTING

Second, the superscriptions often give the historical setting a particular psalm. In examining the title, the expositor will want to ask: When was the psalm written? Why was it written? What was the occasion for the psalm to be written?

EVENTS IN DAVID'S LIFE

Thirteen psalms directly relate to specific incidents in David's life (3; 7; 18; 34; 51; 52; 54; 56; 57; 59; 60; 63; 142). In preaching the Psalms, any expositor will want to become reacquainted with the life of David, rereading the events of his storied career as the anointed king of Israel (1 Sam. 16-31; 2 Sam. 1-24; 1 Chr. 1-29). The superscriptions relating to David's life supply historical background for the psalms listed below and identify important events in David's life:

Psalm 3, when David fled from Absalom his son (2 Sam. 15:13-17).

Psalm 7, concerning the words of Cush a Benjamite (2 Sam. 16:5; 19:16).

Psalm 18, the day the Lord delivered David from his enemies/Saul (2 Sam. 22:1-51).

Psalm 29, at the dedication of the house of David (2 Sam. 5:11, 12; 6:17).

Psalm 34, when David pretended madness before Abimelech (1 Sam. 21:10-15).

Psalm 51, when Nathan confronted David over sin with Bathsheba (2 Sam. 12:1-14).

Psalm 52, when Doeg the Edomite warned Saul about David (1 Sam. 22:9, 10).

Psalm 54, when the Ziphites warned Saul about David (1 Sam. 23:19).

Psalm 56, when the Philistines captured David in Gath (1 Sam. 21:10, 11).

Psalm 57, when David fled from Saul into the cave (1 Sam. 22:1; 24:3).

Psalm 59, when Saul sent men to watch the house in order to kill David (1 Sam. 19:11).

Psalm 60, when David fought against Mesopotamia and Syria (2 Sam. 8:3, 13).

Psalm 63, when David was in the wilderness of Judea (1 Sam. 23:14; or 2 Sam. 15:23-28).

Psalm 142, when David was in a cave (1 Sam. 22:1; 24:3).

THE PSALMS OF DAVID
1ˢᵗ Period (Early life): Pss. 7; 8; 11-13; 16; 17; 22; 23; 34; 35; 52; 54; 56-57; 59
2ⁿᵈ Period (From ascension to throne to great sin): Pss. 8; 9; 10; 15; 16; 17; 18; 19; 20; 21; 23; 24; 26; 29; 36; 58; 60; 68; 101; 108; 110
3ʳᵈ Period (From fall to flight): Pss. 5; 6; 32; 29; 40; 41; 51; 55; 60; 64
4ᵗʰ Period (From flight to restoration): Pss. 3; 4; 27; 28; 31; 61; 63; 69; 70; 143
5ᵗʰ Period (Last period of David's Life): Pss. 139

MUSICAL INSTRUCTION

Third, several psalms carry a musical notation for the worship director and reveal contextual clues. These inscriptions indicate why a psalm was used in public worship (*Gittith* and *Shoshannim*), its special purposes (*Muth-labben, Mahalath, Nehiloth*, and *Al-tashheth*), its topic (*Aijeleth hash-Shahar* and *Jonath elem rehokim*), or special choirs that accompanied it (*Sheminith, Alamoth*, and *Jeduthun*). Some argue that the musical instructions belong at the end of the preceding psalm, not in the psalm titles.[4] These musical inscriptions accompany fifty-five psalms, and include the expression, 'For the Chief Musician.' The Chief Musician served as the conductor of the Temple choir. He trained the choir and led the singing of the psalms in Temple services.

SPECIAL CHOIRS

Some of the musical notations are directed to the singing of special choirs:

1. Alamoth
This term appears only in Psalm 46 [45]. It translates, 'to (the voice of) young women,' indicating that young women sung this psalm (cf. *almah*, Isa. 7:14). A female choir sung this psalm.

2. Sheminith

This term occurs in Psalms 6 and 12. It relates to the Hebrew word for 'eight,' though the exact meaning remains uncertain. It probably means a musical instrument known as an eight-string lyre. In 1 Chronicles 15:20-21, *alamoth* (female choir) parallels *sheminith*, indicating that Psalms 6 and 12 were to be sung by a choir of men.

3. Jeduthun

This term appears in Psalms 39, 61, and 77, referring to one of David's three choir leaders (1 Chr. 16:41-42; 25:1, 6; 2 Chr. 5:12). It is possible it refers to a third choir known as a *jeduthun*, or praise choir. This choir featured songs of praise and thanksgiving (cf. 1 Chr. 25:3).

SPECIAL SEASONS

Other musical notations pertain to the singing of the psalm on the occasion of special seasons:

1. Shoshannim

This term occurs in Psalms 45 and 69 and translates 'lilies,' or 'flowers.' Israel sang these psalms for the Feast of Passover in the spring to remember God's deliverance from Exodus. The expositor must become familiar with the first Passover and the Passover celebration if he wishes to accurately expound these psalms.

2. Sushan Eduth and El Shoshannim

These expressions appear in Psalm 60 in the singular and in Psalm 80 in the plural. They translate, 'Lily of the Covenant,' or 'Lily: Testimonies,' and 'Lilies: Testimonies.' These are psalms for 'a second Passover.'

3. Gittith

This word occurs in Psalms 8, 81, and 84 and translates 'wine-presses' (cf. Neh. 13:15). Three psalms were sung at the Feast of Tabernacles. 'Gittith (Gitt/ith) = 'Winepresses,' recalls the Feast of Tabernacles, the object of which was to commemorate God's great goodness to Israel in their pilgrimage through the wilderness. As the Passover reminded Israel that Jehovah was their Redeemer, so the Tabernacles feast brought to mind that He was also their Keeper. Hence the psalms illustrate reliance on God in times of adversity, and that very plainly.'[5]

DAVID'S SONGS

Still other musical notations surround the life of David. These include the following:

1. Muth-Labben
This term occurs in Psalm 9, and translates, 'The Death of the Son.' Expositors cannot identify with certainty who this son was. Suggestions include Ben (a Levite in 1 Chr. 15:18), an unknown prince, and Absalom. The notation remains obscure. Another reads, 'For the Death of the Champion (Goliath),' rather than 'The Death of the Son.'[6] David penned Psalm 8 shortly after he defeated Goliath to commemorate the event. God had surely 'visited' David on that day (8:4), and Israel had crowned David with 'glory and honor' (8:5). God had 'put under his feet' (8:6) Goliath and 'the beasts of the field' (8:7; 1 Sam. 17:46). Thus, David expresses in Psalm 8 that God gave him dominion in the earth, though he is small and insignificant compared to the majesty of God.

2. Mahalath
This term occurs in Psalm 53 and translates 'dancings.' Israel danced greatly following David's victory over Goliath and the Philistines (1 Sam. 18:6-7). 'One may well conceive David holding in his hand the sword of the fallen giant, and writing this psalm.'[7] In Psalm 88 *Mahalath* is placed next to *Leannoth*, meaning 'dancings and shoutings.' That historical occasion for the dancings and shoutings was David relocating the Ark to Jerusalem (2 Sam. 6:5; 14, 15; 1 Chr. 13:8, 15, 16, 28).

3. Ai Jeleth Hash-Shah Ar

This inscription occurs in Psalm 22, and translates, 'the Hind of the Morning.' 'The "Hind of the Morning" glow — this is an oriental word-picture of the sun as he sheds his rising rays. The traveler watches with keen desire for the first beams of light, and he warmly greets the "Dawn Hind" as he dances on the distant horizon.'[8]

4. Jonath Elem Rehokim

This expression attached to Psalm 56 translates, 'A Dove on Distant Oaks.' David dreamed that he had wings like a dove to fly away and escape the troubles of Absalom's rebellion (2 Sam. 15-19) and the betrayal of his 'familiar friend,' Ahithophel (55:13). In grief, he remarks, 'Oh, that I had wings like a dove! I would fly away and be at rest' (55:6).

HUMILIATION

Another musical notation pertains to a time of personal self-humiliation in the life of the psalmist.

1. Al-tashheth

This term occurs in the title of Psalms 57, 58, 59, and 75, and translates, 'Do not destroy.' In times of sorrow, suffering, and distress, Israel pleaded with God for mercy and deliverance.

OTHER TITLES

There are other musical notations that concern themselves with the playing of a musical instrument:

1. Nehiloth

This term occurs only in Psalm 5 [4] within the Psalter. Because this term lacks a *beth* preposition, it does not mean 'flutes,' but refers to 'inheritances' (as a commemoration). Thus, Psalm 5 is a 'commemoration of Israel's perpetual obligation to God for the inheritance into which the tribes had come.'[9]

2. Neginoth

This term appears in Psalms 4, 6, 54, 55, 61, 67, 76 (and Hab. 3:19). It translates, 'stringed instruments.' Two different stringed instruments, the harp and lyre, accompanied these psalms.

3. Selah

The final musical notation deserving comment is one that is found throughout the Psalter: Selah. This word occurs seventy-one times in the Psalms, particularly in the first three books and served as a musical marker. 'The word SELAH ('life up') gives notice of the beginning of a new section or stanza in a hymn or poem designed for singing. Properly it should be placed at the beginning of such section or stanza.'[10] The word may also mean a lifting up of the voice, or a mighty crescendo. Or it may indicate the lifting up of the mind to ponder and contemplate what was previously said. Thus, it would mean to pause and meditate.

LITERARY CATEGORY

Fourth, other headings of the psalms denote the particular type of literary category into which that particular psalm falls. These are as follows:

1. Psalm

A psalm (*mizmor*) appears in fifty-seven superscriptions and denotes a praise song (3-6; 8-9; 12-13; 15; 17-24; 29-31; 38-41; 47-51; 62-68; 73; 75-77; 79-80; 82-85; 87-88; 92; 98; 100-101; 108-110; 139-141; 143). The root (*z-m-r*) often denoted songs with musical accompaniment (33:2; 71:22; 98:5; 147:7; 149:3), or praises accompanied by musical instruments (30:12; 47:6-7; 68:4, 32).

2. Shiggaion

This designation occurs only in Psalm 7, and indicates a hymn of praise.

3. Miktam

This title appears in six psalm titles (16, 56-60) and may mean a private prayer or personal meditation.

4. Maskil
This heading is found in thirteen psalms (32; 42; 44; 45; 52-55; 74; 78; 88; 89; 142) and related to a root (*s-k-l*, 'to be wise, instruct') and probably signifies a didactic psalm (cf. 32:8).

5. Song
This superscription (*sir*) occurs more than thirty times (30; 45-46; 48; 65-69; 75-76; 83; 87-88; 92; 108; 120-134) and simply designates a song (1 Chr. 6:31-32). Sometimes *sir* is combined with other titles, such as 'A song. A psalm' (48, 66, 83, 88, 108); 'A psalm. A song' (30; 65; 67; 68; 75; 76; 87; 92); 'A wedding song' (45); or 'A song. A psalm of the Sons of Korah… A *maskil* of Heman the Ezrahite' (88).

6. Psalm of Petition
This inscription (*tehillah)* occurs only in Psalm 145 and is derived from the root (*h-l-l)* from which 'hallelujah' (praise Yah [weh]) comes.

7. Petition
This word (*lehazkir*) means 'to remember' and signifies a fervent call to the Lord to remember the psalmist (38).

8. Teaching
This word designates that the purpose of the psalm, only Psalm 60, be used to instruct, i.e., to teach David's fighting men how to relate to one another.

9. For the Sabbath
This title identifies the use of this one psalm (92) in relation to the Sabbath.

10. Giving Thanks
This inscription occurs only in Psalm 100 to indicate that it was used to express gratitude.

11. Prayer

This superscription, appearing only in Psalm 90, emphasizes an important plea to God.

THE PSALMIST'S WORLD

Before the expositor applies his psalm to the congregation, he must discover as much of the original context of the psalm as possible. A key way that he discovers the original context involves assessing the psalm titles and endings. To this very point, Derek Kidner writes, 'It may seem unnecessary to attach much importance to the 'small print' of the psalms [titles]... If we are intended to share the heart-searchings of a man as exceptional and as sorely tried as David, we shall be the poorer if we insist on treating his works as anonymous and divorced from his eventful life.'[11] The psalm headings and endings tip off the preacher to key contextual clues that casual readers often overlook.

The literary and historical psalm headings and the musical endings provide a gateway into the ancient world of the psalmist. That is, the psalm titles help expositors understand Israel's psalms, hymns, and spiritual songs. They contribute significant history for practitioners of grammatical-historical hermeneutics.

MAKE THE
OBSERVATIONS

*Read the individual psalm many times
and scrutinize the text of that psalm*

The next critical step in the expository process is known as the observation phase. By necessity, this stage must precede the subsequent step of interpretation. The observation phase asks the basic question, 'What does the Bible *say*?' Interpretation then focuses upon 'What does the text *mean*?' One must know what the text actually states before it can be accurately determined what it means. This important stage is fundamental in the investigative study process. We cannot determine what Scripture means until we know what Scripture says.

To this very point, noted expositor John MacArthur states, 'Observation includes a broad awareness of the terms, structure, and literary form of a passage.'[1] Such keen observations of the biblical text must be undertaken carefully and persistently. Every part of a passage must be examined. Martin Luther likened this critical step of observation to the determined effort to gather apples from a tree: 'First I shake the whole tree, that the ripest may fall. Then I climb the tree and shake each limb, and then each branch and then each twig, and then I look under each leaf.'[2] In other words, the German Reformer knew if he was to adequately study the truth of Scripture, he must carefully observe every aspect of the biblical text, looking under every leaf of every branch.

DIGGING DEEP INTO THE TEXT

In reading any psalm, the expositor should have an alert eye. He should read the passage repeatedly, being keenly aware of its basic content, message, and parts. He will want to scrutinize it multiple times until he becomes intimately acquainted with its important features and specific details. In so doing, the expositor must identify the biblical context, key people, historical circumstances, and central idea.[3]

Perhaps J. C. Ryle states it best, 'We must read our Bibles, like men digging for hidden treasure.'[4] This is to say, expositors must dig into the text, as miners looking for precious gold, until they extract its riches. Martyn Lloyd-Jones adds, 'You have to question your text, to put questions to it, and especially this question — What is this saying? What is the particular doctrine here, the special message? In the preparation of a sermon nothing is more important than that.'[5] In other words, expositors must tunnel down into the depths of the passage until they discover the buried nuggets of truth that lie beneath the surface.

BIBLICAL CONTEXT

First, the expositor must take note of where the individual psalm fits into the overall structure of the Psalms. It has been well said: a text without a context is a pretext. Even so, a psalm without a context is unattached in one's thinking. Consideration needs to be given to:

INDIVIDUAL BOOK

As has already been discussed in Chapter 4, compiling the Psalms involved a lengthy process of some 1,000 years. The Psalter was arranged in five books, those being Psalms 1-41; 42-72; 73-89; 90-106; and 107-150. Each individual book has its own primary theme. Many believe the central idea is related to the five books of Moses, Genesis through Deuteronomy, respectively. Thus, as an expositor approaches an individual psalm, he must ask himself: In which of these five books is this individual psalm found? What is the overall theme of this book? How does this psalm fit into this general theme? Does this psalm begin one of the five books? Does it conclude one of these books? What psalm precedes it? What psalm follows? Is there any significance to this location?

ENTIRE PSALTER

As the compilers of the Psalter carried out their work, they did so within the context of their own day. For example, Psalm 89 records the fall of Jerusalem at the hands of the Babylonians. It appropriately concludes Book III because it parallels what had occurred in Israel, bringing to conclusion this sad period in Israel's history. Psalm 90 — a psalm written by Moses after their Egyptian captivity during the days of Israel's wilderness wanderings — begins Book IV. This is striking, given the interesting parallel of when Psalm 90 was placed into the Psalter, a time in which Israel has just returned from Babylonian captivity, after their journey through the wilderness between Babylon and Jerusalem.

KEY PEOPLE

Second, the expositor will want to make general observations within the psalm. Specifically, he must begin with the key people. Who is the speaker? Who is the audience?

MAIN SPEAKERS

The first step of observation asks: Who is speaking? David? The sons of Korah? Asaph? Solomon? Moses? Heman? Ethan? An anonymous author? Israel? Or is the Speaker God Himself? An enemy of the psalmist? Generally, the psalmists speak on their own behalf. These psalms use the singular personal pronoun 'I' (89:1-2, 19-20). Yet often within these individual psalms, there is a corporate aspect as well, employing the plural possessive pronoun 'our' (89:17-18). Other individual prayers conclude with a summons to Israel (131:3).

Other times the psalmist speaks on Israel's behalf. The Songs of Ascents (120-134), for example, are corporate psalms in which the psalmist speaks not merely for himself, but for the entire nation, as the plural pronouns indicate (124:1, 7-8). Sometimes the psalmist offers an individual prayer on behalf of the entire nation (25:22). The expositor should remain alert for the shift from the individual perspective (51:16-17) to the corporate perspective (vv. 18-19).

In some psalms God Himself speaks through the psalmist to His people. For example, Psalm 50 contains the first-person pronouncements of God. This is especially characteristic of the Asaph Psalms (50; 73-83): 'Gather My godly ones to Me, Those who have made a covenant with Me by sacrifice' (50:3-5). On other occasions, the psalmist expresses the verbal assaults of his enemies. At other times, the speaker is one of the enemies of God who is taunting the psalmist: 'The kings of the earth take their stand and the rulers take counsel together Against the Lord and against His Anointed, saying, "Let us tear their fetters apart And cast away their cords from us!"' (2:2-3). Thus, the expositor listens for a change of speaker.

ADDRESSED RECIPIENTS

In turn, the expositor should ask: *Who* is addressed? Did the author address God? Israel? His enemies? Himself? Or readers in general? Though each party receives attention, the psalmist primarily addresses God Himself: 'Give ear to my words, O Lord, Consider my groaning' (5:1). This is what makes the Psalter so unique. Every other Bible book is God speaking to man, but the Psalter, on the whole, is largely man addressing God.

At other times, the psalmist addresses Israel: 'But know that the Lord has set apart the godly man for Himself; The Lord hears when I call to Him' (4:3). Or, again: 'O Israel, hope in the Lord From this time forth and forever' (131:3). Occasionally, he addresses his enemies: 'O sons of men, how long will my honor become a reproach? How long will you love what is worthless and aim at deception? Selah' (4:2). Or, on another occasion, 'But it is you, a man my equal, My companion and my [former] familiar friend' (55:13-14). At times, the poet counsels himself: 'Bless the Lord, O my soul, and all that is within me, bless His holy name' (103:1). Frequently his readers are in view: 'The Lord is my Shepherd, I shall not want' (23:1).

HISTORICAL CIRCUMSTANCES

Third, the expositor must give attention to the general circumstances of the psalm. Evidence may be found in the superscription or postscript, a feature discussed in Chapter 7. Also, important clues surface with a casual reading of the psalm itself.

HEART MOTIVATIONS

The expositor should inquire why this psalm was written? Was it written as an expression of praise/thanksgiving? A teaching of divine wisdom? A heart-felt lament? A soul-perplexing dilemma? A plea for deliverance? A confession of sin? An acknowledgement of divine blessing? A declaration of God's majesty? A jarring imprecation? An affirmation of resolute trust?

The psalm titles help immensely to determine purpose, especially with the psalms of David. For example, the heading of Psalm 51 reads: 'A Psalm of David, when Nathan the prophet came to him, after he had gone into Bathsheba.' That title tips off the reader to 2 Samuel 11-12 which records David's tragic downfall and Nathan's bold rebuke. The ending of Psalm 8, 'For the Death of the Champion (Goliath),' directs the preacher to 1 Samuel 17 to discover David's motivation for writing the psalm: his unprecedented victory over the uncircumcised Philistine.

However, most psalms omit background information, leaving the expositor to ask diagnostic questions: What is the problem being addressed? What moved the psalmist to write? In Psalm 117, for instance, God's covenant love and enduring truth (v. 2) motivated the psalmist to write. Psalm 1 possesses no historical ties, so the expositor observes that the psalmist's motivation came from a desire for readers to take the prosperous path of the wise, rather than the destructive path of fools.

Expressed Emotions

The expositor also considers the attitude of the psalmist: How is the psalm spoken? Discerning the psalmist's tone aids interpretation. Is his tone jubilant? Is it sad? Is it confident? Or fearful? Is his voice triumphant? Or is it one of defeat? *How* the psalmist speaks matters as much as *what* he speaks. Praises are upbeat, laments are downcast, instruction is matter-of-fact, and imprecations are fiery and stern. Tone signals literary type.

Many psalms, such as Psalm 13, move from extreme discouragement (vv. 1-2) to great delight (vv. 5-6). In Psalm 87, the sons of Korah overflow with joy (e.g., 87:7), which the musical ending also confirms, 'Song. A Psalm of the sons of Korah. For the choir director; according to Mahalath Leannoth [dancings and shoutings].'

Psalm 88, on the other hand, is the saddest psalm in the entire Psalter. Here Heman the Ezrahite grieves over 'troubles' (v. 3), weakness (v. 4), 'the lowest pit' (v. 6), 'loathing' (v. 8), 'affliction' (v. 9), and 'terrors' (v. 15). In Psalm 108:8-9, David utters a fiery imprecation toward his enemy: 'Let his days be few; Let another take his office. Let his children be fatherless and his wife a widow.'

CENTRAL IDEA

Fourth, each psalm must be read as a literary unit with the overall flow and patterns of development in view. Expositors must not divorce single verses from the whole or isolate ideas from their circles of content. In order to grasp the key ideas, the expositor identifies the repetition, traces the progression, observes the stanzas, and summarizes the psalm:

REOCCURRING THOUGHTS

The preacher must watch for repeated words or phrases. For example, Psalm 8 begins and ends with a refrain which frames the psalm with praise and wonder: 'O LORD, our Lord, How majestic is Your name in all the earth' (vv. 1, 9). Also examine the preceding and following psalms to see if the same refrain, words, or phrase occurs. Psalms 42 and 43 obviously connect, due to the repeated refrain: 'Why are you in despair, O my soul? And why have you become disturbed within me?' (42:5, 11; 43:5). The same could be said of Psalms 1 and 2, which begin and end with the identical 'How blessed' (1:1; 2:12): Likewise, Psalm 119: 'How blessed are those whose way is blameless, Who walk in the law of the Lord. How blessed are those who observe His testimonies, Who seek Him with all their heart' (119:1-2).

BUILDING THEMES

The preacher must then ask: *How* does the psalm progress?

Does it start in the valley of despair and end on the mountain top of triumph? Does it begin with praise for God and then give reasons for that praise? Does it start with defeat and end with victory? Does it begin low in spirit and conclude low? Each of the psalms is characterized by its form. That is, each psalm will share similar structural characteristics with other psalms of its particular type. Thus, the category of each psalm often follows a predictable pattern that is common to the classification of that psalm. In Psalm 6, King David states the problem (6:1), trusts God (6:2-4), complains to God (6:5) and complains against his enemies (6:7, 10). In Psalm 126, sadness turns to singing as the psalmist moves from exile to restoration.

Stanza Divisions

An initial observation of any psalm should always include a survey of the stanzas. How many stanzas are there? What does each stanza say? How do the stanzas relate? What is the high note in this unfolding progression of stanzas? What is the low point? Each stanza contains one central theme. After marking off the stanzas, the preacher should write a tightly-worded sentence that summarizes the main idea of that stanza. This sentence should be a brief, concise statement that crystallizes the core idea of the stanza.

To determine the point of the stanza, six interrogatives deserve attention: (1) *Who*? Who is speaking to whom? (2) *What*? What is the speaker saying? Is he offering praise? Expressing lament? Confessing sin? Requesting help? Voicing complaint? (3) *Why*? Why does the speaker say what he does? Is it gratitude for God's greatness? Hurt feelings for difficulty? (4) *Where*? Where is the speaker? In the wilderness? In the palace? In Zion? En route to Zion? (5) *When*? When does he write? In a time of duress? After a victory over his foes? During a time of prolonged silence from God? (6) *How*? How does the speaker express himself? With celebration? With heartache? With longing? With urgency?

For example, in the literary masterpiece known as Psalm 23, David presents a beautiful allegory (extended metaphor) of the shepherd (vv. 1-4). Employing the six interrogatives to identify the location (open field), the instruments (rod and staff), the scene (pasture, water, restoration), and the adversity ('the valley of the shadow of death'), enables the expositor to identify the key idea of verses 1-4, namely, 'The Lord is my shepherd' (v. 1). In verses 5-6, David introduces a second metaphor — the Lord is my host. As the preacher uses the six interrogatives, he finds that the host metaphor parallels the shepherd metaphor in location (tent), instruments (goodness and covenant love), the scene (table, ointment, wine), and the adversity ('my enemies'). Thus, employing the six interrogatives helps the expositor observe the key idea of each section.

SUMMARY SENTENCE

After writing a summary sentence for each stanza, the expositor crafts a summary statement for the entire psalm. Each stanza summary sentence should be gathered together and compressed in one summary sentence of the entire psalm. In the case of each psalm, identifying its central theme requires the preacher to consider the following:

What is the overriding message of this *entire* psalm? The dominant theme will not necessarily flow from one verse per se. Nor will it emerge from one stanza. Rather, the central idea of the psalm will surface from the whole psalm. In addition, the central theme will often be identified by key words or certain truths that reemerge throughout the entire psalm. The main idea may be stated in the opening verses of the psalm only to be later repeated in its closing verses. Moreover, the big idea of a psalm is often found toward the end of the psalm in the climactic position. In other words, the entire psalm is the unfolding of an idea that is not fully revealed until the end. Also, while most of the psalms are not interconnected, some are. Some psalms are joined together as a two-fold unit and constitute one central idea. Thus, the central idea of a psalm is sometimes discovered by seeing it in relationship to the previous, or following, psalm. For example, Psalms 3 and 4 seem to form a morning and evening devotion. Psalms 9 and 10 form an acrostic,[6] while Psalms 127 and 128 focus upon the family.

This summary sentence captures 'the psalm in a nutshell.' No psalm is ready to be preached until its central thrust is reduced to one short, crystal clear sentence. Stephen F. Olford writes, 'The dominating theme is the truth that the text proclaims. It is the central idea of the text. It is the 'big idea,' and it is the unifying element of the sermon. A message is enhanced by unity and unity is aided greatly if the main idea (also called the subject, the proposition, the sermon in a sentence, the central idea, or the dominating theme) is stated clearly.'[7]

SATURATED WITH PRAISE

The key in this stage of the sermon preparation is reading, reading, and then *more* reading of the biblical passage. The expositor must pour over the text of the psalm to be preached. At this point, the expositor must familiarize himself with the specific particulars of the psalm. Before he consults commentaries and instigates his word studies, he must read and reread the selected psalm, over and over again, until it is lodged into his mind.

He should read the psalm prayerfully, with his heart open to God. He should also read it carefully, with pen and paper in hand, underlining and underscoring what is important. Further, he should read it meditatively, pondering the text and what it says. He should read it devotionally, applying its message to one's own heart. Moreover, he should read it attentively, with an alert mind for the essential parts of the text.

Expositors must be careful readers of the text, like a sponge absorbing the biblical text soaking up its truths.

UNIT III

THE INTERPRETATION PHASE

UNDERSTAND THE LAWS

*Know the laws of interpretation that govern
the meaning of the words and message of the psalm*

After observing what the psalm says, the expositor must determine what it actually means. To this very point, John MacArthur asserts,

> Since all true preaching must be expository, the preacher is called to study in preparation... The Bible is the field you will plow all your life. It is the mine you will dig all your life. And it requires a radical commitment to diligence. You must preach the true sense of Scripture... The meaning of

the Scripture is the Scripture. You have to preach the sense
of it as God has intended it, and He only intended it to say
one thing. You have to discern what that is.'[1]

In other words, as MacArthur often says, the meaning of the text
is the text. Until you have the meaning of the text, you do not have
the text. All you have, he reasons, is black print on white paper.

Discovering the proper meaning of the psalm is the expositor's greatest challenge. He must discern the precise meaning of
what God is saying in his text before he can preach it. Therefore,
the preacher must know the laws of sound interpretation and
be able to apply them in the diligent study and careful research
of his passage. Discovering the meaning of a passage requires
that he implement a method of interpretation that, at its most
basic level, is known as the literal, historical, and grammatical
approach to interpretation. These core aspects will be covered in
greater detail later in this chapter, but at this point let us introduce ourselves to the three main ones.

Literal, Historical, Grammatical Meaning

First, the *literal* approach takes words at face value and seeks
their natural meaning. This differs from the allegorical or spiritual approach, which assigns a figurative meaning to some texts,
one that is concocted out of thin air, subject to the whimsical
imagination of the preacher. Certainly, a literal hermeneutic
acknowledges the use of figures of speech such as idioms and
poetic language, frequently employed by the psalmist. But in
such cases, the expositor simply determines what the figure of
speech means and teaches it literally.

Second, the *historical* approach identifies the historical background in which the author wrote to his original audience.
What is the historical setting of those addressed in the psalm?
The historical context in which the author finds himself? The
historical backdrop being described?

Third, the *grammatical* approach limits the meaning of a text to the precise rules of grammar and syntax. By using these laws, the preacher is one who is 'accurately handling the word of truth' (2 Tim. 2:15) and is able to 'give the meaning' (Neh. 8:8) of the passage. Attention should be given to the relationship of words within a sentence. What is the main verb? What are the subordinate clauses and phrases? What modifies what?

FIXED LAWS OF INTERPRETATION

Hermeneutics is the science of Bible interpretation. Sound Bible interpretation has fixed laws, like science, or rules, like sports. Hermeneutics are the rules of the game in determining the meaning of a passage. The one who wants to win must play by the rules, or he will be disqualified. Different interpretations stem from disregarding these rules, or from playing by different rules. What are the basic rules of hermeneutics? What laws of interpretation should the preacher use with the Psalms? The expositor must discover the:

LITERAL MEANING

First, the Psalms, as with any portion of Scripture, should be understood in its most literal sense. This means that the most normal or natural meaning of words in a sentence should be sought as a matter of primary importance. On the whole, the psalmist speaks in plain terms and, as such, what he writes should be taken at face value. Only if a literal sense is impossible, absurd, immoral, or a compelling reason suggests otherwise, should a figurative sense be pursued.

THE MOST ORDINARY SENSE

Granted, the Psalms contain many figures of speech and literary symbols. But the initial attempt must always be to determine the literal meaning of any biblical text. This is certainly the approach one must take with the Psalms. Words, phrases, clauses, and sentences, first and foremost, are to be understood in their most ordinary sense — that is, seeking their most simple and direct meaning. No expositor is free to read his own meaning into the psalm. Instead, he must draw out of the text its most straightforward meaning.

Regarding the literal meaning of Scripture, Merrill Unger wrote, 'When the plain sense of Scripture makes common sense, seek no other sense; therefore, take every word at its primary, usual, literal meaning, unless it is patently a rhetorical figure or unless the immediate context, studied carefully in the light of related passages and axiomatic and fundamental truths, clearly points otherwise.'[2] Bernard Ramm further adds, 'Whenever we read a book, an essay, or a poem, we presume the literal sense in the document until the nature of the literature may force us to another level. This is the only conceivable method of beginning or commencing to understand literature of all kinds.'[3] So it is with the Psalms. The expositor should always seek its most literal meaning.

The Natural, Obvious Meaning

In the introduction to *Calvin's Commentary on the Psalms*, James Anderson explains that this literal principle of interpretation undergirded John Calvin's basic approach to extracting the proper meaning from any passage of Scripture. This was certainly true of the great Genevan Reformer's approach to the Psalms. Anderson explains:

> Before this time the mystical and allegorical method of explaining the Scriptures was very prevalent; according to which, the interpreter, dwelling very little or not at all upon the literal sense, sought for hidden and allegorical meanings. But rejecting this mode of interpretation, which contributed little to the right understanding of the word of God, and according to which the meaning was

made to depend entirely upon the fancy of the interpreter, Calvin set himself to the investigation of the grammatical and literal sense, by a careful examination of the Hebrew text, and by a diligent attention to the drift and intention of the writer's discourse… [He had a] great aversion to the mystical method of interpretation, and to the absurd and extravagant lengths to which it was carried by the Fathers.[4]

This literal approach to Scripture became the driving force of the Protestant Reformation. Likewise, it is this very same commitment that must govern interpretation today. The expositor is never free to play fast and loose with a biblical passage. He has no license to impose his own meaning upon a text. Eisegesis — which is the practice of reading into a text what the author never intended — violates sound interpretation. Instead, John Calvin asserted, 'The true meaning of Scripture is the natural and obvious meaning.'[5] This should be the goal of the expositor. He must restrict himself simply to discovering the literal meaning of his passage.

AUTHORIAL INTENT

Second, the expositor who would rightly handle any psalm must ask the crucial question: 'What did the psalmist mean when he wrote this to his original audience?' This is called discovering the authorial intent of the biblical text, apart from imposing any self-derived allegorical meaning that was never intended by the author.

WHAT THE AUTHOR MEANT

Walter Kaiser notes, 'The sole object of the expositor is to explain as clearly as possible what the writer meant when he wrote the text under examination.'[6] To answer this, the preacher must determine the intended thought of the psalmist. He must ask himself: What did the psalmist mean by what he wrote? Kaiser asserts, 'The exegete is on the most solid basis when the author himself has defined the terms he uses.'[7] A careful study of the

immediate context along with a comparison with parallel passages in other psalms may especially help the preacher discover
what the psalmist intends.

UNFOLDING THE WRITER'S MIND

Asserting this law of authorial intent in interpretation, John
Calvin explains:

> Since it is almost his (the interpreter's) only task to unfold the
> mind of the writer whom he has undertaken to expound, he
> misses his mark, or at least strays outside his limits, by the
> extent to which he leads his readers away from the meaning
> of his author… It is … presumptuous and almost blasphe-
> mous to turn the meaning of Scripture around without due
> care, as though it were some game that we were playing.
> And yet many scholars have done this at one time.[8]

John Broadus, revered Professor of Preaching at Southern Baptist
Theological Seminary in the nineteenth century, issues the same
warning, 'If we take the passage in a sense entirely foreign to what
the sacred writer designed, as indicated by his connection, then,
as we use it, the phrase is no longer a passage of Scripture at all.'[9]
In other words, the expositor must always seek the precise meaning of what the biblical author meant by what he wrote.

LEXICAL PRINCIPLE

Third, the expositor must devote himself to uncovering the
meaning of the individual words of the psalm. This principle will
be covered more fully in Chapter 11, 'Examine the Language.'
In conjunction with textual criticism and Bible translation, he
must devote himself to a careful study of the key words of the
psalm. To the extent he can, this is best done by working in the
Hebrew language.

THE MEANING OF WORDS

In this consideration, the exegete must target specific words in the psalm that are critical, repetitious, unclear, and emphatic. This involves doing word studies, delving into the etymology of the word and surveying its multiple usages. In order to determine a word's meaning, the expositor will also want to compare with synonyms and antonyms of the word being probed. Further, he will want to parse the key verbs, giving consideration to the nuances of the verb tense. In so doing, he must consult Hebrew lexicons, concordances, theological dictionaries, and commentaries.

Every expositor must answer the key question: How does each word contribute to understanding the passage? Words mean different things in different contexts. One must take into account literary devices, idioms, structure, and genre. At the same time, he must also be on the alert for the pitfalls of word studies. Word study fallacies plague exegesis. Further, a preoccupation with word studies to the neglect of syntactical studies can be a mark of the incomplete study of the preacher. Taken by themselves, word studies, though important, often do not delve deep enough into the biblical text. The word study should always be combined with syntactical and contextual observation.

GRAMMATICAL STRUCTURE

Fourth, the preacher must give attention to the grammar of the psalm. This principle will be discussed at length in Chapter 13, 'Study the Grammar.' This requires that he understand the basic grammatical structure of each sentence. If he can work in the original language, as he does, that is even better.

THE RELATIONSHIP OF WORDS

At this point, the expositor must ask himself: What is the main verb? What is the subject? What are its modifiers? What are the clauses and phrases modifying? How are they connected with the rest of the sentence? What is primary? What is subordinate? What is emphatic? In the Psalms, attention also needs to be given to parallelism, covered in Chapter 12, 'Find the Parallelism,' and to its poetical stanzas.

Every interpreter must ask the basic question: How does each grammatical structure contribute to the argument of the psalmist. He must examine macro syntax (sentences, paragraphs, and entire discourses) in addition to micro syntax (words, phrases, and clauses). That is, he must discover the purpose of the larger portions of text, as well as consider the smaller portions of his text. He must be observant for structural contours. It is difficult to overestimate the importance of grammatical interpretation in discovering the proper meaning of a psalm.

HISTORICAL BACKGROUND

Fifth, the expositor must determine the historical background of the psalm. This hermeneutical principle will be covered more fully in Chapter 14, 'Research the History.' This interpretive key means that the preacher must interpret each psalm according to the facts of history that lie behind it.

DISCOVERING THE BACKDROP

Here, the expositor must ask the basic questions: What was the original background of the psalm? What were the circumstances when it was first written? What was the historical setting of the people and events referenced by the psalmist? What did this psalm mean to the people to whom it was first written? The answers to these questions will help yield the original intent of the psalm.

Every expositor must involve himself with the study of the historical background of his passage. In addition to Scripture, he must also glean important information from the findings of archaeology and ancient extra-biblical sources. When available, these will shed light on the meaning of the text. Grammatical-historical hermeneutics presupposes the historical accuracy of the Bible. Violating the historical principle, accounts for a large portion of faulty Bible interpretation.

GEOGRAPHICAL LOCATION

Sixth, the expositor must also take into account the geographical background of the psalm being studied. This interpretive principle will be covered more extensively in Chapter 16, 'Survey the Geography.' The study of the geography of the individual psalm is absolutely necessary to rightly understanding its proper meaning. Many psalms contain specific names of places that help unlock the right interpretation of the passage. Geography adds yet another dimension to Bible interpretation that moves the preacher toward a closer perspective of life in the ancient Near East.

KNOWLEDGE OF THE LAND

Specifically, the preacher must study the cities, towns, regions, mountains, valleys, streams, rivers, seas, tribal territories, and surrounding nations mentioned in the psalm. Understanding the location, topography, elevation, weather, climate and conditions of these places is critically important in understanding what the psalmist is saying. A significant portion of the Psalter offers predictive prophecies surrounding the first and second comings of Jesus Christ. Those prophecies are intimately tied to specific geographical locations, such as Jerusalem, Zion, the Temple, and the valley of Megiddo. The geographical principle promotes a sound interpretation of prophecy that consistently applies grammatical-historical methodology. Honoring the geographical principle enables the expositor to take the psalm at face value.

CULTURAL CONTEXT

Seventh, the student of Scripture must investigate the cultural background of the psalm. This hermeneutical principle will be covered more extensively in Chapter 15, 'Investigate the Culture.' In short, the cultural setting of ancient Israel provides the backdrop for the book of Psalms. Each psalm must be examined from the perspective of the culture in which it was written.

INVESTIGATE THE CULTURE

In the book of Psalms, this includes a very wide range of cultural categories, involving the worlds of politics, agriculture, society, religions, legal system, economics, military, meteorology, floral variety, precious metals, shepherding, animals, hunting, and more. This requires a breadth of knowledge in many different areas of ancient life in the Hebrew culture. The expositor must always ask: What did this mean in light of the culture of the day?

LITERARY DEVICES

Eighth, the biblical preacher must identify the literary form of the particular psalm with which he is working. The form of language, also called genre, indicates the kind of literature that the biblical author employed. The Old Testament features two basic genres — prose and poetry. Prose includes narrative, history, and law. Poetry includes psalms and wisdom literature. The book of Psalms fits into the broad literary category of poetry, specifically Hebrew poetry.

FEATURES OF HEBREW POETRY

The expositor must be aware of the unique features that are peculiar to Hebrew poetry in the Psalms. These include features such as Hebrew parallelism, stanzas, strophes, refrains, figures of speech, and the rest. As poetry, the Psalms further divide into two basic genres, that of lament and praise. Lament expresses a cry for help, a plea of repentance, or call for God's justice. Praise worships God for who He is and what He has done.[10] The preacher who would rightly handle the Word must have an awareness of the issues involved in the different forms of genres.

Thus, the expositor of the Psalms must ask: What genre of literature am I reading? How did this genre function for the original readers? Ronald Giese notes, 'Genre, though often ignored completely, is actually the level of context to which an interpreter should give the most attention.'[11] Failure to properly classify genre frequently results in misinterpretation. One must discover the form of communication used in the Psalms, and the features that accompany it, rather than imposing upon the text a genre from his contemporary language. He must think like the psalmist is thinking in the literary style he is using.

FIGURATIVE SPEECH

Ninth, the expositor must also seek to understand the meaning of the text using the figurative principle of interpretation. This point will be more fully elaborated in Chapter 17, 'Discern the Figures.' This principle is very important in rightly handling the Psalms because of its many figures of speech. Figurative language is a literary device in which a word or phrase communicates something other than its literal, natural meaning in a way that is vivid, interesting, and memorable.

A Colorful Communication

As a general rule, the expositor should take a passage in its literal sense unless there is good reason for taking it in a figurative way. In the Psalms, this involves the use of many figures of speech, such as the legitimate use of simile, metaphor, allegory, metonymy, synecdoche, hyperbole, personification, apostrophe, anthropomorphism, hypocatastasis, merismus, zoomorphism, and eponymy. These figures of speech convey the normal meaning of a biblical truth in a colorful, picturesque way.

THE LANGUAGE OF POETRY

As poetry, the Psalms employ an exceptional amount of figurative language. The psalmists engage readers with choice figures of speech for dramatic impact and graphic word pictures. Figurative language helps the reader see what psalmist is saying. The Lord knew that the most effective way to communicate His truth was not through abstract, sterile language, but through descriptive word pictures that arrest attention and demand consideration. Thus the interpreter must remain sensitive to the figurative language that frequents poetry.

SYNTHETIC UNITY

Tenth, the expositor of the Psalms must consider the synthetic principle, or what the Reformers called the analogy of Scripture (*analogia scriptura*). The Psalms cannot be rightly interpreted independently of the rest of the Bible. This principle presupposes that the Bible never contradicts itself. Instead, Scripture interprets Scripture. It is *one* Book united in every part. Of this interpretive principle, John MacArthur states: 'Scripture does not contradict itself, but is consistent in its teaching.'[12] Put another way, Scripture is its own best interpreter, and often provides its own commentary on one's text.

SPEAKING WITH ONE VOICE

This principle of the analogy of Scripture is based upon the fundamental presupposition that all Scripture speaks with one voice. That is, the Bible teaches one body of truth, and it nowhere contradicts itself. It establishes one doctrinal standard, one way of salvation, one moral ethic, one plan for human history, one design for the family, and so forth. Roy Zuck writes, 'No interpretation is acceptable if it is contrary to the general tenor of the rest of Scripture.'[13] Thus, no individual passage contradicts the analogy of faith.

Regarding the analogy of Scripture, Milton Terry identifies two degrees of analogy: (1) the positive, which is a truth clearly articulated by numerous passages, so that there is no doubt about the meaning (e.g., sin, redemption, omnipotence), (2) the general, which is a truth not supported by explicit affirmations, but is obvious in its meaning and important to Scripture as a whole.[14] According to this law, every doctrine of the Bible perfectly harmonizes in one accord with every other teaching of Scripture. In other words, Scripture teaches only one system of doctrine. As the expositor interprets the Psalms, this synthetic principle must be carefully maintained.

SINGULAR THRUST

Eleventh, there is only one true interpretation for any passage in the Psalms. There cannot be one meaning for one preacher, and a different interpretation for another preacher. Instead, this assumes there is only a singular meaning for a text of Scripture. This interpretation is the same for all men who enter the pulpit. Martin Luther expressed it this way: 'The Holy Ghost is the all-simplest writer that is in heaven or earth; therefore his words can have no more than one simplest sense, which we call the scriptural or literal meaning.'[15]

ONE ORIGINAL MEANING

For the faithful exegete, Walter Kaiser writes, 'There is only "one sense" or meaning to be gleaned from every passage if the interpreter is true to his mission.'[16] It is not the expositor's job to read into the text what is not there. Nor is it his responsibility to uncover multiple layers of hidden meaning, the first being literal with some deeper allegorical meaning laying beneath the surface. Rather, he is to extract the one true meaning of the text. The author's intention has but one meaning. Robert Mounce notes, 'An interpretation is literal only when it corresponds to what the author intends to convey with his statement.'[17] The singular principle in rightly handling a psalm may be summed up with the popular axiom 'one meaning, many applications.'

MULTIPLE RELATED IMPLICATIONS

At the same time, the New Testament writers often referred to statements in the Old Testament and enlarged upon or extended what was written beyond their original setting to refer to Christ. This is often the case with New Testament use of the Psalms. A psalm passage was sometimes heightened in the New Testament to speak of Christ. The New Testament writer did not contradict the psalm, but expanded its meaning to apply to Christ.

For example, Psalm 78:2 states that Asaph spoke in parables, yet Matthew 13:35-36 applies this to Christ and His public ministry of speaking in parables. In Psalm 41:9, David referred to 'my close friend in whom I trusted, who ate my bread, has lifted up his heel against me,' pointing to a contemporary in his day. Yet in John 13:18, Jesus said that Judas's betrayal would fulfill this Old Testament verse, David's betrayal by a false friend pictures Judas's betrayal of Christ.

In Psalm 35:19, David prayed that 'those who hate me' not be allowed by God to continue acting maliciously. Yet beyond David, Jesus later told His disciples in John 15:25 that the hatred of unbelievers for Him 'filled what was written in their Law,' quoting this psalm. Again, David spoke in Psalm 22:18 of his enemies, referring figuratively to them as bulls, lions, and dogs and as people who 'cast lots for [His] clothing.' Yet in John 19:24, these words were seen to be 'fulfilled' when the soldiers gambled for Jesus' seamless undergarment: 'They divided My garments among them and cast lots for My clothing.' The same fulfillment is seen of Psalm 34:20 in John 19:36. That 'a righteous man,' though having 'many troubles,' is delivered by the Lord and 'not one of [His bones] will be broken.' This was fulfilled in Christ when the soldiers did not break Jesus' legs when He was on the cross.

AN EXTENDED MEANING IN CHRIST

It should be clear that these psalms were not initially written as direct predictions of Jesus Christ. The context in each case reveals that these verses had no initial reference to Jesus. Yet they were 'fulfilled' in Christ in the sense that there was an extended meaning to be found in Him. They had an immediate significance to the psalmist and an enlarged meaning in the New Testament for Jesus Christ. This does not mean that the New Testament writers saw hidden meanings in these psalms. They were not changing the meaning in the psalm. Instead, these New Testament writers and even Jesus Himself had legitimate prophetic purposes when they quoted the Psalms.

It must be admitted that the psalmist did not always fully comprehend all they wrote, though certainly God had more in mind than the psalmist sometimes knew. Thus, some Psalms passages may not have been recognized as prophetic until they were fulfilled. The teaching of the New Testament adds helpful confirmation and needed clarification to one's understanding of the Psalms.

PROPHETIC FULFILLMENT

Twelfth, the preacher must maintain a firm grasp of the New Testament use of the Psalms. Jesus rebuked His followers for not understanding basic Old Testament prophecies, specifically Messianic prophecies (Luke 24:25-27, 44). This included the prophetic nature of many psalms.

To determine if a phrase or passage is prophecy, the expositor must determine if the text resembles a circumstance or event in the psalmist's life. He must scour the historical books for clues. If there is no direct match between the passage and a situation contemporaneous to the psalmist, he should consider its possible prophetic and Messianic implications. He should ask: Could any aside from the Messiah possibly fulfill this portion of Scripture?

Next, the expositor must ascertain how the New Testament writer uses the psalm quotation, paraphrase, or allusion. Does the New Testament writer indicate a direct fulfillment, or does he apply the psalm to a situation? Is the New Testament writer simply comparing a situation in his day to an event that will be fulfilled in the end times? Further, one must also determine when the predictive prophecy is fulfilled. That involves the literal principle and the geographical principle, among others. Was the prophecy fulfilled at the first coming of Jesus Christ? Will the prophecy be fulfilled at the second coming, which is yet future?

PROGRESSIVE REVELATION

Thirteenth, the expositor must interpret the Psalms with an awareness that the whole of Scripture was written over an extended period of 1,600 years. Likewise, the book of Psalms itself required approximately 1,000 years to write. As the five books of the Psalms were written and compiled, God gradually revealed many of His truths over that time. A gradual unfolding of the truth over this extended period must be taken into account.

THE UNFOLDING OF TRUTH

This does not mean that what was stated earlier in the Bible was in error. Nor does it mean that the Old Testament is less inspired or less clear than the New Testament. Rather, it means that what was first written was incomplete. That is to say, what often was initially written was only a partial revelation in Scripture. What followed was later enlarged upon, either by the same author or by a later writer. This means that in the progressive study of the Bible, God added to what He had given in its earlier portions. Instead, it means that what was given as partial information in the Old Testament, including the Psalms, was enlarged upon by subsequent authors so that the latter revelation in the New Testament is more complete.

This principle of progressive revelation is critically important in properly understanding the Psalms in the unfolding of the Old Testament. It must be remembered that the Psalter was written to Israel under the Old Covenant. The Law of Moses prevailed and dictated worship. Corporate worship revolved around the sacrificial system given in the book of Leviticus, involving the priesthood offering animal sacrifices and meal offerings in the tabernacle or the Temple. Many restrictions governed this approaching of God. But all that this represented was fulfilled in the death of Christ. The sacrificial system was the shadow and the atonement of Christ is the substance. It was not until the New Testament that the Lord instituted His church. The church in the Old Testament remained a mystery to Old Testament believers. Thus, the one who interprets the Psalms must exercise great discretion and recognize these differences in the economy of God.

RIGHTLY HANDLING THE WORD

In this chapter, we have covered fourteen basic principles of Bible interpretation that are necessary for every expositor to employ in studying the Psalms. Five of these interpretive principles will be examined more carefully in the following chapters. These sections will address the task of the expositor to bridge the gaps of (1) language, (2) grammar, (3) history, (4) culture, and (5) figures of speech. Each of these interpretive laws are necessary in rightly handling the Word. Every pastor must present himself to God as a workman who labors diligently in the Psalms and in the entirety of God's Word. He must correctly interpret the biblical text before him, not falling prey to the novel or unstable interpretations of many. An approved workman must study the Psalms diligently.

Hermeneutics is one of the most important subjects that an expositor will study. As a foundational discipline, Bible study methods and one's interpretation shape everything. *What* the biblical text means is more critically important than *how* it is to be presented. Substance is always more weighty than style. But a careless pastor handles the Scripture improperly, all too often making it say what he wants it to say. If a skillful handling of a psalm is to become reality, the expositor must present himself to God, as a living and holy sacrifice, applying the proper laws of hermeneutics in properly interpreting His Word. Every preacher must 'cut it straight' with the Psalms. He must be meticulous in the way he extracts meaning from the biblical text, for it remains the divine Word, not the mere message of the preacher himself.

EXAMINE
THE LANGUAGE

Interact with the Hebrew language

Written in the distant world of the Middle East, from 2,400 years to almost 3,500 years ago, the Psalms is an ancient book. This long-ago, written hymn book was recorded in a different language, to a different people, surrounded by a different culture, living in a different land. In order for the modern reader to understand what God meant by what He said centuries ago, several gaps must be bridged. One of the vast gulfs that must be spanned is the language gap. As John MacArthur notes, 'The Bible was written originally in Hebrew, Aramaic, and Greek. Therefore, to interpret

it correctly, one needs to understand the original languages.'[1]
The Psalms were written in Hebrew, and if the expositor is to
best grasp the meaning of his text, he must learn to operate in
the Hebrew language.

It must be admitted that a linguistic proficiency will vary from
one preacher to the next. Some men have been better trained in
the ancient language of Hebrew than others. Still others have a
greater aptitude in Hebrew than others possess. Yet others have
more time available to work in the original language. Some men,
for example, are bi-vocational and have limited time for bridging linguistic gaps. But according to the education, ability, and
time that has been entrusted, the preacher should work in the
original language to the extent he can.

Bridging the Linguistic Gap

When preaching the Psalms, the closer an expositor can access
the Hebrew language, the better he will be able to uncover the
precise meaning of his text. MacArthur again writes, 'Often
understanding the meaning of a word or phrase in the original language, can be the key to correctly interpreting a passage
of Scripture.[2] Given the abundance of Hebrew language tools
available today, the preacher should be able to work, to some
extent, with the original text in his attempt to correctly interpret it.

This chapter focuses on bridging the linguistic gap from the
Hebrew text of the Psalms to the native language of the expositor in order to uncover the true meaning of the text. As the
expositor approaches the psalm to be preached, there are several
key considerations he must take into account: textual criticism,
translation work, key words, and word studies. Uncovering the
riches of Hebrew words in the text will yield a greater understanding of its meaning.

From Blessed to Hallelujah

From the very first word of the Psalter in Psalm 1:1 — 'How blessed (*asher*)' — to the last word in Psalm 150:6 — 'Praise the Lord! (*hallelujah*)' — the individual words of this inspired book await our exploration, explanation, and exclamation. Let us consider now four aspects of bridging the linguistic gap: textual criticism, translation work, key words, and word studies:

TEXTUAL CONSIDERATION

First, the expositor should begin his interaction with the Hebrew text of a psalm by asking the most basic question of all: 'What is the text?' This is the logical starting point in the work of Hebrew exegesis.

Different Variants

In approaching a passage, an awareness of the textual issues in a passage is necessary, especially when the variant affects the meaning of the text. The work of textual criticism demands significant training and expertise by the preacher, but it certainly pays rich dividends. In so doing, the expositor will want to consult the best critical and technical commentaries for additional help. To this very point, James Montgomery Boice writes:

> What is the true text? To what extent should one acknowledge and deal with variants? Generally one does not deal with variants at all. Indeed, the preacher does not even need to deal with variants at all. Indeed, the preacher does not need to spend much time considering them privately. This is because they are inconsequential. They concern word orders, spelling, or insignificant additions or omissions. But from time to time, there are variants that bear upon the meaning of the passage, and they must be handled if the text is to be treated honestly.[3]

A brief summary of the most basic principles of textual criticism would be as follows: One, the textual critic should compare the readings of the ancient text, which are the Masoretic Text, Samaritan Pentateuch, Qumran manuscripts, Greek Septuagint and daughter versions, Aramaic Targummim, Syriac Peshitta, Old Latin, Latin Vulgate, and miscellaneous early versions (e.g., Sahidic, Coptic, Ethiopic, Arabic, and Armenian). Identifying the preferable reading, however, may not be made solely on the basis of external evidence. Two, the textual critic should evaluate internal factors such as graphic, lexical, syntactical, and contextual considerations.[4] This involves considering which textual reading could have possibly given rise to the others. Three, the textual critic should then select the best reading and give reasons for his decision based on internal and external evidence. He should articulate *why* he prefers a particular reading over another.

CORRECT TEXT

A few examples of how helpful textual criticism can be to the expositor can be seen, first, in Psalm 49:11 (Heb. 12), where *qrbm* possesses a potential transposition, or reversal of letters. It appears that the Hebrew text 'as it stands defies a reasonable solution.'[5] One must determine whether the Hebrew reading is correct ('their inner parts' or 'thoughts'), or whether the Septuagint, Peshitta, and Targum are correct ('their graves').

Another example is found in Psalm 18 and 2 Samuel 22, which contain the same psalm with slight variations. 2 Samuel 22:33 reads, 'my strong fortress,' while its parallel, Psalm 18:32, reads, 'who girds me with strength.' One must decide if the two psalms should be harmonized, or if differences should remain intact. Many other examples could be cited, each of which should be sufficient to entice the preacher to a more careful study of this academic discipline.

TRANSLATION EFFORT

Second, the expositor will want to translate the psalm to be preached from the original Hebrew language into his native language. After several years of study in Hebrew, a preacher can often sight-read most passages. A skilled Hebrew exegete can recognize most words without the aid of a dictionary. Further, he can parse most verbs without consulting an analytical key.

TRANSLATION WORK

Not all are at this point though. The pastor who is untrained in Hebrew should not be discouraged. He can consult the various linguistic tools that are available to him that will help in bridging his understanding of the original language. Even the pastor who is untaught in Hebrew can nevertheless make efforts to work in the original language. He can use a parallel Old Testament if necessary to do translation work. The point is: he should attempt to make a preliminary translation of the Hebrew text to the extent that he can.

Regarding this initial translation work, William Barrick writes, 'This step might be accomplished by diligently comparing the original language with a literal translation such as the English Standard Version (ESV), New American Standard Bible (NASB), or the New King James Version (NKJV). Note any translational variations from the original language. Determine to discover the basis for any textual variant followed by the translation or suggested in the margins of the translation. Remember: no translation is perfect.'[6] The expositor should simply do what he can in translation work. At the least, he should become aware of the linguistic issues that are involved in his passage.

SYNTAX AND GRAMMAR

The real benefit of translation work, Kaiser writes, is becoming 'aware of the syntax and grammar in phrases, clauses, and sentences.'[7] Seeing the relationships of Hebrew words to one another in a sentence is invaluable in determining what is primary and what is in a supportive, modifying role. Further, the preacher can see the word order in the sentence and discover what is in the emphatic position.

KEY WORDS

Third, the preacher will want to read through the psalm with an observant eye that is alert for key words in the text. He should note strategic words used by the psalmist. The movement and meaning of a psalm is often enriched by grasping the etymology and meaning of certain pivotal words.

STRATEGIC WORDS

Because the Psalms were originally written in Hebrew, reading the passage in the original language will yield a greater understanding of the text. Old Testament scholar Robert Chishom writes, 'We must examine the biblical usage of words, noting carefully various contextual and linguistic factors that signal precise nuances of meaning in a given context.'[8] Without a knowledge of Hebrew, the expositor will need to rely on good translations and on concordances and dictionaries that refer to the Hebrew. Depending upon the length of the psalm, he will want to notice certain key words, which demand his attention:

1. Crucial Words
Each psalm will contain certain significant words which are loaded with theological importance. Understanding the precise meaning of these individual words will play an important role in determining the authorial intent of the passage. For example, Psalm 46:1 compares God to a 'refuge' and 'strength.' These are key words that must be explored in greater depth if the preacher is to capture the full meaning and impact of the psalm. In this

text, there are three key words — 'refuge,' 'strength,' and 'help' — that should invite the expositor's focused attention and skilled investigation. Great preaching necessitates grasping and explaining the meaning of these words.

2. Repeating Words

In addition, the repetition of a word, or a repeated cluster of words, usually serves to underscore their importance. Careful expositors should pay close attention to words that appear two, three, or more times, either in a single stanza or in the entire psalm. Psalm 103 provides an excellent example of this principle of repetition. The repeated use of the word 'bless' should secure the preacher's attention for further study. Both the first verses and the final verses repeat the word 'bless.' Noting the intentional repetition of 'bless' should invite the preacher's probing into its meaning.

3. Unclear Words

Moreover, if any word remains unclear, the expositor will want to dig deeper in order to more carefully examine it. Rather than pass over it, he must pause and ask: What does this word really mean? Does my listener understand its meaning? For example, Psalm 66:3 uses the word 'feigned,' the exact meaning of which may remain somewhat unclear. A word study reveals that *feigned* means 'to bow down in cringing before another.' The idea is that when God appears as a warrior, His enemies will surely fear being destroyed by Him. They will give 'cringing' or 'trembling' obedience to Him, though granted it may not be a true obedience from the heart.

In pursuing this, the preacher may discover that different translations of the Bible will differ when it comes to a particular word. He should ask: Why have the Bible translators chosen a different word for their translations? What synonyms have they used that may make this more clear? When further clarification is needed, he should carefully study the word and seek to determine: Why is a different word used? Which synonym is best?

4. Emphatic Words

In order to underscore the importance of a particular word,

the psalmist occasionally will move it to the beginning of the sentence. This is the emphatic position, which draws attention to that word. In such cases, the preacher will again want to dig deeper into the meaning of that word. The word 'blessed' in Psalm 1:1 sits in the emphatic position and demands careful attention. It is as if the psalmist is pointing his finger at 'How blessed' in order to underscore its importance.

BIBLICAL CONTEXT

Next, the preacher should then actually study these key words. He will want to investigate the immediate context, as well as compare lexicons, concordances, theological dictionaries, and Bible commentaries. The expositor will want to examine:

1. Immediate Context
Undertaking a word study begins with considering the immediate and larger context of the word. The expositor should ask himself: What immediately precedes the word under consideration? What follows it? Is parallelism involved with a synonym surrounding it? Studying the context involves many things such as identifying grammatical structures, contextual contrasts, poetic parallelism, literary style, rhetorical devices, figures of speech, common idioms, and dialectical distinctions. Investigating the context of a word is critical for several reasons. For one thing, a single word may have different meanings in different contexts. Examining the various contexts in which the word is found will help determine the intended meaning. Further, the expositor will want to know how the same psalmist uses this very word within the same psalm.

In addition, he should consider the theological thrust of the context. False interpretations often arise from ignoring the central theme of the passage. For example, some understand Psalm 2:8-9 as a text to be used at missions conferences. But a more careful examination reveals that the immediate context is actually one divine judgment upon rebellious sinners. Therefore, 'inheritance' refers not to Christ receiving men and women in salvation, but the very opposite. It addresses Christ inheriting the nations to judge them.

2. Larger Context

Then, he should note how the word is used in other psalms by other authors. Further, he should see how other biblical writers use this same word in other books in the Old Testament. In addition, he should note how writers outside the Bible use this word. This is especially needed with Hebrew words that are used only once or twice in the Old Testament. Approximately 1,300 words occur only once in the Old Testament. These are called *hapax legomena*, meaning a word used only once in the Hebrew Bible. About 500 Hebrew words occur only twice in the Old Testament. In such cases, the way these words are used in extra-biblical writings can sometimes help ascertain meaning.

LANGUAGE TOOLS

In determining the meaning of Hebrew words, the expositor will want to consult Hebrew concordances, theological dictionaries, and reliable Psalms commentaries.

1. Hebrew Lexicons

Also, the preacher will want to consult Hebrew lexicons in his study of the passage. After locating the word in a Hebrew lexicon, he should read the entire entry and note correct grammatical information. Lexicons reveal the full range of meaning that a word has, often providing verse references, as well as grammatical information. As the preacher consults a Hebrew lexicon, he should ask: What is the possible meaning of a word? Where do those meanings appear in the Old Testament? What is the gender and number of a noun? What is the stem of the verb?

2. Hebrew Concordances

Moreover, the expositor will want to consult a Hebrew concordance. Concordances provide the statistical usages of the word,

indicate identical forms, reveal word distribution, and reference
parallel passages. The preacher should ask: How often does the
word occur? How is the word used? How often does the identical
form appear? Does this word occur in poetry, narrative, or both?

3. Theological Dictionaries

Likewise, the expositor should consult theological dictionaries,
noting the sources, synonyms, antonyms, and problem passages
related to the word being studied. In so doing, he will want to
determine how an individual word differs from its synonyms.
This distinction can help the expositor narrow the unique meaning of this particular word more carefully. Thus, the expositor
should seek to discover how closely related words carry varying
shades of meaning.

By using a theological dictionary to compare and contrast
different synonyms, the expositor is able to uncover the specific shade of meaning of each word. For example, in Psalm
32:1-2, each word for sin — 'transgression,' 'sin,' 'iniquity,' and
'deceit' — brings its own emphasis regarding its deadly nature.
Investigating many other such synonyms for other words will
greatly enrich our understanding of Psalms.

4. Psalms Commentaries

Further, the preacher should consult Bible commentaries on his
particular passage. He should note the meaning of a passage as
explained by other noted teachers and theologians. He should be
observant of differences in interpretation from one commentary
to the next. The expositor should ask himself: Do the various commentators agree on the usage of a word? How does the translation
of a word affect the interpretation? The preacher should then summarize his findings and incorporate them into his sermon notes.

CUTTING IT STRAIGHT

There is no substitute for cutting it straight with God's Word. No
expositor can properly explain the meaning of a psalm if he fails

to bridge this important linguistic gap. While many preachers today are preoccupied with the theatrics of their delivery, what should be of greatest concern to them is their 'accurately handling the word of truth' (2 Tim. 2:15). In the final analysis of preaching, substance is more important than style. Precision with the text is more important than its packaging in a sermon. This is not to suggest that delivery is unimportant. We will cover the critical nature of pulpit delivery later in this book. To be sure, substance and style are *both* critical. We must be both accurate *and* interesting. But the right interpretation of the text is the sturdy foundation upon which the sermon delivery rests. No house can stand without a strong foundation. Neither can a sermon.

Let all preachers strive with all their God-given abilities to handle the Bible accurately. Let them diligently labor to discover the true meaning of the text of Scripture. May they remember, it is the Word of God that they bring, not their own, nor that of any mere man. Let them give their best effort in discovering the proper meaning of a passage. May every expositor exercise the utmost care to study the Bible properly, knowing that the meaning of the Scripture *is* the Scripture.

FIND THE
PARALLELISM

Note the stanzas, strophes, and parallelism

The Psalms are the very heart of the Scripture, and the very heart of the Psalms is understanding the literary device known as parallelism. This form of communication is the most distinctive characteristic of Hebrew poetry. In this ancient genre, the successive lines of poetry form a powerful means of conveying the divine message. Affirming this very point, C. Hassell Bullock maintains, 'The heart of Hebrew poetry is a device called parallelism.'[1] Here, an initial line is recorded, followed by a second and sometimes a third line or more, with noticeable similarities or dissimilarities between them. More than mere repetition is involved in parallelism. Rather, there is the expansion or advancement of the original line's meaning through either resemblances or contrasts in the following line or lines.

This being so, the Psalms were written, generally speaking, in a literary style called Hebrew poetry. This is a form of communication quite different from the other genres used in Scripture. Robert Davidson notes 'Poetry is the language of emotion and imagination.'[2] It stands distinct from narrative, legal writings, prophecy, discourse, parable, and epistle. Using highly figurative language, Hebrew poetry conveys God's message in vivid expressions that are colorful, emotional, and picturesque. Unlike English poetry, which is based upon rhyming and rhythm, Hebrew poetry is based upon parallelism and meter. According to this genre, poetic parallelism states an idea in the first line and then reinforces it with an array of literary devices in the second line or following lines.[3]

A Distinctive Style

Regarding this style of communication, John MacArthur explains, 'Unlike most English poetry, which is based on rhyme and meter, Hebrew poetry is essentially characterized by logical parallelism.'[4] C. Hassell Bullock further explains, 'It is a literary pattern that states an idea on one line and focuses more closely on the same idea in the following line either repeating the thought in different terms or focusing on the thought more specifically.'[5] Or, as Gerald H. Wilson states, 'The most distinctive characteristic of Hebrew poetry is to be found in the frequent linking of successive lines of poetry in a manner that emphasizes grammatical, structural, and thematic similarities between them. This relationship between lines has been traditionally called *parallelism*.'[6]

Parallelism introduces an idea and then expresses it again in different words. In this distinctive style of literature, the concepts of the two lines closely correspond. The relationship between parallel lines determines the meaning and emphasis of a passage. This chapter considers the main types of Hebrew parallelism in the Psalms. The expositor of the Psalms must be well acquainted with their various kinds. They include:

SYNONYMOUS

The most common type of Hebrew parallelism is known as synonymous parallelism, which repeats the idea of the first line in the second line. That is, the second line simply restates the central idea of the first line using synonyms. The synonymous expression of the follow-up line enhances the clarity, emphasis, and dramatic effect of the lead line. Leland Ryken explains, 'Synonymous parallelism consists of expressing similar content more than once in consecutive lines in similar grammatical form or sentence structure. More often, the second line simply restates the idea in a contrasting way.'[7] For example:[8]

> How blessed is the man
> who does not walk in the counsel of the wicked,   [A]
> nor stand in the path of sinners,   [B]
> nor sit in the seat of scoffers!   [C]
> (1:1)

> Why do the nations conspire   [A]
> and the people plot in vain?   [B]
> (2:1)

ANTITHETICAL

Antithetical parallelism contrasts the second line with the first. The opposite idea drives home the point with added impact. Most often, the word 'but' signals the contrast of the first line with the second line. Ryken explains, 'In antithetical parallelism, the second line states the truth of the first in a contrasting way. Sometimes one line states the idea positively and the other negatively.'[9] Examples include:

For the LORD watches over the way of the righteous, [A]
but the way of the wicked will perish.   [B]
                                                        (1:6)

For by their own sword they did not possess the land, [A]
and their own arm did not save them,
but Your right hand and Your arm and the light of   [B]
Your presence, for You favored them.
                                                        (44:3)

SYNTHETIC

Synthetic parallelism further develops the first line with the second. Here, the proposition stated in the first line is advanced and further developed in the second line. As Ryken notes, 'Synthetic parallelism (growing parallelism) … consists of a pair of lines that together form a complete unit and in which the second line completes or expands the thought introduced in the first line.'[10] Thus, the second line develops or extends the central thought of the first rather than merely repeating it. Here are two prime examples:

Help, Lord, for the godly man ceases to be,   [A]
for the faithful disappear from among the sons of men.[B]
                                                        (12:1)

The law of the LORD is perfect, reviving the soul.   [A]
The statutes of the LORD are trustworthy,
    making wise the simple.   [B]
The precepts of the LORD are right,
    giving joy to the heart.   [C]
The commands of the LORD are radiant,
    giving light to the eyes.   [D]
The fear of the LORD is pure, enduring forever.   [E]
The ordinances of the LORD are sure
    and altogether righteous.   [F]
                                                        (19:7-9)

EMBLEMATIC

Emblematic parallelism joins a literal expression with a figurative one. That is, the first line uses a simile or metaphor to express a synonymous concept. Allen P. Ross states, 'Emblematic parallelism occurs when one of the parallel units is a metaphorical illumination of the other.'[11] This form of parallelism is so potent because emblems or symbols serve as powerful communication tools. They paint a vivid picture of the truth at hand. The psalmists frequently used figures of speech because they transformed abstract truth into concrete terms, and portrayed ideas in graphic, vivid, and memorable ways. Psalms 42 and 44 demonstrate this:

> As the deer pants for streams of water,   [A]
> so my soul pants for you, O God.   [B]
>   (42:1)

> Yet You have crushed us in a place of jackals   [A]
> and covered us with the shadow of death.   [B]
> But for Your sake we are killed all day long;   [A]
> we are considered as sheep to be slaughtered.   [B]
>   (44:19, 22)

CLIMACTIC

Climatic parallelism, also called step or staircase parallelism, begins with a crucial word, phrase, or truth in the first line and then expands it in the second line to a dramatic climax. Ryken explains, 'In climactic parallelism, the second line completes the first by repeating part of the first line and then adding to it.'[12] That is, the succeeding lines carry the idea of the first line forward. Psalm 29 illustrates this:

> Ascribe to the LORD, O mighty ones,
> Ascribe to the LORD glory and strength.
> Ascribe to the LORD the glory due his name;
> Worship the LORD in the splendor of His holiness. (29:1-2)

The voice of the Lord is upon the waters;
The God of glory thunders,
The Lord is over many waters.
The voice of the Lord is powerful,
The voice of the Lord is majestic.
The voice of the Lord breaks the cedars;
Yes, the Lord breaks in pieces the cedars of Lebanon.
He makes Lebanon skip like a calf, and Sirion like a
    young wild ox.
The voice of the Lord hews out flames of fire.
The voice of the Lord shakes the wilderness;
The Lord shakes the wilderness of Kadesh.
The voice of the Lord makes the deer to calve and strips
    the forests bare;
And in His temple everything says, 'Glory!'   (29:3-9)

ALTERNATE

In this form of parallelism, the third line repeats the idea of the first, and the fourth line repeats the second in an A…B…A…B pattern. In Psalm 103, for example, the psalmist describes the immeasurable distance from the heavens to the earth (line one), and then he restates the same idea by mentioning east from the west (line three). In lines two and four, the psalmist parallels God's love with His forgiveness of sins:

For as high as the heavens are above the earth,   [A]
so great is His love for those who fear Him;   [B]
as far as the east is from the west,   [A]
so far has He removed our transgressions from us.   [B]
(103:11, 12)

CHIASTIC

This type of parallelism employs an A…B…B…A pattern in which the second line advances the first, the third line restates the second line, only in the fourth line to return to the truth of first line. That is to say, the lower half of the structure mirrors the upper half in an inverted fashion. Each segment corresponds to its counterpart. The emphases of a chiasm lies in the central element(s), therefore the preacher's explanation should emphasize what the chiasm emphasizes. Chiasms draw the focus to one point, like a magnifying glass. The example below focuses the attention on the [C] portions:

Lord, You have been our dwelling place	[A]
in all generations	[B]
Before the mountains were born	[C]
Or you gave birth to the earth and the world,	[C]
Even from everlasting to everlasting,	[B]
You are God.	[A]
	(90:1-2)

EXTERNAL

This form of parallelism refers to the external or outside portions of a structure, as opposed to the internal segments. For instance, the [A] segments in Psalm 30:8, 10, comprise the external parallel, while [B] and [C] comprise the internal parallel. External parallelism often extends beyond verse boundaries. Thus when the expositor identifies parallelism, he should check the surrounding verses for external parallels.

To You, O Lord, I called,	
And to the Lord I made supplication:	[A]
What profit is there in my blood,	[B]
if I go down to the pit?	[B]
Will the dust praise You?	[C]
Will it declare Your faithfulness?	[C]
Hear, O Lord, and be gracious to me;	
O Lord, be my helper.	[A]
	(30:8-10)

VIVID COMMUNICATION

This chapter showed how parallelism adds luster and colorful effect to the literary quality of the Psalms. The structural patterns of this literary device enhance the artistic beauty of the Psalms, conveying robust pictures of what the psalmist intended to communicate. The beauty of parallelism is that it is a memorable form of communication that effectively teaches truth.

Every expositor should model the psalmists' use of parallelism in his own preaching. Restating truth in a variety of ways makes for vivid expressions of the truth. Repetition communicates truth effectively from the pulpit. Not only should he identify parallelism in the text, but use it to declare what God is saying. Thus, it is important not only *what* he says, but *how* he says it. The message is primary, but the manner with which it is conveyed is vitally important. Such is the value of learning not only to interpret parallelism, but to use it.

STUDY THE GRAMMAR

Investigate the grammatical structure of the psalm

O ne of the most important parts of sermon preparation is this next step, that of studying the grammar. As the expositor analyzes the biblical text of the psalm, he must give careful consideration to the grammatical features of the passage. With this clearly in mind, Roy Zuck notes, 'Since the human instruments used human language in writing the books of the Bible ... we [must] pay attention to the common rules of grammar and syntax. Grammar is the study of words and their function in sentences, and syntax ... refers to how the sentences are put together.'[1] Such a grammatical investigation of the passage requires the understanding of the basic structure of each sentence.

Since every jot and tittle of a psalm is infallible, then attention must be given to every part of the divinely inspired text. This includes the inner-relationship of each word to the other words. Specifically, grammar deals with the way individual words in a sentence relate to one another. This study involves applying the basic laws of grammar in order to plainly understand the precise function of each part of the sentence. Such a discovery is important because the psalmists recorded divine revelation through the grammar and syntax of the original language with which they wrote.

BRIDGE THE GRAMMATICAL GAP

In this chapter, we will focus upon bridging the grammatical gap, which involves digging into the very words of every sentence in order to discover the significance of word relationships. This investigation requires that the expositor give careful attention to: (1) internal structure, (2) poetic strophes, and (3) poetic stanzas. The exegete best visualizes these structures in a (4) block diagram. The expositor must see and understand the inner-relationships within the psalm before he can preach it with clarity and conviction. The more clearly he can view the inner-connectedness of words within his text, the clearer he will be in the pulpit.

Let us consider each of these features that deal with the grammatical structure of the Psalms. This will include the following:

INTERNAL STRUCTURE

The expositor must discover how each part of a psalm relates to the other parts. Understanding the relationships between words and clauses provides essential insight for understanding the original intent of what the psalmist is saying. Studying word relationships within a sentence forces the expositor to address what the author actually says with precision and accuracy. In so doing, the preacher should take note of:

NOUNS

Exegetes of the Psalms must observe the qualities and uses of nouns, pronouns, adjectives, and noun clusters. In so doing, the expositor should ask key questions of the passage: What is the subject of the verse? Is the noun definite or indefinite? Does the noun include an article? What is the gender of the noun — masculine or feminine? What is the number of the noun — singular, dual, or plural? Is the pronoun in the first, second, or third person? An observant eye looks for grammatical discoveries like these. Consideration should be given to:

1. Nouns
These words name something, whether a place ('mountain,' 3:4), a thing ('tree,' 'fruit,' 'leaf,' 1:3), a concept or idea ('salvation,' 'blessing,' 3:8), or an action ('deliverance,' 3:2). A common noun names things generally, such as 'inheritance' (1:8), whereas a proper noun is a name that identifies a particular person ('Jacob,' 81:1) or place ('Hermon,' 42:6). Collective nouns refer to groups of people of things ('nations,' 2:1; 'generations,' 14:5). A verbal noun (also called a gerund) is a form of a verb that ends in *ing*, but acts as a noun ('groaning,' 5:1).

2. Pronouns
These words substitute for nouns. Exegetes will need to ask themselves: Is this a personal pronoun ('I,' 3:4), a demonstrative pronoun ('this,' 44:18), an interrogative pronoun ('who,' 15:1), a relative pronoun ('who,' 3:6), or a reflexive pronoun ('themselves,' 3:6, 'Himself,' 4:3). Pronouns such as *each*, *either*, and *none*, are called indefinite pronouns.

3. Adjectives
These describe nouns. Their placement in the Hebrew, as compared to English is often inverted. For example, in Hebrew,

attributive adjectives normally follow the noun they modify ('His *holy* temple,' 11:4). Predicate adjectives normally precede the noun, and they always appear without an article ('the Lord is *good*,' 34:8). Predicate adjectives make an assertion about the noun they modify, drawing attention to the noun. Because adjectives are rare, Hebrew normally modifies nouns with construct chains and apposition.

4. Noun Clusters

These are back-to-back nouns, which include construct chains, in which two or more nouns are juxtaposed by means of a construct relationship (1,896 occurrences in the Psalter), apposition, in which two nouns are placed side by side and the first noun serves as an adjective to modify the second (660 occurrences), and the less frequent hendiadys, in which two or more nouns are connected by "and" to create intensification in the meaning. Each category of nouns deserves careful consideration and possesses exegetical and expositional significance.

Moreover, the expositor should keep a keen eye for the agreement of person, gender, or number. This agreement reveals the relationship between words. For example, the key to understanding Psalm 110:1 rests in the agreement of person, gender, and number. One notices that the first occurrence of 'my' is a first-person, masculine, singular pronoun referring back to 'David' (also first person, masculine, singular). Who was David's Lord? The Messiah, the second member of the Trinity. Thus, David relays an inter-Trinitarian conversation between the Father ('The LORD') and the Son ('my Lord').

VERBS

Further, the expositor must note the verbs in his psalm. They describe the action ('save,' 'pursue,' 'deliver,' 7:1) or a state of being ('is,' 1:1; 'be,' 1:3). The multi-dimensional function of Hebrew verbs is seen as they perform at least nine different functions. They reveal: (1) the action, (2) the subject, (3) the object, (4) voice, (5) case frame, (6) type of action, (7) time of action relative to the time of speaking, (8) the quality of action, and (9) the mood. Each function may carry interpretive significance. Verbs abound with exegetical insights.

The expositor who wishes to dig down into the depths of the psalm must work with verbal syntax, which involves analyzing the Hebrew verb stems and conjugations. Stem indicates voice — the relationship of the subject of the verb to its action or state. The main verb stems include:

1. Active Verbs
With active verbs, the subject is the person or thing performing the action. In the Hebrew language, the active stems include *qal*, *piel*, and *hifil*. *Qal* verbs occur 3,411 times in the Psalter and express a state or action. *Piel* verbs occur 873 times in the Psalms and primarily cause a state of being and focus on the result of the action. 'Acquit me of hidden faults' (19:12). *Hifil* verbs appear 882 times in the Psalms, which cause an action and focus on the process of the action. The Lord 'causes rain for the earth' (147:8); He 'causes grass to grow' (147:8); 'He causes His wind to blow' (147:18).

2. Passive Verbs
In the passive, verbs are usually formed with *be*, and the person or thing performing the action is introduced by the preposition *by*. Here, the subject is passive, meaning it is being acted upon. The passive stems include *pual*, *hofal*, *nifal*, and *qal passive*. *Qal passive* verbs are more rarely used in the Psalms, occurring only six times (44:23; 73:2; 87:4, 5, 6, 90:2). *Nifal* verbs appear 312 times in the Psalter and reveal passive action (106:22; twice, 25, 28, 30, 31, 42, 45). The psalmists employ *pual* verbs forty-one times in the Psalter (144:12, 13, 14). The *hofal* verb is used nine times in the Psalter (22:11, 16; 37:24; 45:3, 15 twice; 45:16; 69:9; 102:5). Each of these indicate passive action in which the subject is acted upon.

3. Reflexive Verbs
With a reflexive stem, the subject both performs and receives the action. This is indicated by the *hitpael* stem, which occurs

seventy-five times in the Psalter. 'You show Yourself blameless' (18:25); 'You show Yourself pure' (18:26); 'Delight yourself in the Lord' (37:4). 'Will You hide Yourself forever?' (89:46).

4. Conjugations

The conjugation reveals mood and discourse function, not tense. Strictly speaking, tense is indicated by context and context alone. The *Qatal* conjugation occurs 1,411 times in the Psalms. It views the action from the outside as a totality, without regard for duration. The *Yiqtol* conjugation appears 2,704 times in the Psalms. It views the action from the inside, considering its phases. 'How blessed is the man who does not walk in the counsel of the wicked, or stand in the path of sinners, or sit in the seat of scoffers' (1:1). Here the psalmist views the *Qatal* verbs 'walk,' 'stand,' and 'sit' from the outside as a whole, without regard for the internal phases of the actions. The next verse switches to a *Yiqtol* verb: 'But his delight is in the law of the LORD, and in His law he meditates day and night' (1:3). The *Yiqtol* verb, 'meditates,' views the action from the inside, considering the phases or duration of his meditation — consistent or habitual meditation. Thus, a godly man habitually or repeatedly thinks about Scripture, as the grammar indicates and the context confirms ('day and night').

5. Participles

A participle is a verb that can be used as an adjective or noun or used to make compound verb forms ('is going,' 'has been'). These verbal forms occur 797 times in the Psalms and indicate continuous or characteristic action. As with many features of Hebrew, context determines usage. 'The law of the Lord is perfect, restoring the soul; the testimony of the Lord is sure making wise the simple' (19:7).

6. Infinitival Constructs

An infinitive is the basic form of a verb, normally with the word *to*. These verbal forms appear 290 times in the Psalter with a wide variety of uses. Some indicate purpose or manner, or time. 'The wicked have drawn the sword and bent their bow to cast down the afflicted and the needy, to slay those who are upright in conduct'

(37:14); 'And in their heart they put God to the test' (78:18).

PHRASES

The expositor must also be aware of phrases within the sentences of his text. A phrase is a small group of related words forming a unit within a clause. A phrase is without a verb, and, thus, cannot stand alone. There are three basic types of phrases with which the preacher must be familiar:[2]

1. Prepositional Phrase
This type of phrase consists of a preposition and compliment, usually a noun. That is to say, a preposition phrase is a group of words without a verb and introduced by a preposition: 'in His sanctuary,' 'in His mighty expanse,' 'for His mighty deeds,' 'with trumpet sound,' 'with harp and lyre' (150:1-2).

2. Participial Phrase
This particular phrase consists of a group of words introduced by a participle which acts as an adjective modifying a noun. They communicate continuous action or characteristic action. 'The precepts of the Lord are right, *rejoicing the heart*; The commandment of the Lord is pure, *enlightening the eyes*' (19:8, emphasis added).

3. Infinitival Phrase
This kind of phrase is a group of words introduced by the word 'to.' The infinitive phrase may be used as an adverbial phrase to modify a verb, or as an adjectival phrase to modify a noun. 'To make them sit with princes, With the princes of His people' (113:8); 'To which the tribes go up, even the tribes of the Lord — An ordinance for Israel — To give thanks to the name of the Lord' (122:4).

CLAUSES

Moreover, the expositor must investigate his text for the use of a clause which is a coherent group of words with a subject and

verb. These words form part of a sentence.[3] There are three types
of clauses:

1. Independent Clause
This kind of clause is known as a main or principle clause and
serves as the backbone of many sentences. It expresses a complete
idea and can stand alone.[4] Additional phrases or clauses can be
added to make a more complex sentence. 'Ascribe to the Lord the
glory due to His name; Worship the Lord in holy array' (29:2).

2. Coordinate Clause
This kind of clause forms one part of a compound sentence.[5] That
is, a coordinate clause is a coherent group of words that make up
one portion within a larger sentence. Each unit of thought can
be joined together to form parallel ideas, which express totality.
'Wash me thoroughly from my iniquity And cleanse me from
my sin' (51:2); 'Purify me with hyssop, and I shall be clean; Wash
me, and I shall be whiter than snow' (51:7).

3. Dependent Clause
Also referred to as a subordinate clause, this clause is any which
does not express a complete thought and which cannot stand by
itself.[6] In other words, dependent clauses attach to independent
clauses. 'Even though I walk through the valley of the shadow of
death, I fear no evil, for You are with me; Your rod and Your staff,
they comfort me' (23:4).

CONJUNCTIONS

The expositor also should be alert to various words that introduce clauses. The following conjunctions tip-off the preacher to
the relationship between clauses:

1. Coordinating
Coordinating conjunctions serve as connectors that reveal how
the author relates ideas. These words include: *and, or, not, for, but,
neither, nor, either, or, both, not only, but also.* Here expositors

should notice how the psalmist connects his thoughts. How does he flow from idea to idea? Such observations help the preacher trace and follow the argument of the writer. 'And my soul shall rejoice in the Lord; It shall exult in His salvation. All my bones will say, "Lord, who is like You, Who delivers the afflicted from him who is too strong for him, And the afflicted and the needy from him who robs him?"' (35:9-10); 'And now, Lord, for what do I wait? My hope is in You. 'Deliver me from all my transgressions; Make me not the reproach of the foolish' (39:7-8).

2. Adversative Coordinating

Adversative conjunctions contrast a situation or the actions of two characters. They serve as a pivot that allows the biblical author to distinguish differing ideas. These words signal an abrupt shift of thought: *but, except*. The psalmist frequently distinguishes the godly from the wicked, wisdom from folly, and the frailty of man from the greatness of God. 'I hate those who regard vain idols, But I trust in the Lord' (31:6).

3. Emphatic Coordinating

These words serve to underscore what is said. Many of these conjunctions, if removed, have no adverse effect on the structure of the sentence. Instead, their primary purpose is emphasis. 'For, lo, the kings assembled themselves, They passed by together. They saw it, then they were amazed; They were terrified, they fled in alarm. Panic seized them there, Anguish, as of a woman in childbirth' (48:4-6).

4. Inferential Coordinating

These words advance the movement by drawing a summation. They often indicate purpose (what should happen) or result (what actually happened). These words include: *now, therefore, then, wherefore, so*. 'Now therefore, O kings, show discernment; Take warning, O judges of the earth. Worship the Lord with reverence And rejoice with trembling' (2:10-11).

5. Transitional Coordinating

These conjunctions, like joints in a body or seams in a garment, provide a hinge from thought to thought. They serve to transition from one thought to the next: *and, moreover, then.* 'For it is not an enemy who reproaches me, Then I could bear it; Nor is it one who hates me who has exalted himself against me, Then I could hide myself from him' (55:12); 'Moreover, by them Your servant is warned; In keeping them there is great reward' (19:11).

6. Subordinating

These conjunctions introduce ideas that logically fall under a main idea. They introduce secondary or supporting thoughts: *when, because, if, since, although, that, when.* 'Give heed to me and answer me; I am restless in my complaint and am surely distracted, Because of the voice of the enemy, Because of the pressure of the wicked; For they bring down trouble upon me And in anger they bear a grudge against me' (55:2-3).

POETIC STROPHES

After the expositor orients himself to the basic grammar, he should focus upon the strophic structure within each stanza. These inner-clusters or smaller divisions are known as strophes. In Hebrew poetry, the strophe comprises a brief unit of one or more lines — and its importance in interpreting the Psalms cannot be overstated. Walter C. Kaiser, Jr., writes, 'The identification of the strophe is not an optional matter for the exegete. As the paragraph [of prose] stated one central idea and then developed or organized itself around that one theme proposition, so we would contend that the strophe exhibits a central rallying point around which it organizes its content.'[7] Nevertheless, identifying the strophe greatly aids understanding of the biblical text in this unique style of literature.

CLASSIFICATIONS

The one who would find the strophe must be aware that it comes in different lengths. The shortest strophe is one line, and the longest is eight lines. The various lengths of a strophe are as follows:

1. Monocolon

A strophe of a single line is known as a monocolon. Often a monocolon either begins or concludes a psalm. For example, a monocolon occurs in the last line of Psalm 2 and the first line of Psalm 18.

> How blessed are all who take refuge in Him!   (2:12c)

> I love You, O Lord, my strength   (18:1a)

2. Couplet

A two-line strophe is a couplet, which frequently appears in strophic structure. Some estimate that 70 to 75 percent of all strophes in the Psalms form a simple, two line couplet.[8] An example can be found in Psalms 2 and 4:

> Why are the nations in an uproar,   [1]
> And the peoples devising a vain thing?   [2]
>   (2:1)

> O sons of men, how long will my honor
>   become a reproach?   [1]
> *How long* will you love what is worthless
>   and aim at deception?   [2]
>   (4:1-2)

3. Triad

A strophic structure of three lines is a triad and is used less frequently than the basic couplet. A third line is added to a couplet to further expand or more deeply intensify the thought of the first two lines. One such example is Psalm 1:1.

> How blessed is the man who does not walk
>   in the counsel of the wicked,   [1]
> Nor stand in the path of sinners,   [2]
> Nor sit in the seat of scoffers!   [3]

4. Quatrain

This kind of strophe is comprised of four lines and is extremely rare in comparison to the couplet and triad. An example would be found in Psalm 1:3.

He will be like a tree *firmly* planted by the	
streams of water,	[1]
Which yields its fruit in its season	[2]
And its leaf does not wither;	[3]
And in whatever he does, he prospers.	[4]

5. Pentacolon

Here is a more complex strophic structure that uses five lines. It is a more rapid-fire style of communication in staccato fashion. Please note how Psalm 104:29-30 employs this important tool.

You hide Your face, they are dismayed;	[1]
You take away their spirit, they expire	[2]
And return to their dust	[3]
You send forth Your Spirit, they are created	[4]
And you renew the face of the ground.	[5]

6. Sexcolon

This is a strophe with six lines, an even more rare literary structure. One great example of this appears in Psalm 19:7-9, where six titles for God's word are given along with six characteristics and six effects are also listed.

The law of the LORD is perfect, restoring the soul;	[1]
The testimony of the LORD is sure, making wise	
the simple.	[2]
The precepts of the LORD are right, rejoicing	
the heart.	[3]
The commandment of the LORD is pure,	
enlightening the eyes.	[4]
The fear of the Lord is clean, enduring forever;	[5]
The judgments of the LORD are true; they are	
righteous altogether.	[6]

7. Heptacolon

The seven-line structure known as a heptacolon appears infre-
quently but drives home a point, like a nail being struck seven
times and driven into a board. Its first use in this ancient hymn
book is Psalm 12:4-5, where the point being driven home is the
arrogance of the words of the wicked:

Who have said, 'With our tongue we will prevail;	[1]
Our lips are our own;	[2]
Who is lord over us?'	[3]
Because of the devastation of the afflicted	[4]
Because of the groaning of the needy	[5]
'Now I will arise,' says the LORD;	[6]
I will set him in the safety for which he longs.	[7]

IDENTIFICATION

How does the expositor mark off and identify each strophe?[9]
The following help identify strophes:

1. Refrains

First, one should look for repeated refrains which usually signal
the end of a strophe. Nineteen psalms contain these identifying
refrains (39; 42-44; 46; 49; 56; 57; 59; 62; 67; 78; 80; 99; 107; 114;
136; 144; 145). Psalm 42:5, 11, for example, contains an easily recognizable refrain. The refrain signals the conclusion of a strophe,
and what follows initiates the next strophe:

Why are you in despair, O my soul?	
And why have you become disturbed within me?	
Hope in God, for I shall again praise Him	
For the help of His presence.	(42:5)

Why are you in despair, O my soul?	
And why have you become disturbed within me?	
Hope in God, for I shall yet praise Him,	
The help of my countenance and my God.	(42:11)

2. Selah

The preacher should watch for 'selah.' Selah appears seventy-one times in thirty-nine psalms (e.g., 3:2; 24:10; 39:11; 47:4; 60:4; 76:3; 88:10; 140:3). While its exact meaning is debatable, many see a connection with the Hebrew root, *salal*, 'to raise, to lift up.' The question then remains: Raise up *what*? It is possible that as a musical instruction it could mean to signal the raising-up of voices, or a crescendo of instruments, all to make a powerful, underscoring effect at that point of the psalm. Or, quite possibly, it could signal a pause for meditation, i.e., a musical interlude, a pause, or a change of key, as worshipers would lift up their thoughts to God.

> Many are saying of my soul,
> 'There is no deliverance for him in God.' Selah.   (3:2)

> I was crying to the Lord with my voice,
> And He answered me from His holy mountain.
>   Selah.   (3:4)

> Salvation belongs to the Lord;
> Your blessing be upon Your people! Selah.   (3:8)

3. Introverted Parallelism

The expositor must watch for a literary device called introverted parallelism or chiastic parallelism. In this pattern, the logical units develop in an A...B...B'...A' pattern. One such usage is found in Psalm 1:3:

> He will be like a tree firmly planted by streams of water,
> Which yields its fruit in its season
> And its leaf does not wither;
> And in whatever he does, he prospers.

4. Interrogative/Exclamation

Another strophe marker is an interrogative or exclamation. This is a poetic device where a single word ('for') or words ('O Lord,' 'O my God') stand outside of the basic pattern of the strophe. Two examples include Psalm 26:8 and 33:9:

O LORD, I love the habitation of Your house
And the place where Your glory dwells.   (26:8)

5. Distant Parallelism

Another marker of the strophe occurs when parallel paired
words are separated from each other. A slight distance between
parallel words marks the parameters of a strophe. For example,
in Psalm 18, 'I destroy those' (v. 40) and 'I beat them' (v. 42) have
four lines separating them.

> You have also made my enemies turn their backs to me,
> And I destroyed those who hated me.
> They cried for help, but there was none to save,
> Even to the Lord, but He did not answer them.
> Then I beat them fine as the dust before the wind;
> I emptied them out as the mire of the streets. (18:40-42)

6. Particles

Apart from the literary devices mentioned above, the expositor also watches for macrosyntactic particles — emphatic or
attention-grabbing words that mark off strophes. Such particles
help identify units of thought. They often translate *now, therefore, behold, if,* and *thus.* For instance, a particle may begin a new
section. Such an example can be found in Psalm 2:10:

> Now therefore, O kings, show discernment;
> Take warning, O judges of the earth.

Further, in Psalm 73:10, a different discourse level particle, also
translated *therefore*, launches a new section and marks the start
of a new portion of text.

> Therefore his people return to this place,
> And waters of abundance are drunk by them.

7. Introductory Formulas

Expository preachers of the Psalms also alert themselves to introductory formulas such as *wayhi* when it commences a context.

Wayhi, though often untranslatable, carries exegetical significance. In Psalm 94, the poet recounts the corruption of his enemies (v. 21), but affirms God's protection, thus making the transition to a new strophe with the use of *wayhi* (v. 22). Another introductory formula is a statement like 'God has spoken in His holiness' (60:6), which signals to the reader that a new section is beginning.

> They band themselves together against the life
>   of the righteous
> And condemn the innocent to death.
> But the Lord has been my stronghold,
> And my God the rock of my refuge.   (94:21-22)

8. Speaker Change
One identifies strophes by changes in speaker. The most frequent speaker change occurs between the psalmist and God. For example, Psalm 50:4-6 switches from Asaph to God to Asaph.

> He summons the heavens above,
> And the earth, to judge His people:
> 'Gather My godly ones to Me,
> Those who have made a covenant with Me by sacrifice.'
> And the heavens declare His righteousness,
> For God Himself is judge. Selah.

9. Addressee Change
The expositor notices transitions from one addressee to another. He asks: To whom is the speaker talking? For example, Psalm 43:3-4 records the psalmist praying to God for deliverance, but he shifts to address himself in verse 5, signaling a break.

> O send out Your light and Your truth, let them lead me;
> Let them bring me to Your holy hill
> And to Your dwelling places.
> Then I will go to the altar of God,
> To God my exceeding joy;
> And upon the lyre I shall praise You, O God, my God.
> Why are you in despair, O my soul?

And why are you disturbed within me?
Hope in God, for I shall again praise Him,
The help of my countenance and my God.   (43:3-5)

10. Topic Change

The exegete also watches for a shift in topic. A move from one
theme to another distinguishes strophes. Psalm 36, for example,
pivots from the corruption of the wicked (vv. 3-4) to the loyalty
to God (vv. 5-6), thus marking a strophe.

The words of his mouth are wickedness and deceit;
He has ceased to be wise and to do good.
He plans wickedness upon his bed;
He sets himself on a path that is not good;
He does not despise evil.
Your lovingkindness, O Lord, extends to the heavens,
Your faithfulness reaches to the skies.
Your righteousness is like the mountains of God;
Your judgments are like a great deep.
O Lord, You preserve man and beast.   (36:3-6)

11. Form Change

Change in literary type also exposes breaks in the text. Many
psalms move from trouble to triumph, complaint to thanksgiving,
or distress to trust. Such transitions signal strophes. Psalm 28, for
instance, transitions from imprecation (vv. 4-5) to praise (vv. 6-7):

Requite them according to their work and according to
    the evil of their practices;
Requite them according to the deeds of their hands;
Repay them their recompense.
Because they do not regard the works of the Lord
Nor the deeds of His hands,
He will tear them down and not build them up.
Blessed be the Lord,
Because He has heard the voice of my supplication.
The Lord is my strength and my shield;
My heart trusts in Him, and I am helped;

Therefore my heart exults,
And with my song I shall thank Him. (28:4-7)

POETIC STANZAS

Moreover, the expositor must also note the stanzas or major divisions of a psalm. What the paragraph is to prose, the stanza is to poetry. Technically, an entire psalm may consist of only one stanza, such as Psalm 117, but this is rare. Almost every psalm divides into multiple stanzas that represent a series of lines arranged together in a recurring pattern. Thus, in the Psalms, a stanza consists of one or more verses with a focused thought or unified theme. Some translations insert spaces between stanzas. The poem is the house, the stanza is the room, and the strophe is the furniture.[10] To identify stanzas or paragraphs one looks for:

SUBJECT CHANGE

Each stanza conveys one basic thought. A change in topic may indicate a change in stanza. For example, Psalm 19 contains two stanzas: verses 1-6 speak about God's natural revelation in creation while verses 7-14 address God's special revelation in Scripture.

REPEATING REFRAINS

The expositor will want to be aware of recurring phrases, usually at the end of a stanza (cf. 42:5, 11; 43:5; 46:7, 11; 107:1, 8, 15, 21, 31, 43). Refrains determine stanza divisions and enable a listening audience to join in. A primary example is found in Psalm 46. Then, this same refrain is repeated six verses later. Finally, the psalmist repeats the refrain again in the next psalm. This indicates that these two psalms originally belonged together.

The LORD of hosts is with us;
The God of Jacob is our stronghold. Selah. (46:7)

The LORD of hosts is with us;
The God of Jacob is our stronghold. Selah.   (46:11)

INCLUSIONS

The expositor must look for an envelope structure in which a
word or phrase is repeated, once at the beginning of the paragraph and then at the end. This literary device is known as
inclusion or inclusio. This repetition creates a bracket effect that
surrounds the stanza. For example, Psalm 8 begins and ends
with the same identical declaration:

O LORD, our Lord,
How majestic is Your name in all the earth,
Who have displayed Your splendor above the heavens!
                                                   (8:1)

O LORD, our Lord,
How majestic is Your name in all the earth!   (8:9)

INTERNAL PATTERNS

Other literary devices signal a change in stanzas, such as introverted parallelism (6:9), distant parallelism (18:39-41), or
chiasm, an A...B...B...A pattern. Here is an example of distant
parallelism:

For You have girded me with strength for battle;
You have subdued under me those who rose up against
    me.
You have also made my enemies turn their backs to me,
And I destroyed those who hated me.
They cried for help, but there was none to save,
Even to the LORD, but He did not answer them.
                                                   (18:39-41)

SPEAKER CHANGE

The expositor must also observe changes in speaker from stanza to stanza. A shift in speaker may mark one stanza from the next. Psalm 2:3 serves as a primary example. Here God's enemies speak first, taunting God (2:3). Then, God Himself speaks (2:6). Next, God's Son speaks (2:7-9). Finally, the psalmist himself speaks (2:10-12).

'Let us tear their fetters apart
And cast away their cords from us!'   (2:3)

'But as for Me, I have installed My King
Upon Zion, My holy mountain.'   (2:6)

'Ask of Me, and I will surely give the nations as Your
    inheritance,
And the very ends of the earth as Your possession.' (2:8)

Now therefore, O kings, show discernment;
Take warning, O judges of the earth.   (2:10)

SELAH

As with the division into strophes, the preacher will want to be aware of the insertion of 'selah.' This may introduce the end of one stanza and prepare the reader for the beginning of a new stanza. One such place where 'selah' concludes a stanza is in Psalm 7:5:

Let the enemy pursue my soul and overtake it;
And let him trample my life down to the ground
And lay my glory in the dust. Selah.

ACROSTICS

The eight-line structure of Psalm 119 marks off stanzas because of the repetition of the first letter of each word. The first letters of each of the twenty-two, eight-verse stanzas comprise the entire Hebrew alphabet:

(1) Verses 1-8 (*Aleph*); (2) Verses 9-16 (*Beth*); (3) Verses 17-24 (*Gimel*); (4) Verses 25-32 (*Daleth*); (5) Verses 33-40 (*He*); (6) Verses 41-48 (*Vav*); (7) Verses 49-56 (*Zayin*); (8) Verses 57-64 (*Heth*); (9) Verses 65-72 (*Teth*); (10) Verses 73-80 (*Yodh*); (11) Verses 81-88 (*Kaph*); (12) Verses 89-96 (*Lamedh*); (13) Verses 97-104 (*Mem*); (14) Verses 105-112 (*Nuu*); (15) Verses 113-120 (*Samekh*); (16) Verses 121-128 (*Ayin*); (17) Verses 129-136 (*Pe*); (18) Verses 137-144 (*Tsadhe*); (19) Verses 145-152 (*Qoph*); (20) Verses 153-160 (*Resh*); (21) Verses 161-168 (*Shin*); and (22) Verses 169-176 (*Tav*).

BLOCK DIAGRAM

As the expositor notes the basic features of the psalm, he will want to turn his attention to writing a syntactical outline. This step, known as block diagramming, provides a visual layout of the passage. Block diagramming allows the preacher to visualize word and sentence relationships at a glance. The diagram offers a bird's-eye view of the text, as well as a close-up view, to see how each part fits into the whole. The idea is to rewrite the text visually, phrase by phrase, in its exact order. This diagram allows the preacher to trace the divinely inspired flow of thought. It exposes the sermon proposition and outline, revealing what is central and what is subordinate.

It should be noted that block diagramming is much different from the 'line diagramming' taught in most English classes. While a line diagram obscures word order, a block diagram maintains the original wording. One should read Walter Kaiser, *Toward an Exegetical Theology* and *Malachi: God's Unchanging Love* for examples of block diagrams.[11]

Each syntactical unit, which is a line in Hebrew poetry, should be isolated on a separate line of the block diagram. Such diagrams do not divide or subordinate adjectives, construct chains, or direct objects. They do, however, subordinate adverbial phrases and internal segments of chiasms. One should insert a dialogue box for direct discourse to avoid confusion, watch for macrosyntactical particles that mark new sections, and attempt to visually display repetition and wordplay. The purpose of having a block diagram for each stanza in the psalm is to show the interrelationships of whole sentences, giving special attention to the parallelism.

GRASPING THE GRAMMAR

The Bible claims verbal inspiration, even to the smallest letter and stroke (Matt. 5:18; 2 Tim. 3:16). That is, every word of Scripture is breathed out by God and is, therefore, vitally important and profitable. Only grammatical interpretation honors the verbal inspiration of Scripture. As a result, expositors must give careful attention to the grammar of Scripture if they are to rightly understand the meaning of the biblical text.

As we have seen in this chapter, grammar deals with the meaning of words and the relationship of these words in a sentence. Grammatical interpretation gives careful attention to the individual words of Scripture and how they are used. To be sure, this exacting discipline is absolutely essential if the preacher is to understand the Bible properly, specifically, the psalm being studied and preached. May all expositors dig into the divinely-inspired text, rightly handling it in order to extract its God-given meaning.

RESEARCH
THE HISTORY

Delve into the historical setting of the psalm

To be rightly interpreted, a psalm must always be studied within the context of its historical setting. Understanding the ancient background of a biblical passage is absolutely critical for determining its true meaning. The Christian faith is not a religion based upon mere philosophical propositions that are divorced from the time-space backdrop in which it was originally given. To the contrary, the biblical message is rooted and grounded in its original background of real time and space involving real individuals. Contained in the biblical record are actual persons in specific places, individuals who were involved in authentic events of history. If the message of the Bible is to be properly understood, its historical setting must be carefully researched.

John MacArthur speaks to this very point, 'Knowing the historical setting of a passage often helps immeasurably to understand its meaning. A major effort of research to develop the historical background of a passage often is the major key to its interpretation.'[1] This is to say, bridging the historical gap is critically important to accurately interpret the biblical text. Christianity is a historical faith, rooted and grounded in the soil of redemptive history.

CHECKING THE HISTORICAL CONTEXT

This fact underscores the need for understanding a psalm's history. Stephen Olford writes, 'Make sure that you can place the text chronologically, geographically, situationally, and generally within the historical realities surrounding it... How does the "occasion" of the biblical book as a whole impact the text to be studied? What historical factors, within the biblical book or external to it, are relevant to the understanding of the text to be studied? What is the real life situation, as best as can be determined, that surrounds the text?'[2] This being so, if the preacher is to grasp the historical setting of a biblical passage, he must consult the necessary tools, like Bible dictionaries and encyclopedias.

This is especially true in preaching the Psalms. In rightly interpreting this ancient book, a great amount of work must be done in exploring its historical background. With some psalms, the historical setting is readily provided in its superscription that sits atop the text. With other psalms, the historical background is clearly stated or indirectly implied in the main body of the text. In order to effectively preach the Psalms, the expositor must acquire a general understanding of the full breadth of redemptive history. This includes knowing something of the greater flow of God's working from eternity past to eternity future.

A Broad Grasp Required

More than any other book, preaching the Psalms requires a broader grasp of the historical background of the entire Bible. The span of knowledge required extends from before creation to the new creation and beyond. It reaches back to before the foundation of the world and reaches forward into the endless future of the ages to come. The basic periods of history referenced in the Psalms require the knowledge of the following:

ETERNITY PAST

Understanding the Psalms requires a theological awareness of the eternality of God. This includes knowing something of His eternal decree issued before the foundation of the world (Eph. 1:11). As the expositor approaches the book of Psalms, he must be keenly aware of this divine decree in handling selected verses.

God's Pre-existence

God is the eternal God, without beginning. He is the uncreated Creator, the first Cause of all that is. Before the creation of the world, God alone existed. Before the foundation of the world, there was God alone. There has never been a time when God was not. 'Before the mountains were born Or You gave birth to the earth and the world, Even from everlasting to everlasting, You are God' (90:2); 'Your throne is established from of old; You are from everlasting' (93:2).

Eternal Decree

In God's book, He recorded the exact number of days each person would live — a number permanently written long before any individual is born. 'And in Your book were all written the days that were ordained for me, when as yet there was not one of them' (139:16).

This decree of God is His eternal purpose, according to the counsel of His own will, by which He has foreordained, for His own glory, all that comes to pass. There is only one eternal decree, a predetermined plan that is all-inclusive, involving everything that comes to past, including both good and evil. Yet God is not the author of sin. There is a distinction made between His directive and permissive decree, or between what God causes and what He allows. The highest end of the divine decree is God's own glory. Thus, before time began, God foreordained all that would come to pass and recorded it in His book — in His eternal decree.

THE BEGINNING

Bridging the historical gap involves going back to the dawn of civilization with creation (Gen. 1-2), the Fall (Gen. 3), the Flood (Gen. 6-8), and the Table of Nations (Gen. 10). Multiple psalmists reference each of these four foundational events at the beginning of human history. They record how God created everything out of nothing by the word of His power. The psalmists address the plunging of mankind into sin, the worldwide catastrophic flood, and the ancestors and nations of mankind.

CREATION

The Psalms teach that God created the heavens and the earth. He spoke everything into being, out of nothing. Psalmists account for each day of creation, beginning with day one, when the Lord made light and initiated day and night (118:27); describe day two, when the Lord made a firmament and divided the waters (104:2; 136:6); day three, when the Lord made dry land, seas, rivers, and vegetation (24:1-2; 33:7; 95:5; 104:3, 5-9; 136:5-6); day four, when the Lord made the sun, moon, and stars (8:3-4; 74:16-17; 104:19-20; 136:7-9; 148:3, 6); day five, when the Lord made sea and flying creatures (104:24-26; 148:10); day six, when the Lord made land animals (104:14-15, 27-28) and man (100:3; 149:2) in His image (Gen 1:27; Ps. 139:14) to have dominion over the earth (Gen. 1:26;

Pss. 8:4-8; 104:20-24; 115:16). All creation is designed to magnify the greatness of God Himself. The entire universe is a grand theatre, showcasing the glory of God (19:1-6; 8:1; 50:6).

THE FALL

Rightly interpreting the Psalms also requires a theological grasp of the doctrine of original sin and the Fall of the human race in Adam. When the first man sinned, the entire human race sinned. By the disobedience of the one man, the many were made unrighteous. Through the sin of Adam, a sin nature has been subsequently transmitted to all mankind, resulting in the total depravity that affects every part of every man. 'Behold, I was brought forth in iniquity, And in sin my mother conceived me' (51:5). 'The wicked are estranged from the womb; These who speak lies go astray from birth' (58:3). As a result, every human being chooses to rebel against God and turn aside from Him. The extent of man's sinfulness is total:

> The LORD has looked down from heaven upon the sons
>   of men
> To see if there are any who understand,
> Who seek after God.
> They have all turned aside, together they have become
>   corrupt;
> There is no one who does good, not even one'
> $\qquad$ (14:2-3; cf. 104:29).

THE FLOOD

The Psalms also address the universal flood in the days of Noah. The psalmist David clearly sets forth the sovereignty of God as the cause of the Flood. 'The LORD sat as King at the flood; yes, the LORD sits as King forever' (29:10). This worldwide flood is the direct result of God exercising His supreme authority over the earth.

PATRIARCHAL PERIOD

Preaching the Psalms requires a keen understanding of the patriarchal period. The psalmist refers to the historical period when Abram was called out of Ur to a land that God would reveal to him. By this summons, a nation was born, Israel, God's sovereignly chosen people. The Lord created this nation, Israel, to be His special covenant people. Later, Israel was taken down into Egypt, where God's chosen people were held in bondage and misery. If the expositor is to rightly explain many of the psalms, he must be familiar with this period of biblical history.

ABRAHAMIC COVENANT

The psalmist who penned Psalm 105 mentions the Abrahamic covenant and the promise of the land to Abraham. 'He has remembered His covenant forever, The word which He commanded to a thousand generations, The covenant which He made with Abraham' (105:8-9); God confirmed this covenant with Isaac: 'And His oath to Isaac' (105:9); and Jacob: 'Then He confirmed it to Jacob for a statute, to Israel as an everlasting covenant' (105:10). This covenant promised to His people the land of Canaan, saying, 'To you I will give the land of Canaan as the portion of your inheritance' (105:11).

EGYPTIAN BONDAGE

Understanding the Psalms also requires a grasp of the time of Israel's bondage and suffering in Egypt. The Lord providentially led the Israelites into Egypt, where He exalted Joseph (105:16-22). God sovereignly used Egypt to demonstrate His greatness and to judge Israel: 'Israel also came into Egypt; Thus Jacob sojourned in the land of Ham' (105:23). Various other psalms are set against the backdrop of Israel's deliverance from Egypt in the Exodus. These psalmists allude to the crossing of

the Red Sea and the destruction of Pharaoh's army in its waters
(74:12-17). In addition, these psalmists make mention of Israel's
wilderness wanderings.

THE EXODUS

The expositor must also possess a knowledge of the events surrounding Israel's deliverance out of Egyptian bondage. Five
individual psalms (78, 105, 106, 114, 136) address the exodus
of Israel from Egypt under the leadership of Moses and Aaron
(105:26). The expositor must be aware of the severe plagues that
God inflicted upon the Egyptians (78:44-51; 103:6-7; 105:28-36).
This special emphasis on the ten plagues shows God's sovereignty over Pharaoh (105:26-36). The Exodus proved to be a
spiritual deliverance by which God redeemed His people to be
His inheritance through the death of a sacrificial lamb (74:2). As
Israel left Egypt, God provided for their financial and physical
needs (105:37-41).

RED SEA

Moreover, the expositor must understand the historical events
surrounding the powerful parting of the waters of the Red Sea:
'Thus He rebuked the Red Sea and it dried up, And He led them
through the deeps, as through the wilderness' (106:9). This
enabled Israel to walk through on dry ground, ('You led Your
people like a flock By the hand of Moses and Aaron' [77:20; cf.
77:16-19; 106:7-12; 114:3, 5; 136:11-12]). This dramatic crossing, as God parted the waters of the Red Sea, is described by the
psalmist:

> The sea looked and fled;
> The Jordan turned back...
> What ails you, O sea, that you flee?
> O Jordan, that you turn back?   (114:3, 5)

MOUNT SINAI

Further, the preacher must comprehend the circumstances and theological issues involved in the giving of the Law to Moses at Sinai (68:7-10, 16-18; 99:6-7). Sinai, the place where the Law was established, is mentioned as Horeb (106:16-23). Sinai is the mountain where Moses ascended and God descended. There, the God of Israel appeared in blazing holiness, issuing His Law ('The earth quaked; The heavens also dropped rain at the presence of God; Sinai itself quaked at the presence of God, the God of Israel' [68:8; cf. 68:17]). After Israel worshiped idols and committed immorality, the psalmist notes, Moses pleaded with God not to destroy the nation (106:23).

THE WILDERNESS

Also, the expositor must grasp the main events, route, and issues surrounding Israel's experiences in the wilderness. This dismal period of testing serves as a backdrop for several psalms (78:14-72; 95:10-11; 99:7; 105:39-41; 106:13-15, 26-31). Israel rejected the positive report of Joshua and Caleb about taking the promised land, and instead chose to return to Egypt, incurring God's judgment (106:24-27). Israel encountered the prophet Balaam, who counseled Balak to seduce them with immorality and idolatry (106:28-31). When Israel fell into sin, God judged them severely. In the end, Moses became impatient with Israel and struck the rock in anger (106:32-33; 95:10-11).

PROMISED LAND

The Psalms also draw upon the historical account of Israel's entrance into the promised land, including their conquest of their enemies. This was to fulfill the covenant that God had pledged to Abraham and his descendants.

LAND ENTERED

The psalmist speaks of the crossing of the Jordan when God parted the river in order for the Jews to enter the promised land. The waters of Jordan could not resist His sovereign will and irresistible power. This parting of the Jordan was a powerful demonstration of God's unrivaled authority over Israel and this world, as well as His care for them ('He turned the sea into dry land; They passed through the river on foot; There let us rejoice in Him!' [66:6; cf. 114:3, 5]). Yet while Israel entered the land, the never fully inherited it.

CONQUEST

Rightly interpreted, the Psalms require an awareness of the conquest of the promised land ('You with Your own hand drove out the nations' [44:2; cf. 44:3, 20-22; 78:54-64; 80:8-14; 105:11]). Many psalms reflect upon Israelite victories in the land over the Canaanites. Some of Israel's greatest military moments came during the days of the Judges (78:56-58; 83:9-12; 106:34-43). Rebelliousness, though, continued to be Israel's way of life in the promised land. The sin of defiance against God proved to be a recurring theme under the Judges. Israel set up high places to worship false gods in her new land, and God responded with jealousy to this disloyalty toward Him (106:34-39).

DAVIDIC MONARCHY

After the period of the Judges, Israel appointed kings who ruled over them, first as a united monarchy under Saul, David, and Solomon, then as a divided monarchy with two kings, one each over a northern and southern kingdom. It was to David that God made a covenant to establish a king over His people forever. No area of historical background is more necessary for the expositor of the Psalms than the period of the monarchy of Israel.

DAVID ENTHRONED

David, the second king of Israel, authored half of the psalms, making him the key human figure (2; 34-41; 51-65; 68-70; 86; 95; 101; 103; 108-110; 122; 124; 131; 138-145). The psalmist Asaph emphasized God's choice of David as being from the tribe of Judah: 'But chose the tribe of Judah... He also chose David His servant And took him from the sheepfolds' (78:68a, 70). The psalmist Ethan underscored the Davidic covenant which God established with David ('Once I have sworn by My holiness; I will not lie to David' [89:35; cf. 89:37-51; 132:11-12]). This covenant which God established with His anointed ruler elevated David and his descendants to a special position before Him (89:26-27). By the Davidic covenant, God's oath concerning an earthly kingdom was made certain to his descendants (89:35-36).

JERUSALEM ESTABLISHED

At this time, God exalted Jerusalem as His special dwelling place. 'There is a river whose streams make glad the city of God, The holy dwelling places of the Most High. God is in the midst of her, she will not be moved; God will help her when morning dawns' (46:4-5). As the capital of God's kingdom, Zion enjoyed His protection and blessing. God's presence within the holy city made it immune from the raging nations outside its walls (46:1-11). When Israel's enemies advanced against the city of God, they were swiftly destroyed by His devastating power (48:3-8; 76:3-6). God provided the city's residents with the necessities of life (132:15-16). His abundant blessings were like life-giving streams flowing through the city. The Temple was built in Jerusalem by Solomon, which became a uniquely-blessed place for worshipers to come (84:1-12).

RELIGIOUS FESTIVALS

Religious pilgrims made their journey to Jerusalem, finding great comfort and delight ('Walk about Zion and go around her;

Count her towers; Consider her ramparts; Go through her palaces, That you may tell it to the next generation' [48:12-13; cf. 84:1; 122:3]). The expositor must also be aware of the historical background of worship in the Temple, including a knowledge of the sons of Korah (42, 44-49, 84-85, 87) and Asaph (50, 73-83) and the worship they led.

BABYLONIAN CAPTIVITY

The historical backdrop of the Psalms further covers the period of time from the Babylonian exile to Israel's return seventy years later. Once the newly-returned Jews were in their land, they undertook the work of rebuilding the Temple and the wall around Jerusalem. But despite this restoration, the people soon lapsed back into many of the same sins that led to their exile in the first place: covetousness, idolatry, callous hearts, neglecting the poor, and oppressing orphans and widows.

THE EXILE

Expounding the Psalms requires a working knowledge of the Babylonian exile, which was much like a second Egyptian bondage. During this period of captivity, God subjected His people to burdensome labor for their sins. In the Babylonian invasion, the city of Jerusalem suffered a violent overthrow and total ruin. The psalmist lamented that Babylonian soldiers entered the Temple and destroyed it with their axes before burning it to the ground ('Turn Your footsteps toward the perpetual ruins; The enemy has damaged everything within the sanctuary. Your adversaries have roared in the midst of Your meeting place; They have set up their own standards for signs' [74:3-4]). During this dark hour, Israel was carried to Babylon, where they were taunted by their captors and derided for their faith ('By the rivers of Babylon, There we sat down and wept, When we remembered Zion' [137:1]).

THE RETURN

In addition, the expositor must possess a thorough grasp of the historical events, dates, and personalities surrounding Israel's return from Babylonian captivity to the promised land under the leadership of Zerubbabel, Ezra, and Nehemiah ('Save us, O LORD our God, and gather us from among the nations' 106:47a; cf. 107:2-5, 10-12, 17-18). The people cried to the Lord and He delivered them from their exile in this foreign land ('Then they cried out to the Lord in their trouble; He delivered them out of their distresses' 107:6; cf. 107:13-16, 19-22, 28-42). Back in their land, Israel rebuilt the Temple in the holy city of Jerusalem. The Songs of Ascent were sung at this time, during this post-exilic period, when Israel would make their annual pilgrimages to worship in the Temple in Jerusalem. God's people experienced indescribable joy in their return to Judah to the point of laughter and song (126:1-2).

MESSIANIC COMING

The Psalter has much to say about the first advent of Jesus Christ. As pre-written history, many psalms look forward to the focal point of history — the coming of the Messiah to suffer and die upon the cross for sinners. As Jesus indicated, 'all things which are written about Me in the Law of Moses and the Prophets and the Psalms must be fulfilled' (Luke 24:44). The expositor must first interpret each Messianic psalm within its immediate Old Testament historical setting, which provides sufficient interpretive information for understanding the meaning of the psalm. Knowledge of the historical events surrounding Jesus' first coming will enable the expositor to see how Jesus and the apostles comprehended and applied the Psalms, and how Jesus fulfilled predictive prophecies.

INCARNATION

The Psalms clearly address the incarnation of Christ in His first coming. The psalmist David writes that God has a Son, One who will come into the world to rule over and judge it: 'I will surely tell of the decree of the Lord: He said to Me, "You are My Son, today I have begotten You"' (2:7). The writer of Hebrews quotes Psalm 40:7 ('Then I said, "Behold, I come; in the scroll of the book it is written of me"') that finds its fulfillment in Jesus Christ (Heb. 10:5-7). As such, Christ was born the seed of David ('The Lord has sworn to David A truth from which He will not turn back: "Of the fruit of your body I will set upon your throne"' [132:11; cf. Acts 13:23]). After His birth, the psalmist Solomon prophesied, great persons would come to adore Him ('Let the kings of Tarshish and of the islands bring presents; The kings of Sheba and Seba offer gifts' [72:10; cf. Matt. 2:1-11]). Jesus lived a sinless and perfect life, characterized by the eager hearing and obeying of what God says in His Word. Such obedience to the Scripture arose from His willing heart and active obedience to the Law. This qualified Him to be the substitutionary Lamb for sinners in His atoning death (40:6, 8).

PUBLIC MINISTRY

The Psalms, likewise, address the public ministry of Christ. Multiple psalmists repeatedly speak of the world's rejection of Him, His cleansing of the Temple, and His preaching in parables. As Jesus began His public ministry, He drove the money-changers from the Temple. His disciples would later recall the words of the psalmist as directly applying to Christ ('For zeal for Your house has consumed me, and the reproaches of those who reproach You have fallen on me' [69:9; cf. John 2:17]). It was zeal for God's glory that drove Him to cleanse the Temple. Jesus' preaching included the giving of parables ('I will open my mouth in a parable; I will utter dark sayings of old' [78:2; cf. Matt. 13:34-35]). He used parables — earthly stories with heavenly meaning — in order to give moral instruction and spiritual applications. Nevertheless, He was rejected by His brethren, even by His own family (69:8; John 1:11; 7:3). He was hated by the Jews (69:4; John 15:24-25) and rejected by the Jewish leaders (118:22; Matt. 21:42; John 7:48).

PASSION MINISTRY

One psalmist foretold how, the night before His crucifixion, the Lord Jesus would meet with His disciples in the Upper Room. Christ would explain to them the world's unjustified hatred of Him, fulfilling the words of another psalm (35:19; 69:4; John 15:25). Jesus foretold that one of the twelve would betray Him, applying the very words of the psalmist to Himself (41:9; John 13:10-11, 18). Peter later noted that the Scripture had spoken of a betrayer long beforehand (69:25; 109:8; Acts 1:20).

VIOLENT CRUCIFIXION

The psalmist David recorded many of the specifics of the crucifixion of Christ. His hands and feet were nailed to the cross ('They pierced my hands and my feet' [22:16; cf. John 19:18; 20:25]). Jesus was forsaken by God. His very words recorded upon the cross as He experienced extreme abandonment in His crucifixion were from one of David's psalms ('My God, my God, why have You forsaken me?' [22:1; cf. Matt. 27:46; Mark 15:34]). While on the cross, David writes that Christ bore reproach ('But I am a worm and not a man, A reproach of men and despised by the people' [22:6; cf. 69:7, 9, 20; Rom. 15:3]).

Further, various psalmists foretell that On the cross, Christ would suffer intense pain ('I am poured out like water, and all my bones are out of joint; my heart is like wax; it is melted within me. My strength is dried up like a potsherd, and my tongue cleaves to my jaws; and You lay me in the dust of death' [22:14-15; cf. Luke 22:42, 44]). He was offered gall and vinegar to drink ('They also gave me gall for my food and for my thirst they gave me vinegar to drink' [69:21; cf. Matt. 27:34, 48; Mark 15:23, 36; Luke 23:36; John 19:28-30]). His garments were parted and lots were cast for His clothing ('They divide my garments among them, and for my clothing they cast lots' [22:18; cf. Matt. 27:35]). Not a bone of

His body was broken (34:20; John 19:33, 36). In this death, Jesus was a priest after the order of Melchizedek (110:4; Heb. 5:5-6), who offered a perfect sacrifice for sinners.

BODILY RESURRECTION

The psalmist David further prophesied the bodily resurrection of Jesus Christ (16:10). Peter applies these words to the greater Son of David, the Lord Jesus Christ (Acts 2:25-28), as does Paul (Acts 13:35). The resurrection of Christ is certified proof that Jesus is the Son of God.

TRIUMPHANT ASCENSION

The psalmist further foretold of the triumphant ascension of the Lord Jesus, back to the heights of heaven ('You have ascended on high, You have led captive Your captives; You have received gifts among men, Even among the rebellious also, that the LORD God may dwell there' [68:18]). Paul later quotes this text in Ephesians 4:8, where the apostle sees its fulfillment in Christ's ascension to heaven. He depicts Christ as returning from battle on earth with the spoils of His victory at the cross, bestowing them upon His people.

SOVEREIGN ENTHRONEMENT

The psalmist David also described the enthronement of Christ in heaven at the right hand of God the Father. Sitting at the 'right hand' of the Lord speaks of the Son's presence in heaven with the Father and the sharing of His splendor and authority. That Jesus is seated represents His completed work on the cross ('The LORD says to my Lord: "Sit at My right hand Until I make Your enemies a footstool for Your feet"' [110:1]). The Messiah's foes will become His footstool under His sovereign rule over history (Heb. 10:13).

FINAL CONSUMMATION

Preaching of the Psalms requires familiarity with the end of the age. The Psalter contains predictive prophecy regarding the latter days at the consummation of the ages. Thus, one must understand some basic chronology of end-time events, such as the wrath of God, the day of the Lord, the second coming of Jesus Christ, and His future reign.

FINAL JUDGMENT

The Psalms foretell the coming of the great Judge to judge the world in righteousness. When He comes, the whole earth will stand before Him (96:13). This coming Judge has been appointed by God to preside over all. He will pour out His wrath on the nations, instilling them with terror. He will break them with a rod of iron, and squashing them like grapes (2:8-9). The psalmist says that the Lord will burn up His adversaries, and melt the mountains like wax (97:3, 5; 2:4-5a).

FUTURE REIGN

During the Messianic reign, nations and kings will bow down to the Son (2:12) and receive a blessing for taking 'refuge in Him' (2:12). The Lord's enemies will become His footstool (110:1, 5, 6). God's future rule will be a perfectly righteous government in which justice will reign throughout all of the ages to come (45:6-7; John 5:30; Rev. 19:11). In that day, God will exercise universal dominion (72:11; cf. Phil. 2:9, 11). Many psalmists also foretell that He will execute judgment and righteousness in Jacob, and His people will worship at His footstool (99:4, 5; 110:5-6).

A FRAMEWORK FOR HISTORY

It should be obvious that preaching the Psalms necessitates a strategic grasp of the entire sweep of world history, and even eternity past. It requires the expositor to cultivate a full breath of biblical knowledge, both in the Old and New Testaments, that enables him to see how God's covenant love and man's repeated rebellion play out on the stage of human history. The end of history recapitulates the beginning of history, with the cross of Christ in the center.

From creation to the future Messianic reign of Christ, the expositor must have a working knowledge of the unfolding drama of redemptive history. From paradise to the patriarchs, from Egypt to Canaan, from the Babylonian exile to Israel's return, from Bethlehem to Zion, the one who would expound the Psalms must be able to trace the flow of redemptive history and draw out the life-altering, day-to-day applications.

The author of Psalm 33 provides a biblical definition of God's sovereignty over human history: 'The Lord nullifies the counsel of the nations; He frustrates the plans of the peoples. The counsel of the Lord stands forever, The plans of His heart from generation to generation' (33:10-11). That is to say, all human history is the unfolding of God's eternal purpose and sovereign plan. The one who would rightly expound the Psalms must be keenly aware of these various stages of redemptive history, as has been surveyed in this chapter. The fact is, history is *His* story.

15

SURVEY THE GEOGRAPHY

Explore the geographical setting of the psalm

n order to unlock the meaning of the Psalms, there is one more interpretive gap that must be bridged — the geographical gap. The backdrop of every psalm occurred in real places on the earth and affects, to one degree or another, the interpretation of the biblical text. For this reason, John Broadus remarks in general, 'We have constant need of observing facts of geography, which would throw light on the text.'[1] The book of Psalms is no exception. The geographical sites of the Psalter cover diverse locations in Babylon, or present-day Iraq, to the east of Israel; Egypt and Ethiopia to the south; Tarshish, which is modern-day Spain, in the west; and Mount Hebron, in the north. The ancient world of the Psalms served as a grand stage involving three different continents — Asia, Africa, and Europe — and must be taken into consideration when interpreting a particular passage.

The geographical background poses a challenge for every preacher today because they live, for the most part, thousands of miles from the land of the Bible and many centuries removed. Thus, a keen understanding of the geography of this part of the world — ancient Israel, Egypt, Babylon, Assyria, and the Mediterranean coast areas — is critically important in rightly interpreting many passages. A knowledge of the land of the Middle East and surrounding regions helps make the Scripture come alive. In order to bridge this geographical gap, a reliable set of Bible maps, Bible dictionaries, and encyclopedias aid the proper understanding of some Psalms.

WHY STUDY GEOGRAPHY?

Geography is especially important in understanding the Psalms. The center stage for the redemptive drama described in the Psalter was the narrow strip of land in Israel, along with various surrounding nations. The Psalms were compiled to lead Israel in her worship of God, specifically, in the holy city, Jerusalem, where God's people went to praise Him. An understanding of the promised land and the surrounding regions is essential in understanding the message of the Psalms.

Sound hermeneutical principles bridge the geographical gap and help reveal the theological meaning as it relates to real events in concrete locations. A knowledge of the land of the Bible makes the Scripture come alive. Geography adds color and increases the emotional impact of the Psalms. Further, a proper understanding of geography guards against an allegorical interpretation of the Psalms. This chapter will consider the three basic geographical areas mentioned in the Psalms: Jerusalem, Israel, and the surrounding regions.

JERUSALEM

The holy city, Jerusalem, is the prime stage for the message in the book of Psalms. Located fifteen miles west of the northern tip of the Dead Sea and thirty-three miles east of the Mediterranean Sea, Jerusalem is the focal point of redemptive history. The holy city rests 2,700 feet in elevation, making the journey from any direction an upward ascent. Jerusalem was originally the rock escarpment on the ridge between the Kidron and Tyropoeon Valleys.

JERUSALEM

Jerusalem is where the tabernacle resided, where the Temple stood, and where much of the Messiah's ministry was prophesied and occurred. It was here in Jerusalem that the Jewish leaders rejected Jesus (118:22), the Jews and Gentiles combined against Him (2:1-2), Jesus was betrayed (41:9; 55:12-14), crucified (22:16), forsaken by the Father (22:1), mocked (22:7-8), offered gall and vinegar (69:21), that His garments were parted and lots cast for His garments (22:18), that He was buried (22:15), that He rose from the dead (16:10), and that He ascended to heaven (68:18).

ZION

Languages and cultures often use multiple names for a geographical place, and Jerusalem is no exception. Zion is another name for the holy city, Jerusalem. Originally, a Canaanite city conquered by David (2 Sam. 5:7), God Himself became the founder of the city of Zion, as it became the possession of His people (Ps. 87:5; Isa. 14:32). Later, Zion came to refer to the Temple area and then to the entire city of David (126:1). Thus, it constituted a formidable natural fortress for its inhabitants, a refuge for the people of God (46:1). God has a great future for the city of Zion (102:13, 16). In all, the name Zion occurs thirty-nine times in the book of Psalms.

Mount Zion

Jerusalem is also referred to as Mount Zion (125:1). This mount upon which Zion rests is a relatively low hill compared with larger mountains, such as the snow-capped Lebanon range. Jerusalem itself rests upon the southwest mount of Mount Zion (48:2). Concerning the stability of Mount Zion, the psalmist wrote:

> Those who trust in the LORD
> Are as Mount Zion, which cannot be moved
> but abides forever   (125:1)

God's City

Jerusalem is also known as 'the city of God' (46:4; 48:1-2; 48:8; 87:3). This name emphasizes God's special love for this city, the dwelling place of His choosing. Augustine selected this expression as the subject and title of his work, *The City of God*.

God's Hill

Jerusalem is also regarded as 'the hill of the Lord' (24:3). This name designates the place where God uniquely promised to live among His people and to be their God.

God's Mountain

The term 'My holy mountain' is a synonym for the Temple mount area in Jerusalem (2:6; 3:4; 15:1; 24:3; 48:1; 78:54). This was Jerusalem's most prominent hill, where God's Son is to be enthroned after His return. The LORD has set apart this mountain to accomplish His divine purposes. The psalmist also uses similar expressions, such as 'Your holy hill' (43:3), to refer to Jerusalem.

ISRAEL

Jerusalem sits within the land of Israel, which becomes the larger stage for the book of Psalms. Israel is a strategic land bridge, where Europe, Asia, and Africa intersect. All traffic had to pass through Israel, and the people that occupied Israel often influenced the destiny of other nations. No piece of land is more strategic than the promised land.

THE PROMISED LAND

When identifying the boundaries of the promised land, the expositor should note that the geographical extent of Israel ebbed and flowed throughout Israel's history.[2] The promised land was significantly larger than Israel ever occupied. The conquest and possession of the promised land fell far short of the larger territory that God gave Israel in the Abrahamic covenant. The Holy Land as occupied by Joshua divides longitudinally into four natural and distinct geographical regions, from west to east: the Mediterranean coast, the hill country, the Rift Valley, and the Transjordan Highlands.

1. Canaan

This name refers to the promised land (105:11; 106:38; 135:11). God gave this Phoenician land to Joshua and Israel, which had been originally promised to Abraham. The psalmist writes:

> … 'To you I will give the land of Canaan
> As the portion of your inheritance'   (105:11)

2. The Land

The Psalms also refer to Israel as, simply, 'the land' (25:13; 37:3, 9, 11, 22, 29, 34; 44:3; 74:8, 20; 105:11, 44). This title emphasizes the fact that God had promised to give this land to Israel. Faithful to His word, this promise came to pass.

MEDITERRANEAN COAST

The western boundary of Israel and the surrounding western regions is the Mediterranean coastal area. This region has four natural divisions: the Plain of Asher, the Coasts of Dor, the Plain of Sharon, and the Plain of Philistia, from north to south.

1. The Plain of Asher
Along the Plain of Asher was Tyre. Tyre was a Phoenician city-state on the Mediterranean coast, situated northwest of Israel, twenty miles south of Sidon and twenty-three miles north of Acre (45:12; 83:7; 87:4; 83:7; 87:4). The center of Canaanite worship and Baal worship, Tyre was the home city of Jezebel, the wicked queen of Israel, married to Ahab, the wicked king.

2. Lebanon
Also along the plain was Lebanon, the loftiest and best-known mountain range of Syria, forming the northern boundary of Palestine. The mountain range begins at the great valley connecting the Mediterranean with the plain of Hamath. The Psalms refer to the grandest of trees which grew in Lebanon (29:5; 104:16):

3. The Coasts of Dor
En-dor was a town about four miles from the foot of Mount Tabor. It was located the land of Issachar assigned to Manasseh, the site of the defeat of Midian by Gideon, and has many caves in the hill side, a fit place for hiding (83:10).

4. Plain of Philistia
Philistia is 'the land of the Philistines' (60:8; 87:4; 108:9), a fertile coastal plain that stretched from Wadi el-Arish northward to Ekron.

HILL COUNTRY

The hill country falls into five natural divisions: upper Galilee, lower Galilee, the hill country of Ephraim, the hill country of Benjamin, and the hill country of Judah. Josephus divided Galilee naturally into upper and lower Galilee based on a 1,500- to 2,000-foot slope known as Esh-Shagur. South of the hill country lay the Negev.

1. Upper Galilee
Zebulun (68:27), situated near Nazareth and Cana, lay north of Issachar, south of Asher and Naphtali (Josh. 19:10-16), east of the Mediterranean and west of the Sea of Galilee. Naphtali (68:27) lay at the northern angle of Palestine, and was enclosed on three sides by Zebulun (south), Asher (west), and Manasseh (east). The territory exceeded 800 square miles, double that of Issachar, and was positioned on the north side of the Tent of Meeting.

2. Lower Galilee
Mount Tabor appears once in the Psalms. It rests on the border of Issachar in the northeast area of the Jezreel Valley and its steep slopes rise 1,929 feet above the sea. Concerning Psalm 89:12, the expositor must ask, is Ethan the Ezrahite referring to all four directions — north, south, east (Hermon), and west (Tabor) — the whole land of Israel, or does he intend to convey a chiasm — north, south, south (Tabor), north (Hermon)?

3. Ephraim
South of lower Galilee lay the hill country of Ephraim. Ephraim was a large land parcel centrally located in Israel (60:7; 78:9, 67; 80:2, 108:8). It was the primary source of defense to the north of Israel. Ephraim and Manasseh, originally called 'the sons of Joseph' (Josh. 16:4), jointly occupied the central highlands between Jerusalem and the plain of Esdraelon. Ephraim's lot rested south of Manasseh. The open mountains and wide valleys of Ephraim helped agriculture but hindered national defence.

4. Shechem
This strategically-located territory rests on the lower south-eastern slope, or shoulder, of Mount Ebal (60:6; 108:7). Hence, the name Shechem means 'shoulder.' This land controlled every road through the central hill country of Israel, though it lacked

natural defenses. It lay west of the Jordan, near the river itself.

5. Shiloh
An early location for worship since the time of Joshua, Shiloh sat between Bethel and Shechem (Jer. 7:12-14; 26:6, 9). Apparently it was destroyed by the Philistines when they captured the ark or shortly afterward (78:60).

6. Zalmon
This piece of land was a blackened mountain (literally, 'dark one') near Shechem (Judg. 9:48). The expositor should ask: How does 'It was snowing in Zalmon' (68:14) contribute to his interpretation?

7. Benjamin
South of the hill country of Ephraim lay the hill country of Benjamin. This is the small territory portioned to the tribe of Benjamin that lay immediately south of Ephraim (68:27). This designated land extended twenty-six miles east to west and twelve miles north to south. Its eastern boundary was the Jordan. Dan intervened between it and the Philistines. Significantly, Benjamin served as the main access point to Jerusalem from the coastal plain.

8. Judah
South of the hill country of Benjamin sits the hill country of Judah. Judah is a thousand-square-mile territory from which David and his descendants came (48:11; 60:7; 63:1; 68:27; 69:35; 76:1; 78:68; 97:8; 108:8; 114:2). Judah extends from Geba to Beersheba, occupying a strip of mountain land on the central spine of southern Israel, roughly fifty miles north to south, and twenty miles east to west. Jerusalem also rests within the hill country of Judah, as mentioned above.

9. The Negev
Among other things, the Negev was where the Amalekites resided. David fought the Amalekites in the area of Ziklag, which Achish, king of Gath, had given him (83:7; 1 Sam. 27:6; 30:1-20).

The Amalekites declined later, and eventually nomads occupied Amalek, southeast of the Jordan River. Also in the Negev were the Streams in the South. This phrase refers to seasonal brooks in the arid region south of Beersheba, also known as the Negev, or the desert south of Judah (126:4-6). In the dry season, these streams have little or no water but overflow their banks in the rainy season.

Rift Valley

The Rift Valley naturally divides Israel into five regions: the Huleh Valley, the Sea of Chinnereth, the Jordan Valley, the Dead Sea, and the Arabah.

1. Jordan Valley
The Jordan River draws from the Sea of Galilee and drains into the Dead Sea. 'The Jordan turned back' (114:3, 5) when God led Israel across the Jordan River on dry land (Josh. 3:16; 4:23-24). All of the geographical features in 114:3-6, 'sea ... Jordan ... mountains ... hills,' respond to the sovereign control of God during the Exodus and conquest of the Holy Land.

2. Arabah
Within Arabah lay Edom. Edom occurs seven times in Psalms (60:1, 8, 9; 83:6; 198:9, 10; 137:7). Wadi Zered serves as the northern border of Edom and the primary enemy of Israel on the southeast border of Palestine (60:8). The country lay along the route pursued by the Israelites from Sinai to Kadesh-barnea. 'Over Edom I shall throw my shoe' (60:8), which probably refers to the conventional symbolic act by which one claimed posses-sion of land (Ruth 4:7).

3. Gebal
Within the territory of Edom was Gebal. Gebal was most likely a community south of the Dead Sea, near Petra. The Gebalites made a covenant with Moab, Ammon, Amalek and others, against Israel (83:7). The term also refers to a mountain region

whose inhabitants allied with Israel's other neighbors against her.

TRANSJORDAN HIGHLANDS

The area known as the Transjordan Highlands was a portion of land occupied by Israel that lay east of the Jordan River. The King's Highway (Num. 20:17; 21:22), a north-south trade route in the Transjordan, made the most significant contribution to its culture and economics. Four lateral canyons divide the Transjordan into five major geographical regions. The five major regions of the Transjordan from north to south include:

1. Bashan
Bashan appears five times in Psalms (22:12; 68:15, 22; 135:11; 136:20). It lies north of Wadi Yarmuk and east of the Sea of Galilee. The mountains of Bashan refer to the mountains surrounding Bashan, including the towering Mount Hermon. The Lord said, 'I will bring them back from Bashan. I will bring them back from the depths of the sea' (68:22). 'Bashan ... the depths of the sea' (68:22) are therefore opposites, the heights and the depths, showing totality.

2. Mount Hermon
This tall mountain stands 9,200 feet above sea level in the extreme north of current-day Israel (24:6; 89:12; 133:3). Also known as Sirion (29:6), this mount is the highest point in Israel. The glaciers of Hermon are the main source of the Jordan. According to the psalmist, brotherly unity is 'like the dew of Hermon coming down upon the mountains of Zion' (133:3). Even the mighty Sirion (Deut. 3:9), fears 'the voice of the Lord' (29:6).

3. Gilead
Gilead occurs twice in the Psalms (60:7; 108:8). It included the land between the Wadi Yarmuk and Wadi Jabbok. Gilead means 'rugged,' a fitting description of the mountainous area. Gilead was home to half of the tribe of Manasseh. Manasseh occupied both sides of the Jordan River, making it unique in having

two territories, a half tribe on each side (60:7; 80:2; 108:8). Geographically Manasseh was the largest of the twelve tribes.

4. Ammon
Ammon surfaces once in the Psalms (83:7). Wadi Jabbok served as the northern border and Wadi Arnon served as the southern border. Gad and Reuben occupied this area. Within Gad lies 'the valley of Succoth' (60:6; 108:7).

5. Moab
The Psalms mention Moab three times (60:8; 83:6; 108:9). Wadi Arnon served as the northern border, Wadi Zered served as the southern border, and the Dead Sea served as the western border. What is the meaning of 'Moab is My washbowl' (60:8; 108:9)?

6. Valley of Baca
Psalm 84:6 mentions 'the Valley of Baca,' whose location and identity remain uncertain. Some see it as 'the valley of weeping' because it sounds much like the word for weeping in Hebrew, though it is spelled differently. Baca may refer to a type of tree or to a parched place.

7. Miry clay
'Miry clay' appears in two psalms (40:2; 69:2, 14). These treacherous quagmires would imprison travelers as a prisoner in a pit: 'He brought me up out of the pit of destruction, out of the miry clay, And He set my feet upon a rock making my footsteps firm' (40:2).

SURROUNDING NATIONS

Extending outward are the regions surrounding Israel. Israel served as a land bridge between the continents of Europe, Asia, and Africa. Thus traffic had to pass through Israel, and the people that occupied Israel often influenced the destiny of other nations. If one is to exposit the Psalms, it will require an understanding of geography, stretching from Ethiopia in the southwest to the Sinai Peninsula in the south, Babylon in the

east, and Syria in the north. The following are among those
mentioned in the Psalms:

AFRICA

Every mention of every location possesses exegetical significance. The expositor must consider the following locations in
Africa and their impact on interpretation:

1. Egypt
Egypt refers to the ancient dynasty in the northeast corner of
Africa, extending from the Mediterranean Sea in the north to
the first waterfall on the Nile River in the south (68:31; 78:12,
43, 51; 80:8; 81:5, 10; 105:23; 105:38; 106:7, 21; 114:1; 135:8, 9).
In ancient times, Egypt consisted mainly of the narrow strip of
land watered by the Nile, reaching from Cairo or Memphis to
the first cataract on the Nile.

2. Rahab
Rahab, appearing twice in the Psalms (87:4; 89:10; Isa. 30:7), is
another name for Egypt and means one who is proud and arro-
gant. It was applied specifically to Egypt as a proud nation.

3. Ham
This is another name for the area in Egypt where part of the
descendants of Ham settled (78:51; 105:23, 27; 106:22).

4. Seba
Seba was a nation in northern Africa, elsewhere mentioned as
Cush. It may refer to the land in modern Sudan, south of Egypt
(72:10).

5. Zoan
This was both a region in Egypt, as well as an Egyptian city: 'He
wrought wonders before their fathers In the land of Egypt, in the
field of Zoan' (78:12).

6. Ethiopia

Ethiopia was a country south of Egypt inhabited by the descendants of Ham (68:31; 87:4). It was known as the country of burnt faces, for their complexion.

ASIA

The region to the east of Israel is Asia. This massive area possesses key exegetical information, most notably that which surrounds the exile of Israel into Babylonian and Assyrian captivities.

1. Babylon

The Psalms refer to Babylon, or the rivers of Babylon, three times (87:4; 137:1, 8). This ancient land was situated northeast of Israel, in the land between the Tigris and Euphrates Rivers. The nation of Babylon occupied this land and became a fierce enemy of Israel. Following some 500 years of disobedience, Judah was taken captive to Babylon, where they suffered exile.

It is in the midst of Babylonian captivity that Psalm 137 refers to, 'By the rivers of Babylon,' meaning along the Tigris and Euphrates Rivers flowing through the Babylonian kingdom. There the captive Jews sat down and wept, 'When we remembered Zion' (137:1). After suffering seventy years of captivity, they were allowed to return to the promised land in what seemed like a Second Exodus.

2. Assyria

The Psalms also mention the land of Assyria in Psalms 83:8. Assyria was the nation northeast of Israel, a dominate kingdom that captured the ten northern tribes of Israel and forced them into exile in their pagan land.

3. Meshech

Meshech was situated in the mountains on the northern boundary of Assyria, bordering on Tabal and Tubal (120:5).

EUROPE

The book of Psalms even extends as far away as the continent of Europe, specifically Tarshish.

1. Tarshish
This was a notable Mediterranean port of uncertain location, possibly Spain: 'With the east wind You break the ships of Tarshish' (48:7). The ships of Tarshish were large, seagoing ships. 'Once every three years the ships of Tarshish came bringing gold and silver, ivory and apes and peacocks' (1 Kgs. 10:22; cf. 1 Kgs. 22:28; 2 Chr. 20:37).

ARABIA

Although some have debated the boundaries of Arabia, classical geographers considered the Sinai Peninsula as part of Arabia. Located south of Israel, the area of Arabia in the Psalms included:

1. Sinai
This was the place in the wilderness where Moses received the Law from God (68:17).

2. Red Sea
Also known as the Reed Sea, the Papyrus Sea, or simply the Sea, the Red Sea straddles the Sinai Peninsula (66:6; 74:13; 78:13, 53; 106:7, 9, 22, 25; 114:3, 5 136:13, 15). God parted the Red Sea for Israel to pass through miraculously (106:7, 9).

3. Horeb
This was most likely another name for Mount Sinai, where Moses received the commandments of God (106:19).

4. Meribah
This place in the wilderness, meaning 'strife' or 'dispute,' was where Israel tempted God (81:7; 95:8; 106:32).

5. *Wilderness of Kadesh*

Kadesh Barnea is the southern desert country (29:8) where David hid during his flight from Saul (1 Sam. 23) and Absalom (2 Sam. 15). It was described by the psalmist as 'dry and weary land where there is no water' (63:1).

6. *Sheba*

Sheba was the ancient kingdom in southern Arabia, or modern Yemen (72:10).

7. *Kedar*

Kedar was the land now known as Arabia (120:5; Gen. 25:13-14; Isa. 21:17). The people of Kedar were known as aggressive and antagonistic barbarians. The psalmist who wrote Psalm 120 lived, therefore, amongst a heathen and hostile people.

> Woe is me, for I sojourn in Meshech,
> For I dwell among the tents of Kedar!   (120:5)

AN EYE FOR DETAIL

A working knowledge of geography of the land of Israel and the surrounding regions is indispensable for rightly interpreting and preaching the Psalms. Perhaps more than any other book of the Bible, the Psalter requires a broad understanding of the greater area of the Middle East and beyond. The expositor must have a clear understanding of the cities, regions, territories, mountains, valleys, deserts, streams, rivers, and seas. In order to bridge the geographical and topographical gap, the expositor needs a reliable set of Bible maps, atlases, historical geographies, Bible dictionaries, and encyclopedias that will contribute to the proper understanding of the Psalms. As with every area of interpretation, this step requires disciplined, diligent, and detailed study.

May God give His church men who are diligent in their study of these places as they preach this inspired book, the Psalms.

16

INVESTIGATE
THE CULTURE

Know the cultural background of the psalm

W ithin ancient, redemptive history, the psalmists
wrote several millennia ago over a span of one thousand years. This specific millennium stretched from
the days of Moses in Israel's wilderness wanderings (*c.* 1445-
1405 BC) to Israel's post-exile period in Jerusalem (*c.* 400 BC). In
order to understand what the psalmists wrote, expositors must
bridge several gaps in their study and pulpit ministry. Among
these is the culture gap. That is to say, if one is to understand
the text before him, he must understand something of the many
customs in ancient life in the Middle East.

Without an understanding of life long ago in Israel, one thousand years before the first coming of Christ, it is hard to understand many portions of this ancient hymn book. Consequently, it is incumbent upon the expositor to view Scripture in the cultural context of the times in which it was written. With this in mind, John Stott writes, 'A true sermon bridges the gulf between the biblical and the modern worlds, and must be equally earthed in both.'[1] The ancient world of the Psalms differs vastly from the contemporary life in which people find themselves today. Therefore, interpreters must first view each psalm in light of the original culture.

KNOWING THE ANCIENT CUSTOMS

Understanding the Psalms requires a knowledge of the many facets of ancient Judaism. This includes knowing something about its politics, farming, religion, laws, money, wars, trades, animals, and plants. Knowledge of other ancient pagan cultures is also essential. The expositor will have to know something about the ancient ways of the Egyptians, Canaanites, Assyrians, Babylonians, and more. Attempting to explain passages with cultural ignorance will miss the proper interpretation.

To this very point, John Broadus writes, 'One must always observe ... the manners and customs of the Jews, and other nations who appear in the sacred story. These aids for understanding texts are seldom used as diligently as they should be. But there is also much to be learned by taking account of the opinions and state of mind of the persons addressed in a text. The relations between the speaker or writer and those whom he is addressing need to be remembered.'[2] To rightly understand the Psalms, one must bridge the culture gap in several important areas:

NATIONAL LIFE

First, the expositor must have a knowledge of the national life of Israel and the surrounding nations. This begins with a knowledge of ancient political and social practices.

POLITICAL ENVIRONMENT

The expositor must study the background of the ancient politics
— the national, international, and civil landscape of the world in
which the Psalms were written. For example, Psalm 89:27 states
that God will make a descendant of David 'My firstborn, the highest of the kings of the earth.' How could Christ be 'My firstborn'?
Does 'firstborn' mean that Christ was created? To the contrary,
firstborn means He is the Heir of all creation. As the ancient political setting reveals, the firstborn child received special honor and
a double portion of the family inheritance.[3] However, in a royal
grant covenant, a chosen person could be elevated to the level of
firstborn sonship and thus have title to a perpetual gift involving a
dynastic succession (2:7).[4] Thus, an accurate interpretation of this
passage requires a grasp of the political scene.

SOCIAL CUSTOMS

Preachers must also be aware of the social practices of ancient
society. This requires an understanding, for example, of wed-
dings, clothing, hair, beards, and the like from long ago.
Ignorance of these customs could result in misunderstand-
ing the meaning of the passage. One must be alert to standard
customs and what they meant to the people in those original
settings. For example, Psalm 45 describes a royal wedding cere-
mony involving a king-groom and his princess-bride (vv. 8-15).
An awareness of ancient wedding customs is necessary for the
interpreter to grasp the full meaning and impact.

ECONOMIC POLICIES

Further, sound interpretation requires an understanding of
ancient economic practices. The exegete must know about usury

or exorbitant interest rates in loaning money. According to the Mosaic Law, the Israelites were forbidden to take usury from their brothers upon the loan of money, food, or anything else. They were not to demand anything more on the return of the loan. However, interest might be taken from foreigners. Most particularly, usury could not be changed in lending aid to the struggling poor, who desperately needed help but could not afford it. Thus, one must know about usury and interest rates (15:5). Some interest rates reached fifty percent even though God's law forbids it (Deut. 23:19-20; 24:10-13).

MILITARY WARFARE

Precise interpretation requires knowledge of ancient military equipment and practices. Before Israel waged war, they offered a sacrifice and the king or high priest delivered an inspiring address. Following the battle signal, hand-to-hand combat ensued. Mountains provided safety and security from enemies. Thus, the student of the Psalms must know about fortresses (18:2; 144:2), shields (18:2), strongholds (18:2), banners (20:5; 60:4), chariots (20:7), horses (20:7; 33:17), arrows (7:12; 38:2; 45:52; 64:7), armies (44:9; 60:10; 108:11), bows (44:6), swords (44:6; 45:3-5; 59:7), and helmets (60:7).

SPIRITUAL LIFE

Further, the expositor must have a general awareness of the religious practices of Israel. This includes a knowledge of Israel's religious forms, as well as those of false religions. This also involves an understanding of ancient covenants as legal documents.

RELIGIOUS FORMS

Further, one must understand the religious practices of ancient Israel under the Mosaic system of worship. He must also be familiar with the false worship of the surrounding pagan nations, with their Baal worship and the like (106:28). The expositor must know about the tabernacle in Jerusalem (11:4; 15:1; cf. 2 Sam. 6:12-17), as well as the meal offering (20:3), the thank offering (50:14), other sacrifices and offerings (40:6; 51:16), such as the burnt offerings (20:3). One must watch for types such as Melchizedek (110:4; Heb. 7:3, 15-17), Aaron (77:20; 99:6; 105:26; 106:16; 115:10, 12; 118:3; Heb. 5:4-5), and the tabernacle (23:6; 26:8 27:5; 76:2; Heb. 8:5; 9:23-24).

Covenantal Agreements

Another cultural gap to bridge involves the ancient legal setting. This requires one to understand the making of a covenant between two people, the witnesses involved, and the stipulations of the terms. The expositor must grasp how each party bound himself to fulfill certain conditions and was promised certain advantages. In making covenants, God solemnly involved Himself as a witness, and an oath was sworn. Accordingly, a breach of covenant was regarded as a heinous sin. Grasping the meaning of some psalms requires a knowledge of the legal, binding covenant between two parties (25:10; 50:5; 55:20; 103:18).

NATURAL LIFE

In addition, the preacher must know something of the natural conditions of Israel, including the subjects of climate, agriculture, botany, and geology. Each of these areas are mentioned in the Psalms.

Climate Conditions

The expositor must also possess some basic knowledge of nature, creation, and the weather of the Middle East. He must have a basic awareness of thick clouds (18:12), hailstones (18:12), thunder (18:13), the heavens (19:1), the firmament (19:1), and the sun (19:2-6).[5] Psalm 29, for example, describes a storm building over the Mediterranean Sea that blows ashore over Israel into the wilderness (vv. 3-7).

AGRICULTURAL PROCEDURES

Another important gap to bridge involves agriculture. For example, Psalm 1:3-4 reads, 'He will be like a tree firmly planted by streams of water, which yields its fruit in its season and its leaf does not wither; and in whatever he does, he prospers. The wicked are not so, but they are like chaff which the wind drives away.' The godly man, like a tree, bears fruit spiritually because of his proximity to the life-giving source — the Spirit of the living God. The wicked, however, are compared to chaff. This requires an understanding of how a farmer winnowed wheat. As the farmer pitched the wheat into the air, the wind separated the lighter chaff from the heavier wheat. The chaff was absolutely useless, good for nothing. Thus, the farmer did not try to retain it. So are the wicked, worthless and without security. Also, other psalmists speaks of plants taking root (44:22; 80:8-11) and the farm wagon dropping its abundance along the cart path (65:11).

NATIVE FLOWERS

Further, one needs an awareness of various flowers native of Israel. Understanding the indigenous flowers — such as myrrh, aloes, and cassia — enriches the understanding and appreciation of certain passages. For example, the psalmist writes: 'All Your garments are fragrant with myrrh and aloes and cassia; Out of ivory palaces stringed instruments have made You glad' (45:8). The glory of the king is evidenced by these costly perfumes and aromas that come from these flowers.

INDIGENOUS MINERALS

Many minerals are mentioned in the book of Psalms, requiring a general familiarity by the preacher. Minerals in the Psalter include: (1) *brimstone* or sulfur, often associated with the Dead Sea (11:6); (2) *miry clay* (40:2), a clay used in pottery, though it produces pots that are fragile and easily shattered (2:9); (3) *mire*, or mud (69:14); (4) *flint*, the impurities removed from metals (119:119; cf. 12:6); (5) *flint*, a very hard compact rock (114:8); (6) *gold*, a precious metal widely used in the ancient world (19:10; 21:3; 45:9; 68:13; 119:27) (7) *iron*, used for bonds or fetters (105:18; 107:10; 149:8), or for a rod or scepter, capable of smashing fragile objects (2:9); and (8) *silver*, a precious metal used as a medium of exchange, as well as in making idols (115:4), smelted in the furnace and refined (12:6). For instance, Psalm 66:10 reads, 'For You have tried us, O God; You have refined us as silver is refined.' What is the refining process (119:119; cf. 12:6)? What is the temperature of the refiner's furnace? How does the Refiner purify His people?

ZOOLOGICAL LIFE

Finally, the expositor must have a basic knowledge of the animals of ancient Israel. Included in this is an understanding of the practices of shepherding and hunting at the time.

ANIMAL SPECIES

The Psalms mention animals frequently compared to other books in the Bible, including references or allusions to the following animals: (1) *bees*, which produce sweet honey (19:10; 81:16); (2) *shephanim*, common rock badgers living in holes and clefts of the rocks (104:18); (3) *dogs*, which ran wild in the streets (22:16, 20); eating garbage and dead animals (59:6, 14); being treacherous and violent (22:16; 20); (4) *doves*, which migrate great distances (55:6-8); (5) *sea monsters*, which live in the depths of the sea (148:7), such as whales, sharks and other large sea creatures, including dinosaurs — which is used as a poetic description of the proud Egyptians at the time of the Exodus (74:13); (6) *eagles*, swift birds that fly on high with ease (103:5); (7) *flies*, which come in swarms (78:45); (8) *birds*, which build nests in the sanctuary (84:3) and in the trees (104:17), while singing (104:12); (9) *foxes*, or scavenging jackals (63:10); (10) *horses*, which pulled chariots into battle (20:7; 33:17).

Further, the preacher must know something about: (11) *leviathan*, a mighty creature — whether a sea monster or dinosaur — who can overwhelm man but is no match for God (74:14; 104:26); (12) *lions*, the mightiest land creatures (7:2); (13) *mules*, stubborn animals lacking direction (32:9); (14) *owls*, which lived in the waste places (102:6); (15) *wild oxen*, which were most stubborn (22:21); (16) *bulls*, well-fed animals that were fattened (22:12); (17) *pelicans*, which lived in desolate places (102:6); (18) *ravens*, which cry out to be fed when young (147:9); (19) *sheep*, dumb defenseless animals requiring much direction and protection (23:1-3; 100:3); (20) *swallows*, small birds that skim the ground and fly overhead with great rapidity (84:3); (21) *vipers*, the Egyptian cobra, one of the most poisonous snakes (140:3); (22) *jackals*, the terror of sheep, but which flees from the shepherd (44:19); and (23) *worms*, helpless and worthless, also maggots, bred in a wound or sore (22:6).

SHEPHERDING PRACTICES

Many psalms require a familiarity with shepherding as practiced in ancient Israel. Among his many duties, the shepherd led his flock in the morning from the fold by going before them and calling to them. Upon arriving at the pasture, he watched over the flock and should any stray, he searched for the lost sheep until he found it. He led them to water at a running stream (23:2). At evening, he brought them back to the fold, making sure that none were missing by passing them under his rod (23:3). Required of the shepherd was willingness to be exposed to much hardship in the hot and cold. Yet he would do so with great watchfulness, especially toward the young, particularly in driving them to and from the pasture. He faced many dangers from wild beasts, but used his staff as a weapon against these threats, as well as a crook to manage the flock (23:4). Psalm 23 speaks of God as a Shepherd to His people, who are likened to sheep. One must understand shepherding in ancient Israel to fully understand this psalm, as well as other psalms using this emblem (28:9; 49:14; 74:1; 77:20; 78:52; 79:13; 80:1; 95:7; 100:3). This image was also commonly used to refer to kings who shepherded their people, especially the King of kings, God Himself and His Son, Jesus Christ (John 10: Heb. 13:20; 1 Pet. 2:25; 5:4).

HUNTING EXPLOITS

Finally, the expositor must know something about the hunting of wild animals in the ancient world. Providing sustenance and pleasure, hunting was carried out using the bow and arrow (11:1-2), sling, snare (119:110), net (57:6), and pit (7:15; 35:7), especially for larger animals. One must have some further knowledge how a hunter set a trap and used a net or snare in order to capture an animal (66:11; 69:22).

THE ANCIENT WORLD

In short, the preacher's task is to provide a window into ancient Near Eastern culture. The expositor must become well acquainted with the biblical culture so that he can explain what the psalmist is indicating by what he is writing. In effective exposition, he must make the congregation feel as though they were there in the culture and customs of the ancient world.

DISCERN
THE FIGURES

Identify the various figures of speech.

As a gifted artist, the psalmist masterfully paints pictures in the minds of his hearers, using a brush called figures of speech. Such forms of speech communicate what lies beyond the literal, natural meaning of the words. Figures of speech are vivid expressions that illustrate spiritual truth. As the language of the psalmist, these picturesque figures are a compelling communication tool that enables the hearer to see the truth with his mind's eye. Since the Psalter has so many figures of speech, it is important to recognize them and discern their meaning.

Figures of speech bring warmth, vividness, and vitality to any writing or speaking. They add bright colors to an otherwise black and white picture. Further, figures of speech attract attention to what is being said. They also provide vivid understanding in only a few words. That is to say, they help make abstract ideas concrete. Moreover, figurative language aids the memory, etching the truth in the reader's mind. At the same time, it encourages reflection because the form of communication is so picturesque.[1]

Worth a Thousand Words

It is said that a picture is worth a thousand words. Such is certainly the case with the potent literary device of a figure of speech. These are the brush strokes by which the poet paints a picture in the minds of his readers. To this point Leland Ryken comments, 'Poets think in images. When the poetic imagination formulates reality, it does so in pictures… To determine the logic of the images is one of the chief tasks facing the reader of biblical poetry.'[2] In other works, the goal of the poet is to paint a clear and vivid picture in mind of the reader or the ear of the listener, helping him to see what is being conveyed. The same can be said of the poetical language of the psalmists.

Instead of using dry theological concepts and specialized vocabulary, the poets of Israel appealed to the senses of their listeners with engaging word pictures. With figurative language, they used the emotional language of the heart. Such visual communication paints a colorful portrait of the truth and uniquely aids the attention, comprehension, and retention of the reader.

A Vivid Means of Expression

As a rule of thumb, one should always take a passage literally unless there is good reason for doing otherwise. As previously cited, Merrill Unger writes, 'When the plain sense of Scripture makes common sense, seek no other sense; therefore, take every word at its primary, usual, literal meaning, unless it is patently a rhetorical figure or unless the immediate context, studied carefully in the light of related passages and axiomatic and fundamental truths, clearly points otherwise.'[3]

Thus, one should prefer a figurative interpretation if the literal meaning does violence to the subject being addressed. A figurative reading is best if a literal reading is impossible, absurd, or immoral. Sometimes a figurative expression is followed by an explanatory literal statement. At other times, a figure of expression is marked by a qualifying adjective, or a prepositional phrase, that hints that the text is not to be taken literally.[4] Common figures of speech in the Psalms include the following:

SIMILE

A simile makes a direct comparison between two realities by using 'like' or 'as.' The challenge of the simile is to determine the ways in which the two objects are similar. Examples are as follows:

LIKE A TREE

Psalm 1:3-4, for example, indicates that the godly man will be 'like a tree.' That is to say, he will be transplanted from a desert to a place near a river. Thus, he will be, spiritually speaking, healthy, growing, and fruit-bearing. Likewise, the ungodly man will be 'like chaff.' He will be empty, light, worthless, ready to be swept away and burned in the fire. In what sense is the believer like a tree and the wicked like chaff?

AS THE DEER

In another instance, the psalmist compares his soul to a 'deer' panting for water. That is to say, he is thirsty for God. His soul is parched. He is desperate for the refreshing, spiritual oasis that only God can bring. For the psalmist, he is facing a severe divine drought (42:1).

LIKE A RAZOR

Elsewhere, David says that the tongue is like a razor with the power to divide and destroy (52:2). It is sharper than a razor and has the ability to cut deeply and sever life.

METAPHOR

A metaphor compares two realities without using 'like' or 'as.' Instead, it uses a form of the verb 'to be,' such as 'is,' 'are,' 'was,' 'has been.' Here, one thing acts like or represents another, whether implied or directly stated. Leland Ryken writes, 'A metaphor or simile is bifocal, a split-level statement, a form of logic and can profitably be analyzed as such.'[5] Why do poets speak in metaphor?

Ryken adds, 'There are several advantages. One is the vividness and concreteness of the appeal to the reader's imagination.'[6] He continues, 'Above all, poets use metaphor … for the sake of precision [in order to] use one area of human experience to shed light on another.'[7] The following are examples:

MY ROCK

In Psalm 18:2, David uses military metaphors and likens God to a 'rock,' a 'fortress,' a 'deliverer,' a 'shield,' a 'horn,' and a 'stronghold.' Each of these are metaphors, comparing God to a likeness with the verb 'is.'

MY SHEPHERD

In another psalm (23:1), David likens God to a shepherd. When he says that the Lord *is* his shepherd, he means that God is like a shepherd. It is simply more emphatic to say that he is a shepherd. This imagery emphasizes the Lord's loving leadership and protective care of His people.

SUN

Again, in figurative terms, the psalmist compares God to a 'sun' and 'shield', indicating provision and protection (84:11). God is a 'Sun', providing life and energy for growth, and a 'shield', providing a defense from harm.

LAMP

In the same way, the Scripture is compared to a 'lamp' (119:105). That is to say, the Word is a source of light, enabling those who travel the narrow path to see their way in life. The path they are to take is enlightened before them. This text is certainly not saying that the Bible *is* a literal lamp. Rather, God's Word is merely *like* a lamp, sending forth the light of truth.

ALLEGORY

An allegory is a series of extended metaphors built around a central theme. The Psalter contains two allegories: Psalm 23:1-4 and Psalm 80:8-16. Regarding the latter, the psalmist portrays Israel as a 'vine' that was 'planted' and 'took deep root.' Other parts of this prolonged metaphor include clearing the ground, filling the land, mountains, shadow, cedars, boughs, branches, sea, shoots, hedges, fruit, boar, forest, fire, cut down.

METONYMY

Metonymy refers to meaning by association. This manner of speech substitutes one figure for another as the two are closely related, i.e., 'mouth' exchanged for 'tongue.'

Mouth and Tongue

For example, Psalm 73:9 uses 'mouth,' but then exchanges it for 'tongue.' The metonymy here refers to meaning by association. 'Mouths' and 'tongues' are used interchangeably, where one represents the other. Varying the vocabulary results in more vivid communication. Further, it helps secure the reader's attention.

SYNECDOCHE

A synecdoche is a literary device in which a part stands for the whole, or the whole for the part. In other words, one of the parts is taken to represent the whole, or vice versa, i.e., 'tongue' may be substituted for 'words.' Roy Zuck writes, 'A synecdoche is the substituting of a part of something for the whole or the whole for the part.'[8] Samples of synecdoche are the following:

Hands and Heart

This is seen, for example, in Psalm 24:4, where the 'hands' and the 'heart' of a man represent his whole life.

Hand and Lord

Another example is Psalm 109, where the psalmist says that God's 'hand' has accomplished something, but it represents His entire being (109:27).

HYPERBOLE

Hyperbole is a form of communication that conveys a concept using a deliberate exaggeration for dramatic effect. The ancient poets employed hyperbole to arrest the reader's attention, i.e., 'my bed swim[s] … with my tears.' Leland Ryken writes, 'Hyperbole is conscious exaggeration for the sake of effect. It does not claim to express literal truth but instead conveys emotional truth.'[9] We see hyperbole in the following:

SWIMMING IN BED

For example, the psalmist David says his tears flooded his bed and his eyes wasted away. The idea is not literal, but it vividly conveys great 'sighing' and 'tears' on the part of David (6:6-7).

EATING TEARS

Elsewhere, the sorrow-stricken psalmist was distressed to the point that he was unable to eat. His appetite was gone. So he says his only 'food' is his 'tears.' Again, not literally, but relatively (42:3).

PERSONIFICATION

Personification is a figure of speech that assigns human-like qualities, such as intelligence or speech, to inanimate objects or abstract ideas. Ryken defines personification as 'a figure of speech in which a poet treats something non human (and perhaps even inanimate) as though it were a person.'[10] Here are two examples of personification:

BONES SAY

For example, in Psalm 35:10, David says that his 'bones' speak. This simply represents the depth of his thoughts toward God:

RIVERS CLAP

In Psalm 98:8, the 'rivers' are described as clapping and mountains as singing to indicate the emotion of joy in the people.

APOSTROPHE

Apostrophe is a manner of expression that addresses lifeless objects as though they were a living person, heightening the intensity of the communication. 'An apostrophe is a direct address to someone or something absent as though it were present. It is frequently combined with personification, in which an abstract quality or physical object is treated as though it were a person.'[11] Apostrophe is among the most picturesque and powerful forms of communication. Here are some examples:

O GATES

In Psalm 24:7, for example, the psalmist addresses the 'gates' and 'doors' of Jerusalem as if they were alive.

O MOUNTAINS

A further example is when a 'mountain' across the Jordan is figuratively described as being jealous of Mount Zion, which God had chosen to be the special place He would be worshiped (68:15-16).

O CITY

In another instance, the sons of Korah speak to Jerusalem as if it were a person. When the 'city' is addressed, it is, in reality, the inhabitants of the 'city' being addressed (87:3).

O Sea

The psalmist portrays the Red Sea and Jordan River as a living being, commanding them to 'flee' or 'turn back.' This pictures the parting of the Red Sea with Moses and the same with the Jordan under Joshua (114:5).

ANTHROPOMORPHISM

Anthropomorphism is a medium of communication that speaks of God as having a human body in order to convey an important truth about His character or conduct. It uses familiar, human-like conventions to depict the unfamiliar qualities and actions of God, who is spirit, and therefore has no body parts. 'An anthropomorphism is the ascribing of human characteristics or actions to God.'[12] Such is seen in:

God's Fingers

For example, Psalm 8:3 describes God as possessing 'fingers.' This figure of speech simply is intended to show the ease and precision of His omnipotent work in creation:

God's Hand

Further, God is said to possess a 'hand,' which He does not literally have. Instead, this reference to God's 'hand' depicts His eager help, which He willingly lends to the helpless (10:12).

God's Ear

Also, King David describes God as having an 'ear.' But this is meant to communicate that He listens to His people, not that He possesses a literal ear like His creation (31:2).

GOD'S FACE

Moreover, God is represented as possessing a 'face.' This figuratively pictures the focused attention He gives His people. But here, He seemingly has turned away from them (44:24).

GOD'S EYES

In addition, God is represented as possessing 'eyes.' But this conveys in human-like terms that He sees all things. It is accommodating language by which God makes Himself known in ways that we can understand (34:15-16).

HYPOCATASTASIS

Hypocatastasis is a less common figure of speech, which compares likeness by a direct naming.[13] In other words, there is a comparison made without using 'like,' 'as,' or 'is.' The subject is simply directly named. The differences between a simile, metaphor, and hypocatastasis may be seen in the following sentences: A simile says, 'You wicked people are like dogs;' a metaphor says, 'You wicked people are dogs;' a hypocatastasis says, 'You dogs' (22:16).

MERISMUS

Merismus substitutes contrasting or opposite parts for the totality or whole. Roy Zuck notes, 'A merism is a form of synecdoche in which the totality or whole is substituted by two contrasting or opposite parts.'[14] Some examples are as follows:

SEA TO SEA

For example, in Psalm 72:8, 'from sea to sea' represents the whole land mass or the entire nation.

KINGS AND MAN

In Psalm 105:14, 'man' and 'kings' represent the entire populace — from the palace to the home of the common man.

HEAVEN AND EARTH

Another example is joining 'heaven and earth,' which is a figurative way of saying, 'the entire created order,' or 'the entire universe' (121:2).

SITTING AND RISING

Still another example is when the psalmist David says, 'when I sit down' and 'when I rise.' These two opposite activities — sitting and rising — represent *all* his activities (139:2).

DAY AND NIGHT

One last example is the expression 'day and night' which is intended to indicate all the time. The two extremes represent the whole (1:2).

ZOOMORPHISM

Zoomorphism ascribes animal qualities to God in order to convey truth about His divine attributes. 'Whereas an anthropomorphism ascribes human characteristics to God, a zoomorphism ascribes animal characteristics to God (or to others). These are expressive ways of pointing up certain actions and attributes of the Lord in a picturesque way.'[15] Thus, we read:

SHADOW OF WINGS

The psalmist represents God as possessing 'wings.' But this is merely metaphorical language, picturing God's protective care. As a mother bird watches over her young, even so God protects His people under His overshadowing care (57:1).

PINIONS AND WINGS

The psalmist pictures God as possessing 'pinions' and 'wings,' simply to indicate the protective care He provides His people. It is much like the mother bird, except even more so (91:4).

ELLIPSIS

Ellipsis is the phenomenon of leaving something out of the text that the listener or reader must supply by context.[16] The omission forces the reader to involve himself with the text. That is to say, an ellipsis omits a word or phrase that must be supplied to complete the context. An example is:

OMISSION OF 'LORD' AND 'LIKE'

Occasionally, psalmists purposely omit a portion of the text while its presence is implied later. Two such examples are Psalms 12:3 and 36:6.

HENDIADYS

Hendiadys expresses one idea with two words. Roy Zuck writes, 'A hendiadys is the substituting of two coordinate terms (joined by 'and') for a single concept in which one of the elements defines the other.'[17] This is seen in 'infants' and 'babes' (8:2), 'light' and 'salvation' (27:1), fear and trembling (55:5), glory and strength (96:7), and misery and chains (107:10).

INCLUSION

Inclusion is a form of repetition that begins and ends a verse, strophe, section, or psalm. Zuck explains, 'An inclusion is a pattern in which a paragraph or longer portion ends in much the same way in which it began.'[18] That is, inclusion serves as bookends that encapsulate a portion of Scripture (8:1, 9; 118:1, 29; 70:1, 5).

EPONYMY

Eponymy occurs when an individual stands for the whole. It refers to a meaning by association. For example, the one son Jacob represents the entire nation Israel (24:6; 135:4; 147:19).

A TREASURY OF TRUTH

To be sure, the Psalms is a rich treasury in which there is found a multitude of figures of speech. The psalmist is a poet who often speaks in figurative language. The expositor must be alert of these literary devices if he is to accurately handle the meaning of the text. The figurative is a color vehicle for presenting literal truth. It must be understood that figurative language is not contrary to literal interpretation. The actual meaning of the figurative is to be determined, and then it is taken literally.

Every expositor of the Psalms must approach this subject with care and skill. If he is to be an able interpreter of this highly figurative book, he must learn how to identify figures of speech and be efficient in discovering their meaning in the passage being studied and preached. In defense of teaching figures of speech and literary devices to young people in the church, Martin Luther notes, 'Certainly it is my desire that there shall be as many poets and rhetoricians as possible, because I see that by

these studies, as by no other means, people are wonderfully fit-
ted for the grasping of sacred truth and for handling it skillfully
and happily."[19] May there be many such poets and rhetoricians in
this day, those who are able to speak like the psalmist in vivid,
powerful ways.

UNIT IV

THE
ASSIMILATION PHASE

---- **18** ----

CONNECT THE
REFERENCES

Study the cross references from other passages

One of the most important steps in understanding a psalm is the proper use of cross references. These connecting verses help to interpret and support the psalm being studied and preached. Cross-referencing is the practice of using Scripture to interpret Scripture. Thomas Watson wrote, 'Nothing can cut the diamond but the diamond; nothing can interpret Scripture but Scripture.'[1] That is to say, consulting other passages in God's Word is an important exercise in confirming the true meaning of a biblical text. Stated another way, it is important to consider each psalm in light of the whole counsel of Scripture.

Each individual passage must be compared with the rest of Scripture to check and clarify its proper meaning.

Yet while this process is critically important, the expositor should only turn to a cross reference after he has first labored to plumb the depths of his particular psalm. Starting with the text before him, he must attempt to grasp the meaning in its words and immediate context before he looks elsewhere into other portions of Scripture.

Scripture Speaks With One Voice

Regarding the importance of cross-referencing, John Broadus wrote, 'We must interpret in accordance with, and not contrary to, the general teachings of Scripture. These teachings are harmonious, and can be combined into a symmetrical whole. If a passage may have two senses … then we must choose one which accords with what the Bible in general plainly teaches rather than one which would make the Bible contradict itself… But between possible grammatical meanings we are compelled to choose upon some principle, and certainly one important principle to be considered is that the teachings of Scripture must be consistent.'[2] In other words, we must use the passages that are the clearest to understand those that are less clear.

In this regard, the Westminster Confession gives the following helpful counsel: 'The infallible rule of interpretation of Scripture is the Scripture itself; and therefore, when there is a question about the true and full sense of any Scripture, it must be searched and known by other passages that speak more clearly.'[3] That is to say, the rest of Scripture often makes more lucid the passage immediately before the expositor. Each text must be seen in the light of the whole system of revealed truth. To build an entire doctrine based upon one text, A. A. Hodge writes, 'is like balancing a stool on one leg.'[4] This is the principle that by the mouth of two or three witnesses every fact may be confirmed (Deut. 19:15; Matt. 18:16). Such multiple witnesses are especially true in understanding the meaning of Scripture.

ALL SCRIPTURE EQUALLY INSPIRED

As a result, the expositor will want to turn to other passages that address the same truth. Because of the perfect unity of the Bible, the obscure passages are to be interpreted in light of the clearer passages. Disputable passages should be considered in light of those that are indisputable. This is based upon the fact that all Scripture is equally inspired and exceedingly important to every generation. Leviticus is as equally God-breathed and instructive as Romans. Thus, all Scripture is equally relevant and 'profitable' (2 Tim. 3:16). Cross-referencing may involve tracing the meaning of a word or a doctrine throughout the full breadth of Scripture. Yet one must exercise extreme care in cross-referencing, being careful not to lift a verse out of its context and make it say what one wants it to say.

With any particular psalm, the preacher should pursue cross references in a logical order. Like tossing a pebble into a pond and watching the ripple-effect move outward, cross referencing should begin in the psalm that is under consideration and then progress outward, first to other psalms, then to other Wisdom books in the Old Testament, then to other narrative and prophetic Old Testament books, until, finally, the New Testament passages.

PSALMS

When preaching a psalm, all cross-referencing should begin within the Psalms itself. Before widening the investigation and looking elsewhere in Scripture, the diligent study of a psalm should begin in the psalm itself and then in other psalms. Within the Psalms, the order of progression should be:

SAME PSALM

As previously stated, the work of cross-referencing should begin within the psalm being studied. The expositor will want to ask: How does *this* psalmist expand upon the particular verse or word being studied within *this* same psalm? What words, phrases, or themes does this same psalm repeat? What synonyms are used by the psalmist that give additional insight? What parallel phrases are employed? The expositor must remain aware that many English translations obscure repeated words with synonyms for stylistic reasons. Does the immediate context yield clues to word usage or interpretation? Cross-referencing within a psalm serves as the first line of appeal when searching for corresponding truths.

OTHER PSALMS, SAME PSALMIST

Then the expositor will want to consult other psalms written by the same psalmist. How does the same author make similar statements dealing with this same subject? The preacher will want to consider: How else does David use this word or phrase in other psalms that he has written? For example, how does an author like Asaph address the same issue elsewhere? Or how do the sons of Korah use a similar phrase in another psalm? Each psalmist has certain preferences of word choices and patterns in writing that will want to be considered. Similarities in writing by the same psalmist may provide helpful insights into the passage being studied.

OTHER PSALMS, OTHER PSALMISTS

Next, the preacher will want to consider other parallel passages that were written by a different psalmist. He should start with the same book of Psalms. Remember, the Psalms were collected and arranged into five books, Psalms 1-41; 42-72; 73-89; 90-106; 107-150. He will then want to move outward to different books within the psalms. How does this psalmist use similar words or address the same subject elsewhere in the same book of the Psalter? How do other psalmists address the same topic?

OLD TESTAMENT

After checking cross references within the Psalms, the expositor should then proceed to look outward to other books in the Old Testament. He should begin with other Wisdom books and then expand outward to other Old Testament books.

OTHER WISDOM BOOKS

Cross-referencing should next expand to the other wisdom books: Job, Proverbs, Ecclesiastes, and the Song of Solomon. Psalms is a Wisdom book of Old Testament poetry and should be compared with other such similar Wisdom books. The expositor should ask himself: What does Solomon or other wise sages have to say in Proverbs? What does he say in Ecclesiastes? What does he write in the Song of Solomon about this same truth? How does what the psalmist says compare with the writer of Job?

One such example is the study of 'the fear of the Lord,' which is used repeatedly throughout the Psalms (25:14; 33:8; 34:7, 9, 11; 96:4; 102:15; 103:13; 111:10; 112:1; 128:1; 145:19). In order to pursue the meaning of 'the fear of the Lord,' an expanded study would next investigate its usage in other Wisdom books of the Old Testament. These cross references would include Job 28:28; Proverbs 1:7; 9:10; and Ecclesiastes 12:13. In these similar passages it is discovered that 'the fear of the Lord' requires humility before God, departing from evil, and carrying out God's commandments. Further, it gives the true knowledge of God and good understanding. But those who refuse 'the fear of the Lord' are fools who despise divine wisdom and instruction. Each of these cross references provides some unique insight into the meaning and marks of fearing God and should be consulted.

OTHER OLD TESTAMENT BOOKS

The next step is to compare what the rest of the Old Testament has to say regarding the truth of the verse being considered. The expositor will want to ask: What does the Pentateuch have to say about this particular topic? Then, the expositor should ask: What do the narrative portions of the Old Testament say? Finally: What do the prophets say? Do they address the same subject? If so, what understanding can they add to what the psalmist is saying?

For example, in Psalm 23:6, does 'dwelling in the house of the Lord forever' refer to heaven or the tabernacle? Cross-referencing confirms the tabernacle interpretation. The 'house of the LORD' referred only to the tabernacle in David's day. 'Forever' (literally, 'for the length of days') occurs only three times in the Old Testament, the other two passages being Psalm 93:5, and Lamentations 5:20. In Lamentations 5:20, 'forever' means seventy years, or that which is considered to be an average lifespan. Thus, because his Shepherd provided abundantly (23:1-5), David resolved to return frequently to the tabernacle to worship for the rest of his life — or 'for the length of [his] days.'

Another example of this interpretive principle can be seen in interpreting the word 'blessed' in Psalms 1:1; 112:1; 119:1-2; and 128. Does this word (*asher*) merely mean 'happiness, bliss, contentment,' or is there more? Consulting other Old Testament passages reveals there is a fuller meaning. Referencing the Law in Deuteronomy 28 reveals that blessing is contrasted with cursing. The meaning of blessing is deeply rooted in a state of grace or the status of salvation. Jeremiah 17 further confirms that blessing and cursing are set in juxtaposition to each other, contrasting salvation and condemnation.

NEW TESTAMENT

Finally, the expositor will want to extend outward to the furthest reaches of Scripture. He will next want to ask: What light do the New Testament authors bring to a particular text in the Psalms?

PROGRESSIVE REVELATION

With the unity of the Bible, progressive revelation must be taken into account. This does not mean that truth evolves. Nor that truth taught in the Old Testament was imperfect or erroneous. Neither does progressive revelation imply that the Old Testament is less inspired than the New Testament. Rather, it means that the New Testament enlarges upon what the Old Testament teaches. This is to say, there has been a gradual unfolding of the truth from the Old Testament to the New Testament. What was taught often dimly in the Old Testament is placed in greater light in the New Testament. Partial revelation, given at the beginning of the Old Testament, grew brighter with each additional author of Scripture. In addition, some commands were later changed as Scripture advances from the old covenant to the new covenant.

For example, the charge to Abraham to circumcise (Gen. 17:10) was later rescinded in the New Testament (Gal. 5:2). The ceremonial law of Moses with its Levitical sacrificial system has been fulfilled in the death of Christ (Heb. 7:11-19). Lambs and bulls are no longer being offered as sacrifices by New Testament believers. Neither is public worship to be conducted in Jerusalem in the Temple. Care must be exercised in determining where in the Bible a cross reference is approached, depending upon where it finds itself in the unfolding story of redemptive history. All expositors must be aware of this progress of revelation.

MESSIANIC PSALMS

Cross referencing will, at last, require the expositor to turn to specific New Testament passages in which the Psalms are either directly quoted or indirectly alluded to. Regarding those psalms cited in the New Testament, they are as follows: Psalm 2:7 (Acts. 13:33); Psalm 8:2 (Matt. 21:16; Mark 12:36); Psalm 8:4-6 (Heb. 2:6-8; Mark 14:62); Psalm 8:6 (1 Cor. 15:27; Luke 20:42-43); Psalm 16:8-11 (Acts 2:25-28; Luke 22:69); Psalm 16:10 (Acts 13:35; Acts 2:34-35); Psalm 22:1 (Matt. 27:46; Mark 15:34; Heb. 1:13); Psalm

22:18 (Luke 20:17; John 19:24); Psalm 22:22 (Acts 4:11; Heb. 2:12); Psalm 31:5 (Luke 23:46); Psalm 35:19 (John 15:25); Psalm 40:6-8 (Heb. 10:5-7); Psalm 41:9 (John 13:18); Psalm 45:6-7 (Heb. 1:8-9); Psalm 68:18 (Mark 12:10-11; Eph. 4:8); Psalm 69:4 (John 15:25); Psalm 69:9 (Mark 11:9-10; John 2:17; 12:13; Rom. 15:3); Psalm 69:25 (Acts 1:20); Psalm 78:2 (Matt. 13:35); Psalm 89:20 (Luke 13:35; Acts 13:22); Psalm 102:25-27 (Heb. 1:10-12); Psalm 109:8 (Luke 19:38; Acts 1:20); Psalm 110:1 (Matt. 22:44; 26:64; Heb. 1:5; 5:5); Psalm 110:4 (Heb. 5:6; 7:17, 21); Psalm 118:22-23 (Matt. 21:42; 1 Pet. 2:7); Psalm 118:25-26 (Matt. 21:9); Psalm 118:26 (Matt. 23:39); Psalm 132:11 (Acts 2:30). Each of these psalms when preached should be referenced in the New Testament.

SAME TRUTHS

Likewise, the truths taught in the Psalms, whether they be doctrinal standards or moral precepts, can be affirmed and clarified with proper New Testament citations. These essential truths may be verified by the words of Jesus Christ, the apostles, and other writers of New Testament Scripture. A reference Bible can be very strategic in pursuing these verses. Also helpful can be the use of an exhaustive concordance, topical Bible, or some other specialized tool such as *The Treasury of Scripture Knowledge* (Revell, 1973).

THE ANALOGY OF SCRIPTURE

As has been stated in this chapter, Scripture interprets Scripture. This interpretive principle is *analogia scriptura* — the analogy of Scripture — and is built upon the solid foundation of the perfect unity of God's Word. The sure premise upon which this axiom rests is that the Bible speaks with one voice. The Bible never contradicts itself. All cross references teach and affirm the same standard of truth. The Bible possesses perfect unity of doctrine within its many parts.

Consistency of the message within the whole of Scripture is the premise upon which all cross-referencing rests. As we seek to unfold its meaning, each passage must always be interpreted in light of the whole. Each interpretation must harmonize with the whole of Scripture. Thus, the expositor must always take into account the entire Bible when examining any one passage of the Psalms.

CRAFT THE OUTLINE

*Reshape the syntactical outline
into a preaching outline*

B y this point, the exegesis of the psalm has been undertaken, and the interpretation of the text has been made. On many different levels, the psalm has undergone a thorough study by the expositor. He has plunged into the depths of the passage lexically, grammatically, contextually, historically, culturally, and geographically. He has left no stone unturned. No part of the text has been unexplored. He is gaining a solid understanding of what his passage means. Certainly, this insight will deepen and grow throughout this entire expository process. The more he ponders and meditates upon his text, the more insight he will gain. In fact, until the moment he steps into the pulpit, the biblical expositor will be plunging deeper and deeper into the passage. Even then, as he stands over his open Bible in the pulpit and preaches the Word, penetrating illumination by the Holy Spirit continues to be given.

In this next stage, the actual sermon manuscript will begin to take shape. One of the most important steps of sermon preparation will be the preaching outline. The homiletical outline is like the skeleton of a body upon which all the muscles and tissues of the message are placed. The preaching outline serves as the skeletal frame upon which the exegesis, application, and illustrations will be placed. As such, this outline provides not the *substance*, but the *structure* for the sermon.

The Framing of A Sermon

Putting it another way, think of the preaching outline as the frame of a house being constructed. It is upon the frame that all the plasterboard, ceilings, floor, etc. will hang. The frame determines how many rooms there will be and where they should go. Establishing the frame, in many ways, establishes the parameters of the house. So it is with the preaching outline. It is the framework for the psalm upon which the actual sermon is hung.

To this very point John MacArthur remarks, 'Outline points are hooks to hang thoughts on. They are lights along the pathway to enable listeners to stay on the path. They help retain listener attention and facilitate comprehension.'[1] The homiletical outline determines how many headings there will be in the sermon. It determines the placement of the exegesis, as well as influencing the positioning of the application and illustrations. In this sense, the sermon will be built upon and around the preaching outline.

Put yet another way, the preaching outline can be compared to a road map. The road map is not the road, nor is it the journey itself. Nor is it the destination. It is only the piece of paper that shows where you desire to travel, a document that must be followed for a successful, completed trip. So it is with the preaching outline.

THE AIDS OF AN OUTLINE

All this is to say, a preaching outline is of great value, as it will aid the listener in following the sermon, as well as focus the preacher's presentation. Since most people think in logical units, the preaching outline will help the listener grasp the content of the message. Such sermonic structure keeps their minds tracking with the sermon. This noticeable organization is especially needed in the Psalms. A recognizable orderly flow of thought can greatly assist in presenting the psalm to the listener. A clear sermon outline gives discernible structure to the sermon. Moreover, it provides clear direction for the preacher. It helps make the message understandable for the listener and provides unity to the sermon.

So, in this study, we will devote ourselves to this part of the preaching exercise, the first steps in preparing the sermon manuscript. In this fourth unit, the sermon manuscript takes shape as the expositor assimilates his findings. At this point in the process, a preaching outline must be forged and exegetical findings wrapped around it. Further, transitions must be written that weave the manuscript together into a seamless garment. Let us now consider these aspects:

HOMILETICAL OUTLINE

In order to help focus the preacher's presentation and aid the listeners in following the sermon, a preaching outline may prove to be of great value. Since the Western church thinks in logical units, a preaching outline helps them grasp the text and track with the preacher. Detecting an ordered flow of thought in a psalm often presents a major challenge for the listener. Thus, a clear sermon outline gives structure to the sermon, direction to the preacher, understanding to the listener, and unity to the message. To reshape the exegetical outline in a preaching outline, the preacher should:

WRITE MAJOR HEADINGS

As his study continues, the preacher should establish a reasonable number of major homiletical points based upon the structure and number of verses in the psalm. The major points of the sermon outline will help the expositor, as well as the congregation, understand the psalm before him. For the most part, the main points should represent the main clusters of truth. The expositor should make the psalmist's major points his major headings. In other words, the preaching outline should identify and reveal the natural divisions of the psalms. These major headings should be:

1. Relatively Few

In considering the appropriate number of points, the preacher must resist the tendency of having too many major points. A sermon with too many points has no point. The psalm itself dictates the number of sermon headings that you will craft. Most often, the outline will follow the stanzas. The number of stanzas will determine the number of major headings. Two-point outlines provide focus, three-point outlines are standard, but five- or six-point outlines *may* defy thorough treatment or tax the listener.

For example, Psalm 23 has two stanzas and nicely divides into two homiletical points. Each has an adjective and noun preceded by the definite article 'the':

    I.   The Good Shepherd (1-4)
    II. The Gracious Host (5-6)

Or, Psalm 100 could be easily divided as follows, alternating a simple participle, followed by the name 'God':

    I.   Approaching God (1-2)
    II. Apprehending God (3)
    III. Adoring God (4-5)

2. Obviously Clear

The main points or divisions should be crystal clear to both the preacher and the listener. Here, the use of alliteration or similar sounding words often helps. Obviously, abuses can occur at both ends. Taken to an extreme, some outlines draw too much attention to themselves and not to the text itself. On the other hand, ill-developed outlines obscure the flow of thought and leave the listener groping in the dark. Practice and experience help the preacher here. A clear, simple outline of Psalm 49 is as follows:

    I.   The Psalmist's Call (1-4)
    II. The Psalmist's Counsel (5-15)
    III. The Psalmist's Caution (16-20)

A clear outline of Psalm 93 could be a modifier and noun, followed by a preposition or adverb and 'God':

    I.   The Sovereign Reign of God (1-2)
    II. The Sinful Rebellion Against God (3-4)
    III. The Sure Revelation of God (5)

3. Logically Coherent

Effective outlines reflect logical, coherent, cogent thought. Each major point should support the central theme of the psalm and the main idea of the sermon. Repeating a word or phrase throughout the sermon outline achieves continuity. In addition, well-constructed outlines avoid abstract thought, but instead use concrete language. For instance, Psalm 147 calls for three reasons to praise God:

    I.   Praise for God's Restoration (1-6)
    II. Praise for God's Provision (7-11)
    III. Praise for God's Protection (12-20)

The outline of Psalm 150 shown below provides another example of well-structured, major headings. This one is an adverbial outline, distinguished by 'where,' 'why,' and 'how':

I.   Where to Praise God (1)
II. Why to Praise God (2)
III. How to Praise God (3-6)

4. Tightly Concise

As a general rule, the shorter the wording of the outline, the better. A tightly worded main heading aids note taking, and even encourages the congregation to write the point in the margin of their Bibles. Likewise, a 'shorter' point is easier to repeat later in the sermon when reviewing the various headings. Further, few words are easier for the preacher to remember. In homiletical outlining, less is more. The following outline of Psalm 55 gets straight to the point of the psalm:

I.   David's Anguish (1-8)
II. David's Anger (9-15)
III. David's Assurance (16-23)

A tightly-worded outline, such as the one for Psalm 117, may look similar to this one. The last word 'praise' remains constant, while the first noun changes:

I.   The Call to Praise (1)
II. The Causes for Praise (2a, b)
III. The Crescendo of Praise (2c)

5. Symmetrically Balanced

As the pastor constructs his outline, he should lay it out in a symmetrical fashion, reflecting a proportionate balance. For instance, a psalm of, say, ten verses that comprise three stanzas should not have four homiletical points in the first two verses and only one heading for the remaining eight verses. A preaching outline, like a skeleton, provides structure to support the flesh. The sermon can become an information overload without the symmetry and balance that a good outline helps provide. The following outline of Psalm 43 shows an even distribution of headings throughout:

I.   A Prayer for Vindication (1)
II. A Prayer of Lamentation (2)
III. A Prayer for Restoration (3-4)
IV. A Prayer of Introspection (5)

A balanced outline is important especially in longer psalms. The following is an example for Psalm 51. Both the first and last noun change:

I.   A Cry for Forgiveness (1-2)
II. A Concession of Sin (3-6)
III. A Call for Cleansing (7-9)
IV. A Commitment to Holiness (10-12)
V.   A Consecration of Life (13-17)
VI. A Concern for God's Glory (18-19)

USE VARIED STYLE

1. Simple Observation

This type of preaching outline succinctly states the kernel of truth for each main section of a psalm. The wording is brief. Each outline point appears as an incomplete sentence, usually a solitary noun with a modifier. For example, a preacher could outline Psalm 3 using the simple observation method:

I.   David's Trial (1-2)
II. David's Trust (3-6)
III. David's Triumph (7-8)

Another example is Psalm 34. 'David' remains the same and the noun that follows varies:

I.   David's Worship (1-3)
II. David's Witness (4-7)
III. David's Wisdom (8-14)
IV. David's Wonder (15-22)

Psalm 44 provides another example. Both the modifying adjective and the noun change:

I. A Prosperous Past (1-8)
II. A Painful Present (9-22)
III. A Positive Prospect (23-26)

Yet another example comes from Psalm 75. The first noun remains unchanged, followed by a prepositional phrase in which the last word changes:

I. A Word of Thanksgiving (1)
II. A Word of Triumph (2-3)
III. A Word of Threat (4-5)
IV. A Word of Trust (6-8)

2. First Person

Another style of preaching outline is the first person outline, which allows the psalmist, as it were, to directly speak through the homiletical points. Thus, this genre of outline will have the words 'me' or 'I' repeated throughout. Along this line, a first person outline of Psalm 17 unfolds as follows:

I. See Me! (1-2)
II. Search Me! (3-5)
III. Show Me! (6-7)
IV. Shield Me! (8-12)
V. Save Me! (13-14a)
VI. Satisfy Me! (14b-15)

3. Practical Application

One example of preaching outline is the practical application outline. In this type of heading, the main application of each major division receives priority of place, and becomes the featured heading. Thus, this kind of outline is worded as an action point, calling the listener to step out and follow the major point itself. It implies the second person, 'you.' One example of such an outline is Psalm 65:

I.   Praise God for His Grace (1-4)
II. Praise God for His Greatness (5-8)
III. Praise God for His Goodness (9-13)

Psalm 66 serves as another model of a practical application outline. The action verb changes and what follows, 'to God,' remains the same:

I.   Sing to God (1-4)
II. See God (5-7)
III. Shout to God (8-12)
IV. Sacrifice to God (13-15)
V.   Savor God (16-20)

4. Full Sentence

Another alternative is to word each major point as a complete sentence. Here, the outline, rather than being a mere noun and modifier, or simply a phrase, contains a subject and verb with possibly an object. In such cases, less is more. Such a sentence should be short, compact, and tightly worded. A sample outline using this style for Psalm 36 could be:

I.   Man Is Sinful (1-4)
II. God Is Supreme (5-12)

FOLLOW THE STANZAS

As the expositor crafts the preaching outline, he should follow the structure of the stanzas. Each stanza contains one major truth. Similarly, each homiletical point should contain the same. Most psalms contain relatively few stanzas, which simplifies the outlining process. Thus, a psalm of three stanzas easily divides into the three headings of the outline. However, longer psalms with multiple stanzas require the preacher to group the main clusters of verses. Regarding this, the preacher will want to:

1. Compare Translations

Bible translators decide where to divide the stanzas. A blank space separates each stanza from the previous unit. For the most part, translations agree on how to divide the text. But such is not always the case. The well-prepared expositor consults several Bible translations, looking for discrepancies over the divisions. For those adept in Hebrew, they should look at the Masoretic divisions, and determine paragraphs according to the Hebrew itself.

2. Consult Commentaries

In addition, sound exegetical commentaries aid in resolving disputes over major heading divisions. Good commentators provide evidence for identifying how clusters of verses group together. The preacher can trace the arguments of able scholars in print and see how they have made divisions in the biblical text. Consulting a reliable study Bible can be helpful with this, as well.

3. Compress Divisions

Some psalms significantly exceed others in length, containing many stanzas (Pss. 18, 22, 31, 33, 34, 35, 37, 37, 44, 68, 69, 71, 73, 74, 78, 89, 94, 102, 103, 104, 105, 106, 107, 109, 118, 119, 136, 139, 145). In such cases, if the expositor wishes to preach the entire psalm in one sermon, an eight-point outline is probably not wise, although it is possible. The skill of the preacher will determine the number of the points. In psalms with multiple stanzas, effective expositors will want to compress several stanzas together into one homiletical heading. For the expositor may choose to outline Psalm 109 as follows:

I.   David's Lamentation (1-5)
II. David's Imprecation (6-20)
III. David's Desperation (21-25)
IV. David's Petition (26-29)
V. David's Adoration (30-31)

To account for length, outline points for longer psalms may span several verses. A suitable outline for Psalm 136 may resemble:

I.   Thanks for God's Creation (1-9)
II. Thanks for God's Conquests (10-22)
III. Thanks for God's Care (23-26)

WRITE SUBHEADINGS

Each major point may require subpoints depending upon the number of verses and content. If the preacher opts for subpoints, he may or may not announce them to the congregation, depending upon the number of main headings. What is true of the main headings is true of subheadings, namely, that they are clear, concise, and cover a manageable amount of text. It is critical that supporting points actually *support* the major point under which they find themselves. Skilled expositors keep subpoints to a bare minimum, if they use them at all. A sermon can easily become too congested with a heavy use of subpoints, confusing the listener. Not every major point needs subpoints; indeed, it is not necessary for a sermon to have any at all. Preachers should enlist subpoints at their discretion, only when it enhances the communication of the passage.

Subpoints, if used, should remain as abbreviated as possible. One-word subheadings are best. Single adjectives or adverbs effectively summarize subpoints. Sometimes a prepositional phrase communicates in a clear and clean manner. For example, in Psalm 93, the first stanza consists of verses 1-2. The subheadings could describe the sovereign reign of God as listed below. The Lord reigns:

A.   Exclusively (1a)
B.   Constantly (1a)
C.   Actively (1a)
D.   Infinitely (1a)
E.   Majestically (1a)
F.   Powerfully (1b)
G.   Immutably (1c)
H.   Eternally (2)

At other times, subpoints consist of prepositional phrases,

where the noun changes with each move. For example, in Psalm 47:2-4, God calls people to worship Him because He reigns:

A. Over the Earth (2)
B. Over the Nations (3)
C. Over Israel (4)

Also, the preacher can change one word of a short sentence, such as a verb. For instance, in Psalm 46:4-7, the sons of Korah affirm that:

A. God Satisfied His People (4)
B. God Sustains His People (5-6)
C. God Saves His People (7)

A FINAL THOUGHT

In outlining a psalm, one thing must be kept in mind. The preacher must not force the outline, but instead find it. He must never impose his outline upon the text, causing an unnatural division or improper emphasis. Rather, the outline should arise naturally from the passage. The expositor should always follow the clear flow of thought established by the biblical author. He must never twist the text to fit his outline. Let the passage dictate the text.

Regarding the sermon outline, Eric Alexander observes, 'The structure must never obtrude so as to be admired for its cleverness or originality. It needs to represent the content of the passage and must never be an ill-fitting box into which the truth is thrust, as if we are more concerned with the packaging than with the content. It is the finished building men want to see and not the builder's scaffolding'[2]

Never allow the outline to dictate the text. Better to be true to the flow of the passage at the expense of the outline than force an outline upon the text. If one keeps this in mind, an outline can be a helpful guide in establishing clear and memorable communication.

---— 20 —---

GATHER THE
FINDINGS

---

*Distill and merge the exegesis
into the preaching outline*

Having established a preaching outline, important questions now arise for the expositor. He must ask himself: Should I prepare a manuscript? What do I take into the pulpit? Should I preach from a manuscript? Or from a skeletal outline? Or neither? As it relates to a manuscript, is less more? Or is more even more helpful? Certainly, no verse in the Bible directly speaks to what is the right practice for an expositor. God has wired every preacher differently, and no one solution is the answer for all. This chapter is designed to help think through assimilating one's exegetical findings into a preaching manuscript.

As a basic point of principle, expositors should draft a manuscript, whether or not they use it in the pulpit. The discipline involved in writing out a set of full sermon notes is a healthy exercise. On the whole, good writing improves both the substance and the style of one's preaching. Good preachers are those who understand clear, concise, and compelling language. They grasp the essentials of sound logic and the tight organization of their own thoughts. As Martyn Lloyd-Jones notes, 'If my sermon is not clear and ordered in my mind, I cannot preach it to others.'[1] This begins with incorporating such clarity of thought into their manuscript. As a general rule, if one can write well, he can think clearly in pulling together his preaching notes.

BENEFITS OF A MANUSCRIPT

Manuscripting the sermon forces accuracy in the choice of words. It also expands one's vocabulary and causes a wider variety of expression. Further, writing the sermon produces an ever-growing body of work for future reference and preaching. The discipline of writing a sermon manuscript ensures the careful preparation of the preacher and helps him internalize the message. These benefits and more make the time involved well worth the effort.

But using a manuscript in the pulpit is not a necessity. Many great preachers have chosen not to preach with extensive sermon notes. John Calvin, for example, brought no manuscript into his pulpit — not even notes. No one would dare say that the expository genius of the Genevan Reformer was hindered because he had no manuscript. Charles Spurgeon used only a brief outline which he placed inside his English Bible — and he remains the Prince of Preachers. Jonathan Edwards used a full manuscript early in his prolific ministry, but later began to preach with only a brief outline. R. C. Sproul uses no notes whatsoever, much less a manuscript, and he remains one of the great preachers of our day. But on the other hand, John MacArthur continues to preach from what is essentially a full manuscript. Every preacher has his own style, and there is no right or wrong answer. The key is: What works for *you*?

ADVANTAGES OUTWEIGH DISADVANTAGES

Personally, I believe that the advantages of writing a full manuscript and taking it into the pulpit outweigh the 'no manuscript' option. Why do I say this? First, a fully written sermon helps a verse-by-verse preacher have a command of a wide range of information while he is in the pulpit. Such a practice enables the preacher to address grammatical observations, historical background, cross references, quotes, carefully-worded statements, and speak with accuracy, depth, and confidence. Second, a manuscript ensures that careful attention is given to sermonic structure, sequence of thought, and symmetry. Third, a manuscript helps keep the preacher on message and prevents rambling. It also prevents him from unnecessarily repeating himself. Thus, in my estimation, extensive sermon notes are not a luxury, but, for most, a necessity.

However, there are dangers in using a full manuscript. A full set of notes can cause poor eye contact with the congregation and limit rapport with them. It can hinder the preacher's spontaneity and give him a tendency to speak in written style. It can promote a tendency to speak with a coldness of manner. Nevertheless, the advantages of using a manuscript are many. It promotes solid preparation and good structure. It yields a well-developed introduction, smooth transitions, improved vocabulary, and so forth.

Having said this, it is certainly possible to preach with fewer notes — or no notes at all. This requires, however, a personal command of the biblical text, systematic theology, and compelling language. Further, the preacher must have at his beck and call pastoral application, smooth transitions, engaging illustrations and the like. There are, admittedly, excellent preachers who use minimal notes and still deliver weighty substantial messages. It simply depends upon the individual preacher.

EXCEPTIONS TO THE RULES

Spurgeon, who was mentioned earlier, preached from merely a thin outline. He had no manuscript before him, nor one left behind in his study. But two things must be kept in mind. One, Spurgeon was blessed with a photographic memory — unlike most of us. He was a prolific speed-reader with a steel-trap mind that retained far more information than we do. And, two, he was not a classical verse-by-verse expositor, preaching through books in the Bible. Instead, he was largely expounding one verse, or merely a phrase in a text. Spurgeon did not give as much supportive information in his sermon as a sequential expositor. The fact is, he preached with fewer notes because he drew from a deep well. All this is to say, most expositors, I feel, should use a fuller set of notes than did Spurgeon.

EXEGETICAL FINDINGS

After the preacher writes his outline, he must begin the process of incorporating his exegesis into the appropriate place in the outline. As stated earlier, the homiletical outline serves as a skeleton upon which the preacher places the meat of his study. Now it is time for him to integrate the findings of his study of the biblical text into the outline itself. This requires the preacher to:

CONSOLIDATION

In this phase, the preacher must place his exegetical findings into his preaching outline. He must gather together what he has written concerning the explanation of the text. He must revisit his word studies, verb parsing, grammar and syntax, history and cultural background, cross references, context, book theme, geography and the like. He must make judgments regarding what should be incorporated into the final manuscript. Not everything will be placed into his pulpit document. He will only place what is essential to communicate in the course of his message. The fruit of one's exegetical study should fit logically into the newly created homiletical outline.

In so doing, the expositor must rewrite his findings into concise, understandable statements. Preachers must sift their work like wheat in order to separate the chaff. When reducing one's exegetical findings, the expositor must prayerfully ask, how relevant is this nugget of information for the sermons? Following this compressing process, he now assimilates his exegetical insights into the homiletical outline. It is critical that minor facts not inhibit the major flow of the sermon. Peripheral matters should not detract from the primary thrust of the sermon.

Clarification

After the expositor has extracted his exegesis and put the raw material in place, he needs to rewrite his findings so that they are stated in clear, understandable terms, while remaining biblically and theologically precise. This was one of the strengths of the expository preaching of John Calvin, who intentionally chose to preach with what he called 'familiar' language. This practice should characterize all preachers. He should write out the thrust of his sermon in contemporary language that is understood by the common person. There is no virtue in speaking over the heads of the listener. He should not use the stifled, archaic language of heady theologians or ancient Puritans, though they be deeply loved and admired. Outdated or vague words hinder effective communication of the truth. They lack meaning to the listeners. On the other end of the spectrum, one should avoid colloquialisms and slang that trivialize the message.

At the same time, expositors should strive to make biblical truth understandable, memorable, and applicable. With that goal, low idioms and gutter jargon have no place in the pulpit. Further, Shoptalk must remain in the study, though preachers should employ theological words as they appear in Scripture, such as propitiation, justification, sanctification. Common theological words that do not appear in Scripture also have a place. These would include words like incarnation, trinity. In either case, congregations understand less than preachers think. So preachers should briefly or extensively define unfamiliar terms whenever possible.

TRANSITIONAL BRIDGES

After the exegesis of the passage has been built into the preaching outline, each of these various parts must be sown together into one garment with the silky threads of smooth transitions. Abrupt changes of thought often leave listeners behind. A transition serves as a natural pivot where the preacher moves from point to point or truth to truth. Thus, as the sermon unfolds, hearers are carried along with the preacher. Further, transitions profit preachers and congregations alike because they break the entire message into palatable pieces of information. They provide a clear, concise, reasoned, logical connection from one point of the argument to the next.

According to John Broadus, 'Transition may be formally defined as both the act and means of moving from one part of the sermon to another, from one division to another, and from one idea to another. Transitions are to sermons what joints are to the bones of the body. They are the bridges of the discourse, and by them the preacher moves from point to point.'[2] As with any road, these bridges are both helpful and necessary in order to move forward and arrive at the destination.

CONNECTION

The expositor must give careful thought regarding how to best move from one main heading to the next. These transitions are necessary because they 'pull forward' the listener throughout the sermon, allowing them to follow the preacher's progression of thought. As the preacher builds his argument, he will want to use key transitional words in moving from point to point in order to assist a progression in thought.

1. Transitional Words

The preacher must use transitional words that indicate order. These include words such as 'first,' 'second,' 'third,' 'finally,' 'again,' 'moreover,' 'furthermore,' 'next,' 'further.' For smooth delivery, the preacher will want to use short phrases that signal a move-ment to the next thought or the next outline point. These help the listener 'connect the dots' in what is being said and move with the preacher from one unit of thought to the next. Other helpful transitional phrases include: 'in the next place,' 'what is more,' 'in addition,' 'David goes on to say,' 'the next feature we see,' 'an additional mark is,' 'let us consider further,' 'I also call your attention to,' 'not only, but also.'

2. Explanatory Statements

After announcing his next point, the preacher may want to set up what follows with a few sentences. Before he reads and explains the next verse or verses, he may want to transition by saying something like, 'The psalmist Asaph now provides insight into his soul-searching struggle by describing...' or, 'What will follow in these next verses is a stunning statement that provides for us even greater insight into this important truth.' These preliminary statements help make the transition effective.

3. Repeat Points

Another way to alert the listener that the preacher is moving forward to the next major heading is by repeating the previous main points. This is by way of review. The preacher may say: 'Not only have we seen David's Troubles in verses one and two, and David's Trust in verses three through six, but now, finally, David's Triumph in the concluding two verses.' A brief summary alerts the people that the time has come to move on in the next unit of thought.

4. Interrogative Questions

Also, by asking simple questions, the preacher is able to alert the listener that he is moving forward to the next main point. He may choose to inject: 'So how will David respond in the midst of this trial? The next verses will tell us.' Posing questions also heightens anticipation of what lies ahead. Leading questions ensure that listeners board the train before it moves to the next stop. In Psalm 15, for example, David himself provides the leading question. He asks, 'O Lord, who may abide in Your tent? Who may abide on Your holy hill?' (v. 1). Moving from his first thought to the next, David provides a natural transition for the preacher. He may choose to ask the congregation: What does a godly man look like? How can you identify a spiritual individual? How can you mark your spiritual progress?

CONTINUITY

Transitions within major points help the progression from one statement to the next. Here is where the message becomes even more tightly woven together. After a truth has been stated, it may be helpful to restate or further clarify such propositions. Therefore, the expositor will want to have certain phrases ready, such as: 'that is to say,' or 'in other words,' or 'that is,' or 'to put it another way,' or 'it could be restated like this.' Also, as the message advances, other phrases will be helpful to propel the arguments forward. The preacher will want to have selected phrases in his arsenal: 'What is more,' 'In addition,' 'But that is not all,' 'More than that,' 'This all leads to the following.' Other emphatic phrases are: 'To be sure,' 'Simply put,' 'To this end,' or 'Mark this well.'

GOING THE EXTRA MILE

This chapter has considered the initial steps of pulling a sermon manuscript together. Admittedly, this is hard work that requires an extra allotment of time (1 Tim. 5:17). Surely, this is one reason why many fall short of being great preachers. It is not because they lack sufficient gifts, but because too few are willing to pay the price. They settle for a lower level of excellence in their pulpit ministry. Bottom line, great preaching requires maximum effort to be ready to preach.

Thorough preparation requires extensive effort. Too many cut corners in their sermon preparation and, tragically, too many congregations suffer for it. Going the extra mile often results in the difference between merely a good sermon and one that is great. In matters of good, better, and best, let us always strive to do our best for the glory of God.

Are you willing to pay the price for excellence in the pulpit? Are you ready to make whatever sacrifice is necessary to be properly prepared to preach? God's Word deserves the best we have to give. This is not an area where we can afford to scale back. Let us study, practice, and preach as if lives depend upon it. The fact is, they do.

INTEGRATE THE APPLICATION

Write the timeless principles
to be applied to the listener

A sermon is never complete until the text is practically applied to the individual lives of the hearers. This is no less true for an exposition of a psalm than it is for any other portion of Scripture. The relevancy of the text must be shown by the expositor and made known to the listener. To this end, John Broadus writes, 'Preaching is essentially a personal encounter, in which the preacher's will is making a claim through the truth upon the will of the hearer. If there is no summons, there is no sermon.'[1] This is to say, the preacher must be exhorting his congregation throughout the message to pursue the path laid out in the passage being expounded.

In other words, the preacher must always ask himself: How does this truth relate to the lives of the listeners? What is God requiring of them? What specific actions does God expect from the hearers of this truth? This is where preaching moves beyond teaching. Application is one of the features that distinguishes a sermon from a lecture. Lloyd-Jones writes:

> A sermon is not to be confused with giving a lecture...
> A lecture starts with a subject, and what it is concerned to do is to give knowledge and information concerning this particular subject. Its appeal is primarily and almost exclusively to the mind; its object is to give instruction and state facts. That is its primary purpose and function. So a lecture, again, lacks, and should lack, the element of attack, the concern to do something to the listener, which is a vital element in preaching.[2]

PREACHING AND TEACHING

In a related story, Lloyd-Jones was once approached by a young minister and asked, 'What is the difference between preaching and teaching. The Doctor gave a memorable answer. He said, "If you have to ask me the difference between preaching and teaching, you obviously have never heard preaching. If you have heard preaching, you would not ask me the difference between the two."' One way in which preaching differs from teaching is in this very area of application. Preaching is accompanied by application and makes demands upon the listener.

Application answers the question: How does this truth relate to me? The following questions will help apply the truths discovered in Bible study:[3]

1. Are there *examples* to follow?
2. Are there *commands* to obey?
3. Are there *errors* to avoid?
4. Are there *sins* to forsake?
5. Are there *promises* to claim?
6. Are there *new thoughts* about God?
7. Are there *principles* to live by?

In order to answer these questions accurately, the expositor should consider the following principles:

TIMELESS PRINCIPLES

Every psalm contains key theological principles and timeless truths. These propositions and doctrines extend to every believer in every place in this present age. These timeless principles are one-sentence statements of the relevant truth in a biblical text. They must be discovered, stated, and applied. The expositor must determine which implications of the psalm are relevant for the lives of his listeners. He must find the timeless truths taught in this psalm.

ROOTED IN THE TEXT

All theological principles must be rooted and grounded in the psalm being studied. The principle must never be read into the text, nor imposed upon it, but flow out of the Scripture itself. The expositor does not have to make the Scripture relevant; the Bible *is* relevant. He merely shows its relevance. The expositor must ask himself: What demands does this psalm make upon those who will hear it expounded? What does *this* text require of the listener? What is the reasonable implication of what it says? What is its life application? What is its clear relevance? What does this psalm teach about God, man, salvation, and eternity? What practical truths are taught in this psalm?

Rise Above Time

Further, the theological principles extracted from the Psalms are timeless. That is to say, they are not restricted to the ancient world of the psalmist. They are not bound to any one specific previous era, but rise above the centuries and apply to all people in all places in all times. These timeless principles are broad enough to transcend the centuries and reach to the present hour. So, the expositor must ask himself: What are the timeless, permanent principles here that are true for every generation? How should they be applied and lived?

Transcend Beyond Cultures

Moreover, the relevant principles found in any particular psalm must transcend ancient cultural distinctives. The relevance must not be bound to any one particular civilization or society. Instead, the practicality of the passage rises above the customs and times of the ancient world and possess equal relevance for modern people who find themselves in an entirely different culture.

Consistent with all Scripture

A timeless principle extracted from a biblical passage must be general enough to consistently harmonize with the full counsel of God. In discovering the principle, the expositor must recognize the development of progressive revelation from the Old Testament to the New Testament. He must allow for old covenant/new covenant differences. In so doing, he must make application that does not contradict any other passage of Scripture that speaks to the same issue.

PERSONAL NEEDS

The expositor must not study the Bible simply to construct a sermon. Such a man will soon become a 'professional' in the worst sense of the word, and his preaching will devolve into a mere job rather than the fulfillment a divine calling. As the expositor studies the Bible, he must do so, first and foremost, that he might grow in the grace and knowledge of the Lord Jesus Christ. Before he can think about applying the Bible to others, he must first administer it to his own heart. He must ask himself: What does this passage have to say to *me*? How should *my* life be impacted? The answers to these questions will require:

PERSONAL AUTHENTICITY

Every expositor must have an authentic transparency before the psalm he is studying. He must lay bare his own soul before the written Word of God. With deepest humility and sincerity, he must apply the biblical text to his own needy life. He must examine his passage in light of his own life. He must expose his own heart before God as this passage speaks to his own spiritual condition. Such honest vulnerability of his own soul before the text being studied is absolutely essential. No preacher should require of others what he has not already sought to pursue in his own life.

INWARD APPLICATION

Having humbled himself before his text, the expositor must carefully apply it to his own life. How does this passage relate to his own spiritual walk? What sin does he need to confess and repent of? What comfort and encouragement needs to be drawn? What promises need to be claimed? What example needs to be emulated? What path needs to be pursued? What attitude needs to be adjusted? What practice needs to be implemented? What praise needs to be offered to God? What thanks need to be given to Him? This is to say, the text must be first self-applied by the expositor to himself before it is brought to others.

LISTENER NEEDS

Having inwardly applied the psalm, the preacher must anticipate the needs of the listeners to whom he will be speaking. If
not specific individuals, he must, at least, visualize representative individuals from the group or congregation who will be
present. This involves knowing something of the following:

HUMAN NATURE

The expositor should know human nature — its tendencies,
weakness, and struggles. He should know the basic needs and
conflicts of people. He should be familiar with their areas of
temptations, discouragements, and sins. This requires being 'in
touch' with his congregation. It is with difficulty that one makes
application in a vacuum. Likewise, reading books, magazines,
newspapers, and watching television will reveal current trends
and tensions in the world in which the congregation lives which
the preacher may want to address.

SAMPLE LISTENERS

In addition, the preacher may want to picture five or six members of the congregation to whom he will be preaching. Each of
these people should represent a cross section of those to whom
he preaches. How will the truth of this message intersect with
their lives? He should ask himself: What does this text have to
say to a businessman? A single parent? A college student? A
retired grandparent? A young couple contemplating a move?
How does this Scripture impact their lives?

CURRENT ISSUES

Taking a step further, the expositor must know the critical
concerns and outside pressures that are impacting the lives of

his congregation — or those that soon will be. He must know the times in which he and his flock live. In response, he must speak to the pertinent issues of the day. He must bring the Word of God to bear upon the many problems and mounting pressures that confront the church. Like a watchman on the wall, the expositor must faithfully blow the trumpet when he sees the enemy approaching. He must warn those under his care. This involves:

KNOWING THE TIMES

The expositor must know not only the ancient times of the biblical world, but the present-day world in which his listeners live. He must know the false ideologies of the hour that seek to squeeze his congregation into its mold. Accordingly, he must read current literature periodicals in order to discern the relevance of his text for the listener. What secular philosophies are pressing upon the thinking of his people? What world views are competing for his flock's attention?

ADDRESSING THE TIMES

More than merely knowing the times, the expositor must speak to the times. He must address the threatening issues of the day with God's Word. Like a prophet of ancient times, he must declare, 'Thus says the Lord.' He must confront the secular world views and false ideologies that war against the truth. The preacher must make known the mind of God in light of the counterfeit beliefs of the day. He must point out the dangerous philosophies that are seeking to capture his listeners' attention and ensnare their lives. Moreover, he must show how they are in conflict with the biblical plumbline. This is the role of the preacher of God's Word. He must allow the Bible to speak to the issues of the day.

WRITTEN APPLICATION

Rather than consider this to be a spontaneous part of the sermon, the preacher should manuscript even the application he makes. This discipline in writing forces him to be accurate and thoughtful in connecting the sermon to the listener. He should probably not spontaneously ad-lib the application any more than he should the interpretation. Along this line, the application should be:

PERSONALLY POINTED

The application should have been directly pointed to the heart and life of the listener. Sometimes it should be couched in 'we' terms, or vaguely as 'some people.' But often, the application needs to have more of a directness to it. Sometimes, it needs to be spoken in terms of 'you.' In such cases, rather than having a shotgun approach with scattered buckshot, the application needs to be more like a rifle shot with a direct bullet hitting the target. A variety between first and second person plural pronouns is best. 'We' reflects the preacher's humility, including himself in the application. But 'you' communicates the direct, personal thrust of the point.

STRATEGICALLY PLACED

The application of the psalm needs to be strategically placed into the manuscript at the proper place. As a general rule, revealing what this text requires of the listener needs to be placed throughout the message. It should preferably be located soon after the particular verse has been preached. As a general rule, the preacher should strike while the iron is hot. This is to say, he should drive home the particular application immediately after the verse or group of verses has been explained. By and large, he will not want to allow unnecessary distance to come between the explanation of the text and its application. Generally speaking,

placing application at the end of each major homiletical heading is a good position to put it. Before moving to the next point,
the present section should be applied. Certainly, leaving some
application until the end of the sermon is also very appropriate.
It can serve as a final action point.

EVENLY DISTRIBUTED

The best place for application is to place it throughout the message. Each major movement of the sermon should be seen in
light of its relevancy to the listeners. If the preacher gathers
together all the application at the end of the sermon, his listeners may learn to tune him out while he is teaching the 'meat' of
the passage. Or if he runs short of time at the end of the sermon,
all application would be forfeited. Instead, the preacher should
weave 'action points' throughout the entire sermon. While the
Puritans reserved all application for the end of the sermon, most
expositors today, I would say, should apply the truth immediately after they explain it.

SPECIFIC DIRECTION

If application tells people what to do, implementation tells people how to do it. Application without implementation, it has
been said, leads to frustration. So, what should be considered in
showing the implementation of a passage?

ACTION STEPS

One reason some congregation members carry around heavy
burdens on their backs is because, after hearing weekly sermons
where interpretation and application are correctly explained,
they know what God requires, but do not know how or where
to begin. By not knowing what specific steps to take, guilt often
heaps up and frustration sets in. Without implementation,

church services with strong teaching can become a place where guilt is heaped upon listeners. Pastors must actually show their people how to unload their burdens on the Lord. Congregations need the specifics of personal and practical implementation.

PRACTICAL CONSIDERATIONS

This is where practical tips for implementing the truth come in. If the application, for example, is to 'let the word of Christ dwell richly within you' (Col. 3:16), people must be shown *how* to overcome everyday obstacles such as busy schedules, competing demands, growing family, and physical exhaustion. Positive steps of implementation might include carrying Scripture memory cards in one's pocket throughout the day, listening to an audio recording of Scripture while driving, following a Bible reading plan, and the like.

THE MOST RELEVANT BOOK

Many times, modern-day preachers feel the self-imposed pressure to make the Bible relevant to their listeners. They perceive, and wrongly so, that this ancient Book is out of step with the times and needs help in being modernized. Thus, they try to add to the message of the Bible the ideas of many contemporary philosophers of the day in an attempt to make the Bible applicable to the listeners. Many other ideologies are thus added to their sermons, theories and findings from secular psychology, the self-improvement movement, the business boardroom, and the media-driven market-place. They assume that the Bible is not relevant without supplementing its message from the world today.

LIVING AND ACTIVE

But the fact is, the Bible is the single most relevant book in the world. As already stated, the preacher does not need to make it relevant — it *is* relevant. The Bible is living and active, full of the power of God. It is a life-changing book, unequaled in its ability to transform those who receive its message. I have read many books, but this Book alone reads me. It cuts to the core of my being and reveals me to myself for who I truly am. It allows me to see myself as God sees me. It shows me what I must become by God's grace. No other book in the world can do this. No other book but the Bible can work at the deepest level of who I am and effect change from the inside out. No other book can reroute my eternal destiny, from the depths of hell to the heights of heaven. No other book can change my character into Christlikeness.

Bringing the living and active Book to his flock is the God-given role of the expositor as he expounds God's Word. He must show the practical relevance of his text and apply it pastorally to the individual lives of people. Commenting on the sermons of Jonathan Edwards, R. W. Dale remarks, 'In the elaborate doc-trinal part of Jonathan Edwards' sermons, the great preacher was only getting his guns into position; but that in his "applica-tions" he opened fire on the enemy.'[4] So it must be with every preacher today. Having explained a passage of Scripture, the expositor must bring about a transforming effect in the lives of God's people.

CHANGING THE ENTIRE PERSON

The expositor must be constantly seeking to change the way the people think. He must be conforming their minds to think God's thoughts. He must be enabling them to see all of life from God's perspective. He is to give them a Christian world view, causing them to see everything from God's vantage point. To change one's life, the preacher must change their minds — and the Bible does this, giving the divine vantage point on time and eternity.

But more than that, the Bible changes the heart. It alters what a person feels about the world around them. The Scripture causes people to love what God loves and hate what God hates. It brings their emotions into alignment with God's heart. And, yet further, the Bible challenges a person's will. It alters the criteria for the choices a person makes. It shapes the volitional impulses of a person's life. Their will is radically redirected and transformed.

This is the life-changing power of the Psalms. This is the effect that the expositor brings about when he preaches this ancient hymn book in the power of the Holy Spirit. Expository preaching changes lives, simply put, because the Bible changes lives. The Scripture is undeniably the most relevant book ever written, full of life-change. This phase of application is a critical part of the preacher's arsenal because we preach for changed lives.

22

WRITE THE INTRODUCTION

*Write an opening that will
effectively launch the sermon*

First impressions *are* lasting impressions. This timeless adage is true not only in various walks of life, but in preaching as well. Every sermon needs a strong and compelling beginning. As the message begins, the preacher wants his listeners on board. He will want to secure their attention and cause them to want to make the journey with him through the biblical passage. If the listener's attention is not captured at the start of the sermon, he may not be won along the way. Therefore, it is critically important to start the sermon well. Few preachers are gifted enough to overcome a poor start.

Think of the introduction as a rocket launch. An initial burst of energy is needed by a rocket to get it up and off the ground. If the launch fails, the spaceship is going nowhere. But with the proper lift-off, the rocket will be successfully on its way for a successful journey. So it is with the sermon. Every message needs a strong launch to get it up and going and flying strong. A weak beginning loses people, often without recovery. But a striking beginning most often leads to a strong sermon.

FRONT PORCH OF THE HOUSE

Then again, think of the introduction as the porch of a house. Proportionally, a porch is smaller than the house itself. Yet it serves to provide easy access for all guests to enter the main structure. How strange a house would look if the front porch were too large or, worse, if it were larger than the house itself. Too large a porch would draw too much attention to itself. Rather, it should compliment the beauty of the house. In the same way, the introduction should be large enough to gain the interest of the listener to the sermon, but at the same time, small enough not to distract from the main body of the message. Proportion is critical. An introduction that is too large and too long has ruined many a sermon, even before it gets started.

The oft-repeated three 'I's of a good introduction are well stated: interest, involvement and identification. Ideally, the introduction should create interest, engage involvement, and cause the listener to identify personally with the subject matter. After the introduction, it has been said that the preacher ought to be able to sit down and have thoroughly stimulated the congregation to want him to get back up and finish the rest of the sermon.

This is certainly true in preaching the Psalms. As with expounding any portion of Scripture, the expositor must begin his sermon with an introduction that orients his listeners to the psalm that is to be expounded. Despite the richness of the truths and vivid language of the Psalms, every sermon from this inspired book nevertheless still needs a carefully developed introduction. The following are considerations to be taken into account.

READ VERSES

In the introduction, the expositor will want to read the psalm that he will preach. According to 1 Timothy 4:13, this reading should take place, preferably, somewhere at the beginning of the message. The reading of the text should certainly be before the text is explained or applied. This places the psalm before the listeners, introducing them to the verses to be expounded in the sermon. Even the mere reading of the text draws attention to its importance and underscores its authority. It must be recognized that many of the psalms are so lengthy that reading the entire text may not be practical. In such cases, merely a portion of the psalm should be read. Preferably, it would be the opening stanzas of the psalm. In reading the text, the preacher will want to:

READ CLEARLY

As the preacher reads his psalm, he must do so in a way in which he is clearly heard and intelligently understood. Careful pronunciation must be given to the words. He should familiarize himself with the phonetics of unfamiliar words. Further, he must not read this text so rapidly that he cannot be easily understood — as if rushing to get on with the rest of his sermon. Better to read the passage deliberately than too fast. Moreover, he should vary his pace and tone as he reads. An unchanging pace with a flat monotone voice leads to a boring, monotonous reading of the passage. Like a book in which every line is highlighted with a yellow marker, nothing stands out. Instead, the preacher should read his text so that key words and phrases are noticeably distinguished. Often a soft voice is even more dramatic than a loud voice. And sometimes, slower is more powerful than faster.

READ PASSIONATELY

Further, the psalm should be read not as one would read a phone book, that is, routinely and clinically. Rather it should be read with deep conviction. It should arise out of an enflamed heart that *loves* this passage and *believes* this text. A passionate heart for God and His Word should come through, loud and clear, in the preacher's voice as he reads the Scripture. For this day, it should be as though he is *married* to this portion of Scripture. It is *this* particular text that has won his heart and captured his soul. This should be conveyed as he reads his text. Sadly, in some churches, the announcements are read with greater enthusiasm than the Scriptures.

READ REVERENTLY

Whenever the Bible speaks, as Augustine once said, *God* speaks. The reading of the psalm becomes the direct mouthpiece for God in the sermon. Thus, the preacher should read his passage reverently, as if God were speaking through him — because He *is*. In heart attitude, the preacher should be as Moses before the burning bush. As he steps forward to read God's Word, he should remove his sandals. It should be read with a heart gripped with awe for God.

CAPTURE INTEREST

In one way or another, the introduction should secure the listener's attention. The opening of the sermon should enlist eager, alert listeners. The beginning should draw them into the message. This is one goal of the introduction of the sermon. Capturing the listeners' attention may be done in any number of ways:

Current Events

One way of 'bridge building' from the biblical text to the congregation is to begin the introduction with some recent occurrence drawn from the modern world. This could involve using a current event from the contemporary world. A breaking news item that is on people's minds can draw the focus of the listener to the text. Then the preacher can move from the present-day scene back to the ancient world of the biblical text.

Historical Account

Another way of securing the listener's attention is to begin with an incident from history. This could be from world history, church history, national history, sports history, or whatever aspect of history. To be sure, an introduction from church history or world history can supply *gravitas* for the message. Such a weightiness most often transcends the present moment. Further, if an encounter in church history is used, it has the added advantage of teaching truths that listeners need to know to be well taught.

Striking Quote

Yet another way to begin an introduction can be to start with a poignant quote. This can be especially effective if the citation comes from someone who is well known to the listeners. However, it is critical that the quote be relatively short, pithy, and even have a punch. A long quote tends to lose people. The preacher should narrow it, preferably, to one or two sentences. Further, the quote needs to be striking. One that turns a phrase is preferable, especially one that is memorable. The quote should be followed by a striking statement of how the biblical text relates to that quote.

ASKING QUESTIONS

Still another way of creating interest and connecting with the listener is by asking a thought-provoking question. Sometimes raising a series of rapid-fire inquiries is effective. Asking well-worded questions can draw in the listener to the preacher and cause the congregation to think.

ANECDOTAL DESCRIPTION

Also, the telling of a story can make for a strong beginning. It is a universal truth that people love to hear a story. Even most average preachers can tell a personal experience well. A striking story can immediately engage the listener in the sermon. Again, the story should be followed by a statement that connects it to the passage and topic to be preached.

COMMON PROBLEM

Furthermore, addressing or creating a crisis in the introduction can have dramatic impact upon the listener. Beginning with a controversy or raising a problem common to the listener can cause the congregation to pay attention to the message in order to learn the solution to the proposed problem. This may also involve addressing a felt need that is common to the listener.

CONVEY IMPORTANCE

Further, in the introduction, the preacher should show the listener the practical relevance of the psalm to be exposited. In other words, he must demonstrate the obvious importance of this text to the congregation. Why must they hear this portion of God's truth explained and applied? The importance conveyed is communicated by being:

PERSONALLY CHALLENGING

The importance of what is to be said in the sermon needs to hit home with each congregant. It must be clearly perceived that the message applies to each person. This may require that the preacher refer to the listener in the second person singular 'you.' In the least, he should make the personal connection of the text to their lives abundantly obvious. He should indicate how the importance of the subject matter at hand applies to the individuals of his congregation.

CORPORATELY IMPACTFUL

Likewise, the biblical text calls for the preacher to make application to the larger church family in general. How does this passage relate to the entire body of Christ of which the listeners are a part? Or, it could involve the preacher making the specific connection with the listener being a parent, or a citizen of the community or nation.

REVEAL DIRECTION

Moreover, the introduction should also announce the subject matter to come. There should be no confusion about what this text or sermon will be about. People are likely to go with you if you will tell them where you are going. On the front end, the expositor should tell them where the sermon will be headed and what will be taught. The introduction, at this point, should reveal the 'big idea' of the psalm. That is to say, the core thrust of this message should be stated.

CENTRAL THEME

The preacher will want to state in clear terms what is the central idea of this psalm. This central thrust has also been called the exegetical idea, the core essence of the text, or the dominating theme. The preacher should clearly state the proposition in the introduction of the sermon. This becomes the announced structural framework for the sermon. It provides the mental organization upon which not only the preacher but the listener will hang their thoughts. What is the core idea? What is the central truth? The preacher should let his listeners know the central proposition of the sermon. Most importantly, this main idea should arise from the text itself. It should be faithful to the Word, never imposed by the preacher upon the passage.

Main Points

The expositor may even want to give an overview of the psalm to be preached by stating the main homiletical points. This is a device that Charles Spurgeon, the Prince of Preachers, most often employed at the close of his introduction. He would state the three or four homiletical points at the outset of the message. This alerts the listener where the message is headed. At the same time, it shows organization and encourages note-taking. It also piques interest.

A POWERFUL LAUNCH

This chapter has focused upon the important step of writing the introduction. Perhaps Spurgeon put it best, 'You must attract the fish to your hook, and if they do not come you should blame the fisherman and not the fish. Compel them to stand still awhile and hear what God, the Lord, would speak to their souls.'[1] By adding a strong introduction, what results is more than a mere running commentary of consecutive verses. What results is more than a mere Bible study. What results is the most powerful form of communicating God's Word — an *expository* sermon.

There are only two things going out of this world — the Word of God and the souls of men. Wise is the preacher who pours

his life into both. His life should be primarily given to the diligent study and proclamation of God's Word, faithfully applying
it to the souls of men. Ten thousand years from now, much of
what concerns ministers will not even matter. The tyranny of
the urgent too often drives pastors, rather than the eternal. But
in the ages to come, what surely will be of greatest importance is
the investing of God's Word into the souls of men and women.
Here is wisdom.

The main thing is to keep the main thing the main thing. And
what is the main thing? For the preacher whom God has gifted
and called into the ministry of proclamation, the main thing is
to preach the Word to saints and sinners alike. Proclaiming the
Scripture is job number one. Thus, may we be found faithful to
do this one thing supremely above all else.

23

DRAFT THE
CONCLUSION

Write a clear and concise closing to the sermon
that seals the message and calls for a decision

L ast words *are* lasting words. That is to say, the end of the
message carries great importance. The conclusion of the
sermon has been called the 'most vital part of the sermon.'[1]
The end of the message should never merely wind down to a
standstill. Instead, the presentation of the truth with its demands
upon the listeners should rise to a powerful climax, much like
the concluding crescendo of an orchestra.

As the end approaches, a sermon should serve as a 'fork-in-the-road' before the listener, calling them to choose one of two courses. Either they will continue living as they are, or they will pursue the biblical path as presented in the passage preached. These two paths, one the narrow way and the other the broad, must be clearly marked out for the listener. The congregation must be urged to follow the right path — the path laid out in Scripture. The conclusion of the sermon should bring the listener to answer the question, 'As a result of this message, what does God want me to do?'

ENDING WITH A CLIMAX

An effective conclusion should serve to end the sermon with dramatic impact upon the listeners. It should motivate them to choose to move out and embrace what this passage calls for. Martyn Lloyd-Jones strongly asserts, 'You must end on a climax, and everything should lead up to it in such a way that the great truth stands out dominating everything that has been said, and the listeners go away with this in their minds.'[2] This is to say, a strong finish should summarize the main truths, specify the application, motivate the heart, comfort the soul, and challenge the will. All these are important elements of a compelling ending.

Think of the conclusion as a pilot landing a large plane on the runway. As the flight comes to an end, the plane cannot keep circling the airport. The flight is not successful until it has landed. Neither is the sermon effective until it is properly concluded. The preacher must successfully land the sermon upon the runway of the listener's heart. As he does so, he must have in mind two basic groups of people — believers and unbelievers. Every sermon should conclude with a moving and motivating call to action to both groups.

CALLING FOR ACTION

The Word of God always demands a decisive response and should culminate in a call for such action. It is at this point that the main theme of the message is brought to completion. Yet tragically, a good summation is often neglected. Many students of preaching agree that it is the most likely to be neglected apart from sermon preparation. Walter Kaiser has a helpful word: 'Every … sermon should include one or two concluding paragraphs that issue a summons to action, a challenge to change, an appeal to the conscience, comfort for the present and future, or an indictment for unrepentant lifestyles. The question we should ask is this: 'What is it that God wants us to do, say, or repent of, based on this text?'"[3] This should always be the primary focus of a strong conclusion.

What is true for any sermon is equally true for a message from the Psalms. There must be a striking conclusion to the exposition. In drafting such a conclusion, the expositor will want to consider how the final appeal should affect both believers and unbelievers. The following dual thrust should be taken into account:

IMPACT BELIEVERS

The text of most psalms is addressed primarily to believers. Thus, most sermons from the Psalms will include a strong appeal to believers. Like a lawyer during closing arguments presenting his case to the jury and calling for a verdict, so the effective preacher should summon believers to decide and act favorably toward what God requires in this psalm. Based upon the truth submitted, the closing appeal of the sermon should exhort the listener to:

KNOW SOMETHING

In the conclusion, the expositor needs to remind believers of the main thrust of the psalm itself. The preacher will want to review the main idea of the message and reinforce its relevancy. A succinct summary of the core truth needs to be restated. Likewise, he needs to make known the core thrust of what the listener must *do* based upon what he has been told.

As the message is being reviewed and summarized, it is vital that there not be new material added. G. Campbell Morgan wisely says, 'A conclusion must include the things which have been said, as to their spiritual and moral impact and appeal; it must preclude the possibility that those who listen may escape from the message, so far as is possible.'[4] Neither should the conclusion be lengthy and extended. This wrap-up must be clear and specific, direct and brief. A prolonged conclusion is lethal to the effectiveness of any sermon.

FEEL SOMETHING

Further, the preacher must conclude the message by raising the affections of believers for God, Jesus Christ and the truth. He will want to conclude with an element of sincere, legitimate inspiration. He should motivate his congregation to love and obey God with new resolve and determination. But having said this, carnal motivations should be avoided. Base appeals such as manipulation, intimidation, and imposing guilt should never be used. To be sure, these are illegitimate means. Dynamic preaching is dependent upon the Holy Spirit to strike the hearts of the listeners. By this supernatural power, the preacher should conclude by seeking to lift up, hold up, and fire up believers.

In order to feel the truth preached, the preacher may want to consider concluding the message with a moving illustration that helps drive home the message to the heart. There may be an impactful quotation with which to conclude. Or perhaps there are some key questions that can be asked that help the listener sense the impact of the sermon more deeply. Here is the time 'to encourage, comfort, or build up the flock.'[5] End with emotions. Here is the appropriate moment to help put the wind into the sail of the congregation.

DO SOMETHING

The preacher should also call his listeners to make a decisive choice to follow these prescribed steps of application as stated in the psalm and clarified in the sermon. He should appeal for their immediate response. He should issue a plea and exhort the congregation to act. As per the preacher's appeal, believers must choose to live the truth.

The conclusion should be directional and call for people to change their beliefs and behavior. That the listener might 'do' something as a result of the message is the goal of the sermon. Richard Mayhue writes, 'Call for some sort of decision to mark the beginning of the required obedience.'[6] The preacher, Mayhue adds, should 'Exhort the audience to obey the sermon's appeal.'[7] Care must be exercised not to look back and reproach the sermon, but look ahead to the implementation of the truths contained in the message.

IMPACT UNBELIEVERS

The preacher must also call listeners who are spiritually lost to repent and believe upon Christ. As Paul challenged Timothy, the expositor must 'do the work of an evangelist' (2 Tim. 4:5). This begins with his own congregation. He must urge unbelievers to be reconciled to God (2 Cor. 5:19). The pinnacle of expository preaching must be to preach Jesus Christ and Him crucified (1 Cor. 1:23). It is said that all roads lead to Rome. So, likewise, all biblical texts and sermons must lead to Christ. All passages may not contain Christ, but all sermons should contain Christ. The person and work of Jesus Christ — who He is and what He did — should be the heart of all expository preaching (1 Cor. 1:26-2:5; Col. 1:28). This involves the preacher's call for unbelievers to:

KNOW SOMETHING

In his conclusion, the expositor must present the saving gospel of Jesus Christ to his unbelieving listeners. Even if his passage does not contain the gospel, it does relate, in one way or another, to the good news of Jesus Christ. The faithful preacher must announce in his sermon what the gospel is and what is required of the listener to rightly respond. This requires a summation of the gospel message (1 Cor. 15:3-4). Spurgeon said, 'I take my text and make a beeline to the cross.'[8] So must every expositor be gospel-focused and cross-centered.

This final inclusion of the truths and terms of the gospel are especially true if the passage preached has been a text without the gospel. Not every cluster of verses contains the gospel in it. But it is important that the saving message of Jesus Christ be in every sermon. Every preacher is a minister of the new covenant, one who has been set apart to the gospel of God. If the good news of Christ has not yet been stated in the message, here is the place for it to be clearly and succinctly stated. Without the gospel being in the sermon, the preacher has failed to discharge his duty before God and, to some extent, has blood on his hands (Acts 18:6; 20:26).

FEEL SOMETHING

Further, the preacher must call the unbeliever to repent and mourn over their sin. They must be told to confess their iniquities to God and to turn away from them. They must be exhorted to die to self before Christ can live within them. They must come to the end of themselves before Christ can begin in them. This is the reality of true repentance. Only the Holy Spirit can cause unbelievers to feel deeply about their sin and to sense their desperate need for repentance and faith. All expository preaching must drive the truth of the gospel home to the heart of the unbelievers present. Rather than trying to pacify the unconverted, the preacher must seek to provoke the unsaved to the point of true repentance where they desire saving faith.

DO SOMETHING

Pointing the sinner to Christ, the preacher must call his unbelieving listeners to trust the Lord Jesus. All who are without Christ must place themselves under the lordship of Christ. They must surrender their lives to Him. The expositor must issue the climactic call to unbelievers to commit themselves to the truth *now*. The gospel is a command to obey, not a suggestion to consider. The gospel command is always in the present tense. The unbeliever must immediately respond to the free offer of Christ. As a result, the preacher must command his unsaved listeners to look to Christ and commit their lives to Him. They must be urged to trust the Lord Jesus for salvation. The proclamation of the gospel truth demands an immediate decision for Christ.

If the preacher is to truly preach the gospel, he must do more than set forth the main truths of the good news in Jesus Christ. He *must* go further. He must call sinners to repent and believe on Him. He must exhort and persuade them as those in great danger. Therefore, Lloyd-Jones warns, 'The main danger confronting the pulpit in this matter is to assume that all who claim to be Christians, and who think they are Christians, and who are members of the Church, are therefore of necessity Christians. This, to me, is the most fatal blunder of all.'[9] In other words, the preacher must never assume that all his listeners are personally converted to Christ. All sermons *must* lead to the Lord Jesus, who is the heart and substance of the gospel (1 Cor. 1:26-2:5; Col. 1:28).

Charles Spurgeon, addressing his students who were being trained for the ministry, says concerning this need for gospel appeal in our sermons:

> God has sent us to preach in order that through the gospel of Jesus Christ the sons of men may be reconciled to Him ... for the most part, the work of preaching is intended to save the hearers... The glory of God being our chief object, we aim at it by seeking the edification of saints and the salvation of sinners... Our great object of glorifying God is, however, to be mainly achieved by the winning of souls. We *must* see souls born unto God. If we do not, our cry should be that of Rachel 'Give me children, or I die.' If we do not win souls, we should mourn as the husbandman who sees no harvest, as the fisherman who returns to his

cottage with an empty net, or as the huntsman who has in vain roamed over hill and dale. Ours should be Isaiah's language uttered with many a sigh and groan — 'Who hath believed our report? And to whom is the arm of the Lord revealed?' The ambassadors of peace should not cease to weep bitterly until sinners weep for their sins.[10]

Such passion to reach souls for Christ and to see conversions must mark our preaching.

THIS ONE THING I DO

The focus of this section has been on the completion of the sermon manuscript. The application has now been added. The illustrations included. The introduction written. And the conclusion has been crafted. What results is now more than a mere running commentary of the consecutive verses of a psalm. What results is more than simply a Bible study. What results now is the most powerful form of communicating God's Word — an *expository* sermon.

It has been well said: There are only two things going out of this world — the Word of God and the souls of men. Wise is the preacher who pours his life into both. His life should be primarily given to the diligent study and proclamation of God's Word, faithfully applying it to the souls of men. Ten thousand years from now, much of what concerns us in the ministry will not even matter. The tyranny of the urgent, rather than the eternal, too often drives us. But in the ages to come, what surely will be of greatest importance is the investing of God's Word into the souls of men and women. Here is wisdom.

The main thing is to keep the main thing the main thing. And *what* is the main thing? For the preacher gifted and called by God to a ministry of proclamation, the main thing is to preach the Word to saints and sinners alike. Proclaiming the Scripture is job number one. Thus, may we be found faithful to do this one thing supremely above all else. Let us say: This one thing I do.

---— UNIT V ———

THE
PROCLAMATION PHASE

---------------| 24 |---------------

EVALUATE THE
MANUSCRIPT

---

*Review the manuscript for both balance
and completeness*

What often separates a good sermon from a great one?
What frequently makes the difference between an
acceptable sermon and a sermon that is exceptional?
What often distinguishes between a message that is merely
accurate in content and possessing both divine authority in substance and delivery? The answer may surprise you.

Some time ago, I was talking with John MacArthur about a
certain, well-known preacher of our day. In the course of that

conversation, MacArthur explained that the last time this individual preached for him, the sermon fell flat. The message, he
explained, lacked supernatural power. 'Why?' I asked. 'Because
he failed to *own* the manuscript,' MacArthur answered. In other
words, this noted preacher had simply pulled the sermon manuscript of a message that had worked well in the past, put it in his
briefcase, and stepped into the pulpit with it — without reviewing it and without being possessed by it in his mind and heart.

I have never forgotten that comment. MacArthur then explained
how easy it is to pull a set of sermon notes out of a file, put them
in a notebook, and presume that they will be successful again.
But if the preacher remains unfamiliar with them and unaffected
by them, the message will surely fail to be a demonstration of
power in the Holy Spirit.

A GREAT DIFFERENCE

The difference between a mighty sermon and one that is merely
mediocre often lies in whether or not the preacher *owns* his pulpit notes. By this, we mean that he must intimately know not
only his biblical passage, but the material that he takes with him
into the pulpit. Moreover, he must deeply feel the truth that he
is to preach. To be sure, he cannot be emotionally disconnected
from its content and yet preach with power and authority. At
the same time, there must be a close connection between what
he preaches and how he lives. He must be a living epistle of the
sermon. In the fullest sense, *this* is the man who truly owns his
manuscript.

Admittedly, it is one thing to possess a manuscript, but something else entirely for the manuscript to possess the preacher. If
he is to be gripped by the truths he is to preach, additional time
is required to evaluate and embrace the message. It is often the
one or two additional hours that the preacher invests to be alone
with the manuscript that make the difference in the success of
the sermon itself. There is the world of difference between a

preacher who has the notes in his notebook and one who has them in his head and heart.

With this in mind, we turn our attention to the final step in the process of preparing an expository sermon, that of reviewing and internalizing the manuscript.

FINAL EVALUATION

At this point, the preacher has completed the manuscript — at least, the first draft. He has written the introduction, the main body, the conclusion, applications, illustrations, and transitions. Now the preacher must assess the overall flow and feel of the message. The unexamined manuscript is often not worth preaching.

PROPER LENGTH

First, in light of the allotted time to deliver the message, the preacher should review the length of his manuscript. He should ask himself: How much time do I have to preach? In light of this, what parts of the sermon notes need to be pruned? Which sections need to be 'beefed up' and intensified? Is there too much explanation? Is *more* explanation needed? Are there too many illustrations? Are *more* illustrations needed? Are *more* applications needed? Does the message need encouragement for those discouraged?

Commenting on the proper length of the sermon, Martyn Lloyd-Jones writes that it differs from preacher to preacher and from congregation to congregation.

> What determines the length of the sermon? First and foremost, the preacher. Time is a very relative thing, is it not? Ten minutes from some men seems like an age, while an hour from another passes like a few minutes

… it is therefore ridiculous to lay down a flat rule with regard to the length for all preachers… The capacity of congregations, as we have seen, varies tremendously… If some congregations were the arbiter in this matter every sermon would be of ten minutes' duration only. The preacher must not pay heed to that type of 'worshipper' but make his own assessment of them.[1]

Each expositor must know himself and the context in which he ministers. Given his abilities and the congregation's capacity, he must come to his own conclusion on what is an appropriate length for his sermon. But reviewing the length of his preaching manuscript is a necessary discipline. This is to say, he should attempt to have the right length of notes that fit his style.

PROPER CLARITY

Second, the expositor should review the manuscript for clarity. Are the preaching notes readable and laid out well for use in the pulpit? Or are they too dense? Too cluttered? An old adage says, 'Just because a river is muddy does not mean it is deep.' Sermon notes should be simple, orderly, and clear, not complex, confusing, or murky. The expositor should arrange his notes in a straightforward way for easy reference and quick access while standing in the pulpit. Notes should enable the preacher to see main blocks of information at a glance. Regarding its detail orientation, the preacher must remember that this is a sermon to everyday people, not a lecture to doctoral students. Lloyd-Jones urges:

> Keep on reminding yourself right through from beginning to end that what you are doing is meant for people, for all sorts and kinds of people. You are not preparing a sermon for a congregation of professors or pundits; you are preparing a sermon for a mixed congregation of people, and it is your business and mine to be of some help to everybody that is in that congregation. We have

failed unless we have done that. So avoid an over-academic theoretical approach. Be practical. Remember the people: you are preaching to them.[2]

PROPER SYMMETRY

Further, the preacher should review the balance of the presentation in his sermon manuscript. As he surveys his notes, he should ask: Did I distribute the material evenly? Did I weight each point appropriately? Does the overall message have proper balance and symmetry? Is the introduction too long? Are there too many points? Is one section too heavy and needs to be compressed? Did I distribute the illustrations evenly? Did I position the application strategically? All these factors should be taken into consideration.

On the whole, the sermon should be heavier on explanation rather than application. That is to say, the manuscript should be weighted toward explaining the biblical text far more than conveying its application. What the passage says and means is foundational to what it requires. The sermon manuscript should resemble a pyramid, wide at the base and narrow at the top. That is, it should be broad in the basic explanation of the passage and tapered toward the top in its application. Explanation supports application; doctrine determines duty; principle precedes practice. Thus, instruction and application should receive proportionate attention.

PROPER QUALITY

Finally, the preacher should review the manuscript for excellence. He asks: Is the main idea crystal clear? How well did I express the major points? Are the sub-points helpful or distracting? Is the explanation of each verse accurate and precise? Do the illustrations actually illustrate the point? Do the quotes fit? Are the implications expressed? Is the application supplied? Is the conclusion strong and compelling? Is the introduction well developed and engaging? What areas need an upgrade?

I have felt that the difference between a good sermon and a great sermon lies often here. This final review of the manuscript is critical. Investing a block of time at this point, assessing the quality of the sermon notes, is strategic. What final analysis of the biblical text needs to be made? What parts of the manuscript need to be better groomed? What alternate works need to be used in order to prevent needless repetition? What sentences need to be more emphatic? What transitions need to be smoother? What bottom-line conclusions need to be more obvious? All this and more needs to be reviewed at this stage.

PERSONAL INTERNALIZATION

After finishing the manuscript, the preacher must internalize the message. He must allow it to sink deep into his mind and heart. Of course, internalization occurs throughout the entire sermon preparation. But it must intensify now that the manuscript is complete. What seeds have sown into his notes through his personal study must take root in his own life. The expositor must become one with his sermon. He must become, if you will, married to his message. He must know, feel, and live the truth if he is to deliver the sermon effectively. His entire being — mind, emotion, and will — must be bound to the sermon. In the final analysis, the best method of internalizing one's manuscript is to pray through it. The preacher should offer each truth to God for His approval. Before he can look into the face of men, the preacher must, at this time, first look into the face of God.

KNOW THE MESSAGE

In order for this to occur, the preacher must become intimately acquainted with his manuscript. He must thoroughly refresh his memory with the psalm as printed in his preaching Bible and the sermon as printed in his manuscript. Each man has his own method by which he intellectually absorbs and retains the message before he steps into the pulpit. Certainly praying through the psalm and the manuscript helps etch the message upon the preacher's mind. Beyond that, every preacher should discover what works best for him. Here are a few suggestions:

1. Preaching Bible

In his preaching Bible, the preacher may want to reread the psalm with fresh eyes to refamiliarize himself with typeset and page layout. Further, write the outline in the margin to help him visualize the main divisions and overall flow of the psalm. After focusing on individual 'trees' in his text, he must recapture sight of the entire 'forest.' Moreover, it is helpful to mark key words for easy and quick reference. The preacher may want to underline repetition, circle key words, or draw arrows to show cause and effect. Finally, writing key thoughts in the margin triggers key ideas. It is amazing how a single word along the edge of one's Bible can jog the memory and catapult the mind in the right direction.

2. Sermon Manuscript

As for the manuscript, the preacher should consider highlighting the manuscript to reinforce content and layout. He could highlight in yellow, underline in red, or draw arrows. In addition, he will want to hear the sermon being delivered in his own mind as he reviews his notes. As he reads the manuscript, he should anticipate what it will sound like being presented to the congregation. As he rehearses the notes in his mind, he should project ahead in his thinking to the tone and thrust of the sermon.

FEEL THE MESSAGE

In addition, the preacher must feel deeply the truth to be preached. Deep down within his soul, he must become one with the passage. This psalm must become *his* psalm. There must be a sense of ownership. He must internally embrace the text. He must be emotionally connected to the psalm, sensing the magnitude of the message. His convictions, rooted and grounded in the text, must compel him to speak. The best way to ignite a church is to build a fire in the pulpit. And the best way to ignite a fire in the pulpit is to light one in the pastor's study. Fire in the study quickly spreads to the pulpit, and then leaps to the church. The message must be a fire in his bones. Are you on fire for the truth?

Regarding this need for passion in preaching, Lloyd-Jones writes that the expositor must be deeply moved within. The psalm must grip his heart before he can benefit the congregation:

> Can a man see himself as a damned sinner without emotion? Can a man look into hell without emotion? Can a man listen to the thunderings of the Law and feel nothing? Or conversely, can a man really contemplate the love of God in Christ Jesus and feel no emotion? The whole position is utterly ridiculous. I fear that many people today in their reaction against excesses and emotionalism put themselves into a position in which, in the end, they are virtually denying the Truth. The Gospel of Jesus Christ takes up the whole man, and if what purports to be the Gospel does not do so it is not the Gospel. The Gospel is meant to do that, and it does that. The whole man is involved.[3]

Lloyd-Jones further comments that the preacher who is not moved by these truths obviously does not truly know them as he should. He writes:

> A man who is not moved by these things, I maintain, has never really understood them. A man is not an intellect in a vacuum; he is a whole person. He has a heart as well as a head; and if his head truly understands, his heart will be moved... Where is the passion in preaching that has always characterized great preaching in the past? Why are not modern preachers moved and carried away as the great preachers of the past so often were? The Truth has not changed. Do we believe it, have we been gripped and

humbled by it, and then exalted until we are 'lost in wonder love and praise.'[4]

As he prepares to step foot into the pulpit, the expositor must
be consciously aware that he does so with the pleasure and
approval of God. He must be persuaded that the Lord is with
him. Regardless of how men receive the message, he must know
that he has the Lord's approbation (1 Cor. 4:3-4). Likewise, he
must be aware that the discharging of his duty affects eternal
destinies. This psalm being preached *is* the Word of God unto
salvation. This message *is* able to convert the soul (Ps. 19:7). This
sermon *is* 'the way of the righteous.' It exposes 'the way of the
wicked' (Ps. 1:6). He must wrestle with God in prayer for the
souls of those to whom he will preach. He must intercede on
their behalf pleading for their salvation. Such *weightiness* must
sober the heart of the expositor.

LIVE THE MESSAGE

Third, the preacher himself must live his message. Before he
calls others to obedience, he himself must, first, obey. With all
his heart, he must become the living incarnation of his message.
That requires diligent self-examination and soul-searching.
Prayer is the key here. A humble preacher will pray through the
psalm to be preached and ask God to reveal areas in his life that
do not square with the message. Does his love for God need to
be replenished? Should he recommit to his calling in the ministry? Does he need to repent of a hurtful attitude? Is there a sin
he must confess? Does the psalmist possess an eternal perspective upon which he must refocus? Is there a burden in his life or
ministry that needs to be committed to the Lord?

As the searchlight of the psalm shines into the preacher's soul,
the Holy Spirit reveals sin, and hurtful attitudes and actions
surface. Under such scrutiny, he must acknowledge his iniquities and turn from his sin. As best it can be, his heart must be
clean and pure as he stands to preach. A pure message in an

impure vessel will not do. Instead, the preacher must pursue holiness as commanded and modeled in the psalm. With holy abandonment, he must embody the message of the psalm. The psalmist's trust must become *his* trust. The psalmist's passion must become *his* passion. The psalmist's God-ward focus must become *his* intent gaze.

FOCUSED ANTICIPATION

The biblical text has been studied, and the sermon manuscript has been written, reviewed, adjusted, and absorbed. At this point, as John MacArthur writes, 'An expositor is like an athlete who has finished his last practice, but now must endure the tedious wait until the game. True champions can maintain their concentration and intensity; other athletes cannot. The best expositor, like the winning athlete, must not forget why he prepared: to deliver a soul-searching, life-changing exposition of Scripture with all of the authority and power of a spokesman for God.'[5]

As the time of the sermon approaches, the preacher should focus his heart and mind upon the glory of God. The sermon will be preached *coram deo*, that is, in the presence of God. The Lord Himself will be the true Judge of his message. All the expositor's thoughts and passions must be riveted upon Him, who is over all.

A LIFELONG PURSUIT

How long does it take to prepare an exceptional expository sermon? Ten hours? Fifteen hours? Twenty hours? The reality is, preparing an exceptional sermon requires an entire lifetime. Every hour of study in the past is brought forward and becomes a dynamic part of sermon preparation in the present. Every time the preacher prepares to preach, he draws upon an entire life of study in the Word. Every time he steps into the pulpit, he preaches out of the overflow of his many years of study. With each sermon, his entire life has been a preparation for this one moment in time. As always, the most important sermon he will ever preach is the one that is immediately before him.

All this study has an accumulative effect. Every time the preacher comes to a new passage, he draws from the deep wells he has dug in previous sermon preparation. With each sermon his mind sharpens, his skills develop, and his command of Scripture advances. The twilight years of ministry should be his most effective, most insightful, most pungent, and most poignant. Athletes plateau in their thirties, but the preacher is different. Over time the expositor advances to deeper levels of ministry in his latter years. The more he masters the Scriptures, the more the Scriptures master him. The result is a man of God who is well trained to preach as time progresses.

Let us, by God's grace, pour ourselves into this work of expository preaching to which we have been called.

25

DELIVER
THE MESSAGE

Preach the psalm in the power of God's Spirit

The demanding process of preparing an expository sermon is now concluded. The moment of preaching the message has finally come. 'It is not enough just to have a message,' John MacArthur writes, 'You must also deliver it powerfully.'[1] As the preacher steps into the pulpit, he does so, John Stott reminds us, 'with God's Word in his hands, God's Spirit in his heart, God's people before his eyes, waiting expectantly for God's voice to be heard and obeyed.'[2] To stand behind an open Bible means the preacher handles sacred truths from above. As he opens his mouth to preach the Word, he speaks the very utterances of God.

In this moment, he becomes the chosen mouthpiece of God through whom He speaks. As he declares, 'Thus says the Lord,' he must please a congregation of one, namely, God Himself.

The expositor must be mindful that there are *two* standing in the pulpit. He is never alone. The expositor *and* the One who has enlisted him to preach, God Himself, stand together. As the Son of Man appeared in the fiery furnace with Shadrach, Meshach, and Abed-nego (Dan. 3:25), God likewise draws near to His servants in the pulpit. As they teach all things that Christ has commanded, He has promised, 'I am with you always, even to the end of the age' (Matt. 28:20). Spurgeon believed the closest any man stands to the Lord is when he steps behind the sacred desk to preach. The great Baptist preacher asserted, 'Draw a circle around my pulpit, and you have hit the spot where I am nearest heaven. There the Lord has been more consciously near me than anywhere else.'[3] It is in this closeness to God — really, God *in* the preacher — that he speaks.

Ready to Preach

As every expositor is unique, so each man has his own style and method of sermon delivery. He must cultivate his own manner of delivery. He must decide for himself whether he reads his notes, recites them from memory, uses them as a launching pad, or preaches without notes. Probably, the last two methods are best. Personally, I bring my manuscript into the pulpit and use it as a foundation for what I say. In so doing, I am trusting God to enable me to 'go beyond' my notes during the sermon. This allows the Holy Spirit to use my preparation to the maximum. With freedom and liberty, He guides me, spontaneously, through the sermon. With the help of the Spirit, the preacher should be marked by:

DIVINE AUTHORITY

First, the expositor must preach with divine authority. This authority, of course, resides not in himself, but is delegated to him from God and is found in His Word. This authority was seen in the preaching of Jesus. After the Sermon on the Mount, it was noted that this is how Jesus preached. It was said of Him that He spoke not as the scribes and Pharisees, but 'as one having authority' (Matt. 7:29). Regarding such command, MacArthur notes, 'Authority comes from the preacher's mandate to proclaim the King's Word as a herald with all the authority of the throne behind him (2 Tim. 4:2). A herald is dispatched by a sovereign regal authority as long as he faithfully presents his King's message. The preacher's authority likewise depends upon an accurate relaying of the message of God's Word.'[4] In this manner, expository preaching demands preaching with such authority.

THUS SAYS THE LORD

By nature of this God-given authority, the expositor must preach with deep conviction in the truth. To this point, MacArthur pleads, 'Preach with conviction. The Bible is God's authoritative word to man. As someone remarked, "God did not give us the Ten Suggestions; He gave us the Ten Commandments." We could define authority as "soft confidence." If we believe what we say is true, we should say it with confidence and authority. We say *soft* confidence, because we cannot resemble a spiritual drill sergeant, barking commands at our people.'[5] Instead, the preacher must speak the truth as a loving shepherd to his flock, but without equivocation regarding the essential truth of Jesus Christ. John Calvin says that every preacher must speak with two voices, one that is tender toward the flock and the other tenacious for the wolves.

As the expositor preaches, he must do so with 'boldness' (1 Thess. 2:2). The word 'boldness' means 'full speech.' The idea is that the preacher speaks 'all' the truth for all to hear. He holds nothing back, but expounds the text with a full disclosure of the truth. God's servants must openly proclaim and declare the Word with courage and conviction. The message is not to be mumbled, as if the preacher is uncertain. Nor is it to be whispered, as if he is ashamed. Rather, it must be pronounced as if he is compelled to speak. Charles Spurgeon maintained, 'I cannot help feeling that the man who preaches the Word of God is standing, not on a mere platform, but on a throne.'[6] There must be a fire in his bones, a burden in his soul that *must* be released.

THE WHOLE COUNSEL OF GOD

Exercising such authority involves speaking the entire truth of God's Word, namely, the full counsel of God (Acts 20:27). If one is to speak with authority, no truth should be withheld. No rough edges should be smoothed over. No hard sayings should be made easy. No offense removed. In the Reformation, the battle cry of *sola scriptura* captured the day — Scripture alone. The Reformers were also committed to *tota scriptura* — all Scripture. They preached all the truth in the Bible, withholding no part. So every preacher must commit to preach *all* the truth of the Psalms — salvation *and* destruction, blessedness *and* cursing, heaven *and* hell. A *full* disclosure of the truth in the pulpit is the essence of boldness.

LOWLY HUMILITY

Second, though the expositor speaks with authority, he must also be clothed with humility. He must be bold as a lion and gentle as a dove. The apostle Peter states, 'God is opposed to the proud, but gives grace to the humble' (1 Pet. 5:5). This is to say, as every preacher stands in the pulpit, he must lower himself before the Lord. God is the Sovereign, and he, the expositor, is only the servant. This is the humility every preacher must have. He must realize he has nothing to say apart from God's Word. God is the Author, and he, the preacher, is but the messenger. The entire message belongs to God.

PROMOTING GOD'S GLORY

In order to speak with humility, every preacher must speak with his chief concern being the glory of God. God alone must be in the spotlight, never the preacher. Our Lord is a jealous God, and He will not share His glory with another — not even with one of His gifted preachers. There must be no eclipsing of the Son in the pulpit by His spokesman. The best of preachers is merely a lampstand, and the Word of God is the only true light. May every preacher enter the pulpit in the same manner as Moses did before the burning bush, removing his sandals, for the ground upon which he is standing is holy ground.

A young Scottish preacher, quite self-confident and sure of himself, literally bounded up the steps into the pulpit one Sunday filled with self-esteem. As he stood to preach, he lost his way in the middle of the message and became confounded and disoriented as his memory suddenly failed him. He forgot the rest of the message, quite a humiliating experience. As he came down from the pulpit, entirely humbled, it was in a very different manner from his ascension up into the pulpit. An old Scottish elder came to him, put a hand on his shoulder and said, 'Son, if you had gone up into the pulpit the way you came down, you would have come down the way you went up.' This is true for every preacher. He who exalts himself will be humbled, and he who humbles himself will be exalted (Luke 18:14).

DYING TO SELF

George Whitefield, the great English evangelist of the 18th century, who preached the gospel on both sides of the Atlantic, was a genuinely humble man. When urged to make a name for himself, Whitefield said many times, 'Let the name of Whitefield perish, but let Christ be glorified.' Or 'Let the name of Whitefield die so that the cause of Christ may live.' 'Let the name of George Whitefield be forgotten and blotted out as long as the name of the Lord Jesus Christ is known.' In like manner, let every preacher clothe himself with such humility. Pride is the chief sin of great preachers. Therefore, humility is the chief virtue.

TOTAL DEPENDENCY

Third, the expositor must preach with total dependence upon God. No matter how well scripted the manuscript, the preacher must never trust in the arm of the flesh. His total reliance must be upon the Lord. As Jesus prepared to send out His disciples, it was necessary that He remind them, 'Apart from Me, you can do nothing' (John 15:5). If they failed to abide in Him, their preaching would fail. But as they would humble themselves, they would be empowered to deliver the message. Great is the Spirit's power in the one who abides in Christ. In the pulpit, the Holy Spirit is present to give the fullness of His power.

BEING WEAK ENOUGH

Let every expositor be dependent upon God's power to quicken his mind, enflame his heart and direct his words as he preaches. Concerning this power of the Holy Spirit, Lloyd-Jones writes:

> It is the Holy Spirit falling upon the preacher in a special manner. It is an access of power. It is God giving power, and enabling, through the Spirit, to the preacher in order that he may do this work in a manner that lifts it up beyond the efforts and endeavours of man to a position in which the preacher is being used by the Spirit and becomes the channel through whom the Spirit works.[7]

Lloyd-Jones further describes the ministry of the Holy Spirit in the preacher as a man under His influence:

> You are a man 'possessed', you are taken hold of, and taken up. I like to put it like this — and I know of nothing on earth that is comparable to this feeling — that when this happens you have a feeling that you are not actually doing the preaching, you are looking on. You are looking on at yourself in amazement as this is happening. It is not your effort; you are just the instrument, the channel, the

vehicle: and the Spirit is using you, and you are looking on in great enjoyment and astonishment.[8]

YIELDING TO THE LORD

Regarding this utter dependency, Lloyd-Jones maintains that every preacher must be supernaturally empowered by the Spirit:

> Seek this power, expect this power, yearn for this power; and when the power comes, yield to Him... Let Him use you, let Him manifest His power in you and through you ... nothing but a return of this power of the Spirit on our preaching is going to avail us anything. This makes true preaching, and it is the greatest need of all today — never more so. Nothing can substitute for this.[9]

SIMPLE CLARITY

Fourth, the clarity of the message is an indispensable key to its success. Though the preacher speaks truths that are profound, nevertheless, he must do so in a manner which is easy to understand. His sermons must be lucid, clear, and coherent. There is no virtue in being an enigma in the pulpit. Philip Ryken notes, 'Expository preaching means making God's Word plain.'[10] The Reformers spoke of the perspicuity of the Scripture, that is, the teaching that the Bible itself is lucid and clear in affirming its basic truths. This being so, then so should the preaching of the Word be marked by simple clarity.

THE PLAINER THE BETTER

William Perkins, the gifted Puritan, wrote in his classic book on preaching, *The Art of Prophesying*: 'Preaching must be plain... It is a by-word among us: "It was a very plain sermon." And I say, the plainer, the better.'[11] Such plainness in preaching is a must for effective sermons. The gospel is a simple message, and this clarity should be evident in expository preaching.

Concerning this need for clarity, MacArthur writes, 'Good preaching begins with *clarity* of content. And clarity begins with a single, easy-to-recognize theme.'[12] This necessitates a simple structure to the sermon with a streamlined progression of thought. MacArthur continues, 'Avoid complex outlines; they cause your listeners to miss your major points. The most helpful way of emphasizing your theme and outline is repetition. As you move from one point to the next, use brief transitional sentences to review the points you have already covered. Restate the central idea of the message as often as appropriate.'[13] In other words, one mark of effective preaching is that it is easy to follow and understand.

Communicated With Clear Language

Then MacArthur summarizes, 'Use clear language. Clear ideas need to be communicated in understandable ways. If ten people in your congregation will not understand the word "felicity," use "happiness" instead. Being scholastically impressive at the expense of the listener understanding is counterproductive.'[14] Biblical words should be used, but a clear explanation should be given for them. Otherwise, for the most part, use the words of the common person.

INTENSE PASSION

Fifth, the expositor must deliver the sermon with a burning passion and fervency of soul. He must feel deeply about the truth he is delivering. Passion is a strong emotion that rises up from one's heart due to an enthusiasm for the glory of God and the supremacy of Christ. Passion manifests itself in an intense enthusiasm for the truth. Passion arises out of deep convictions about God, Christ, and the gospel. Passion is a non-negotiable mark of all preaching. If there is no passion, there is no preaching.

THE NEED FOR PASSION

Walter Kaiser explains the indispensable place of passion in preaching. Where there is passion in the sermon, the truth becomes contagious. Kaiser writes:

> From the beginning of the sermon to its end, the all engrossing force of the text and the God who speaks through that text must dominate our whole being. With the burning power of that truth on our heart and lips, every thought, emotion, and act of the will must be so captured by that truth that it springs forth with excitement, joy, sincerity, and reality as an evident token that God's Spirit is in that word. Away with all the mediocre, lifeless, boring, and lackluster orations offered as pitiful substitutes for the powerful Word of the living Lord. If that Word from God does not thrill the proclaimer and fill [him] … with an intense desire to glorify God and do His will, how shall we ever expect it to have any greater effect on our hearers?[15]

COMPELLING URGENCY

Sixth, the expositor should be marked by a compelling sense of spiritual urgency as he preaches. He should speak as one whom men must hear. Moreover, they must hear him and respond *now*. He must convey that the truth of his message requires action immediately. Thus, he should be earnest and insistent as he preaches. The prophets called it 'the burden of the Lord' (Zech. 9:1). This sobriety is a 'blood-earnestness', which flows from a proper understanding that God's message must be heeded now.

IN LIGHT OF ETERNITY

A preacher should convey this sense of urgency as he understands that life, eternity, heaven, and hell hang in the balance. The preacher must preach like Richard Baxter, who once said,

'I preached as never sure to preach again. I preached as a dying man to dying men.'[16] Perhaps earnestness is the most missing characteristic of the modern-day pulpit. Concerning this sense of urgency, John MacArthur notes, 'Feel deeply about the truth you are to preach. If you were giving a book review or reciting an autobiographical vignette, it would be different. Remember that expositors have a mandate from God to preach the truth and that eternal consequences hang in the balance.'[17]

Indicting all indifferent preaching, John Stott sounds a much-needed alarm, 'To handle issues of eternal life and death as if we were discussing nothing more serious than the weather, and to do so in a listless and lackadaisical manner, is to be inexcusably frivolous… For one thing is certain: if we ourselves grow sleepy over our message, our listeners can hardly be expected to stay awake.'[18] To the contrary, let us preach with urgency.

A Sense of Urgency

Martyn Lloyd-Jones speaks to this point of urgency in preaching. He argues that if there is no passion, there is no preaching:

> If the preacher does not suggest this sense of urgency, that he is there between God and men, speaking between time and eternity he has no business to be in a pulpit. There is no place for calm, cool, scientific detachment in these matters. That may possibly be all right in a philosopher, but it is unthinkable in a preacher… Surely the whole object of this act is to persuade people. The preacher does not just say things with the attitude of 'take it or leave it.' He desires to persuade them of the truth of his message; he wants them to see it; he is trying to do something to them, to influence them. He is not giving a learned disquisition on a text, he is not giving a display of his own knowledge; he is dealing with these living souls and he wants to move them, to take them with him, to lead them to the Truth … if this element is not present, whatever else it may be, it is not preaching. All

these points bring out the difference between delivering a lecture and preaching, or between an essay and a sermon.[19]

DIVERSIFIED DELIVERY

Seventh, the expositor should have variety in his delivery. His pitch should alternate according to the thrust of his text. There should be an ebb and flow of a natural delivery, like the tide coming in and recessing out. The expositor must maintain a balance in tone. When Nehemiah stood on the wall, he held a sword in one hand and a trowel in the other. With one he built up the wall, and with the other he fended off the enemies. So the preacher must do both in the pulpit. He must build up the people of God and defend against the enemies of God. He must build up and tear down, console and convict, offer mercy and threaten judgment.

CUTTING IT BOTH WAYS

To be sure, God's Word is a sharp, two-edged sword that cuts both ways. As this sword is unsheathed, the preacher must wield it both ways. He must both uproot and plant, both tear down and build up. He must comfort the afflicted and afflict the comfortable. The book of Psalms certainly does both. This inspired worship book both convicts and comforts. It encourages the faint-hearted, strengthens the weak, consoles the hurting, restores the broken, and emboldens the fearful. Its soothing words bring hope to those weakened by the blows of life. Preaching this book disturbs the wicked and brings pastoral solace to the righteous. Thus, as the expositor unfolds the psalms, he lifts up, holds up, and fires up those under his voice.

The book of Psalms admonishes the unruly, warns the wicked, and condemns the corrupt. But the text and tone of the Psalms is also provocative to the one who is at ease in this world. The psalmist blows a trumpet in the ear of those who are spiritually sluggish, applying a healing balm to the hurting. This is precisely what the preacher does who proclaims this book.

UNIQUE PERSONALITY

Eighth, every expositor is uniquely gifted by God with a one-of-a-kind personality and gift to preach. It is imperative that he preach in his own individual style. This individuality should come out in the pulpit. One mistake that some preachers make, especially younger men, is they try to emulate, if not copy, other noted preachers. While we learn from other gifted men, each expositor, nevertheless, must develop his own preaching style that is consistent with who God has made him to be.

TRUTH THROUGH PERSONALITY

In his famous 1877 Yale *Lectures on Preaching*, Phillips Brooks defined 'real preaching' as 'divine truth through personality.'[20] Each expositor must be careful in the pulpit not to be someone who he is not. He must not try to be someone else, with a different disposition and personality. Certainly, there will be strengths in other preachers worth noting. Some admirable qualities in one man are transferable and worth emulating. But at the end of the day, every preacher must be exactly the man whom God made him to be. In other words, every preacher should be himself!

FORGET YOURSELF COMPLETELY

As a gifted expositor, Lloyd-Jones urged all preachers to be natural in their delivery. While not being overly focused upon other preachers, neither should they be focused upon themselves. Instead, more importantly, they should be riveted upon the greatness and glory of God. The preacher should be Christ-focused, not self-conscious. In other words: 'Be yourself without thinking about yourself.'

Be natural; forget yourself; be so absorbed in what you are doing and in the realization of the presence of God, and in the glory and the greatness of the Truth that you are preaching ... that you forget yourself completely... Self is the greatest enemy of the preacher, more so than in the case of any other man in society. And the only way to deal with self is to be so taken up with, and so enraptured by, the glory of what you are doing, that you forget yourself altogether.[21]

ALL FOR GOD'S GLORY!

All that the expositor does, whether in study or in the pulpit, he does for the glory of God. *This* must be the ever-shining North Star by which the preacher charts his course and expounds the Word. We preach not for men's approval, but for God's approbation. We expound the Word not for men's applause, but for heaven's amen. *This* is our heartbeat. *This* is our passion. And *this* is our motivation. When we come to the end of our lives, may we be able to say with the apostle Paul, 'I have fought the good fight, I have finished the course, I have kept the faith' (2 Tim. 4:8) — all for the glory of God!

THE FULL SPECTRUM SURVEYED

With this lesson, we conclude our brief overview of the strategic steps involved in the expository preaching of the Psalms. We have surveyed the full spectrum of this process from the consecration of the preacher to the proclamation of the psalms. Obviously, much more could be said regarding this important subject. But we have provided a framework by which each preacher may develop his own system and prepare his own notes.

In many ways, preaching is a highly individual and personal endeavor. It requires each man to seek God for himself. Ultimately, no class or school or book can make a preacher. In the final analysis, only God can make a preacher. Yet He has chosen to use a class like this to sharpen our skills. 'Iron sharpens iron, so one man sharpens another' (Prov. 27:17). When iron contacts iron, it creates friction, heat, grinding, smoke, and loud noise. Yet in the end, the iron is *sharp*.

It is to God that each one of us must turn in this high and holy calling of preaching the Psalms. May He who has called us into this ministry of proclaiming the Psalms infuse a yet greater grace into our hearts to fulfill what He has called us to do. And may we preach His Word in order to receive His approval and His approbation: Well done, good and faithful servant.

PREACHING THAT CONNECTS

I n conclusion, we want to reiterate that powerful, life-changing dynamics are unleashed whenever the expositor faithfully
expounds the book of Psalms. Certainly, each book in the
Bible brings its own unique impact upon those who hear it, and
the Psalms are no exception. Here is a book that is intended to
connect the human soul with the heart of God with the result
being that the soul of man becomes conformed to the heart of
God. So great is this spiritual influence that the one who sits
under the preaching of Psalms soon becomes like David, a man
after God's own heart. Here is preaching that connects.

So, what are the potent effects of preaching the Psalms? Several
dynamics should be noted when the Psalms are preached:

First, *expository preaching of the Psalms is God-glorifying.* As perhaps no other book in the Bible, the Psalms unveil a towering, majestic view of God's blazing glory. A high view of God is revealed through every psalm. The infinite character of God is put on display in this book in a grand, theo-centric fashion, as the psalmist is inevitably pointing upward to God, Creator of heaven and earth, Sovereign Lord over history, the One who irrevocably stands by His people. As expositors are to be always magnifying God's glory before their hearers, the Psalms promote this in breathtaking fashion.

> Ascribe to the LORD, O families of the peoples,
> Ascribe to the LORD glory and strength.
> Ascribe to the LORD the glory of His name;
> Bring an offering and come into His courts.
> Worship the LORD in holy attire;
> Tremble before Him, all the earth.
> Say among the nations, 'The LORD reigns;
> Indeed, the world is firmly established,
> It will not be moved; He will judge the peoples
>   with equity'   (96:7-10)

Second, *expository preaching of the Psalms is awe-inspiring.* The Psalms were originally written and compiled to lead Israel, God's chosen people, in worshiping God. Should it surprise us that preaching the Psalms should inspire praise for God in the hearts of His people? The exposition of Psalms leads God's people to the adoration of Him who is worthy of our praise. *This* is our ultimate priority, and the Psalms uniquely help us fulfill it.

> The LORD reigns, let the peoples tremble;
> He is enthroned above the cherubim, let the earth shake!
> The LORD is great in Zion,
> And He is exalted above all the peoples.
> Let them praise Your great and awesome name;
> Holy is He.   (99:1-3)

Third, *expository preaching of the Psalms is passion-igniting.*

Passion in the preacher is absolutely necessary for effective exposition. The Psalms contain the fiery zeal and emotional intensity of the psalmist for God. Thus, when preaching expositionally, the preacher vicariously enters into the same spiritual pursuit of the biblical writer. The strong feelings of the psalm become the earnestness of the preacher. Thus, the Psalms, full of passion for God, become injected into the preacher's soul. The psalmist's spiritual heartbeat is contagious. The fiery fervor soon spreads to the preacher's study and, then inevitably, to the pulpit.

> Give ear to my words, O LORD,
> Consider my groaning.
> Heed the sound of my cry for help, my King and my God,
> For to You I pray.
> In the morning, O LORD, You will hear my voice;
> In the morning I will order my prayer to You and
>   eagerly watch.   (5:1-3)

Fourth, *expository preaching of the Psalms is heart-searching.* As sin and hypocrisy is uncovered in the life of the psalmist, so it is exposed and addressed in those who sit under the preaching of this penetrating book. Here is a collection of songs that sifts through the hearts of a congregation, purging and purifying the individual spiritual lives of the hearers.

> O LORD, who may abide in Your tent?
> Who may dwell on Your holy hill?
> He who walks with integrity, and works righteousness,
> And speaks truth in his heart.   (15:1-2)

Fifth, *expository preaching of the Psalms is practically-relevant.* There is nothing remotely abstract, or distantly theoretical, in this book. No ivory-tower thinking that is disconnected from real life emerges here. Rather, this ancient book is relevant and applicable as it contains highs and lows of human experience, the victories and defeats of human life, the mountain tops and valleys of one's spiritual journey. From the pinnacle of praise to the pit of despair, the full spectrum of human emotions is captured and communicated in this book. No wonder it is a favorite of people everywhere.

> Turn to me and be gracious to me,
> For I am lonely and afflicted.
> The troubles of my heart are enlarged;
> Bring me out of my distresses.
> Look upon my affliction and my trouble,
> And forgive all my sins. (25:16-18)

Third, *expository preaching of the Psalms is soul-comforting.* No book comforts hurting hearts quite like the Psalms. Here is a healing balm for the broken spirit, heart-lifting encouragement for the downcast soul. Thus, preaching the book of Psalms uniquely restores and renews the crushed heart. The old adage is true: Preach to broken hearts and you will never lack for a congregation. People are hurting everywhere. There is, ultimately, only one true remedy to heal the wounded heart, that being God Himself.

> Why are you in despair, O my soul?
> And why have you become disturbed within me?
> Hope in God, for I shall again praise Him
> For the help of His presence. (42:5)

GOD BLESSES HIS WORD

May the Lord abundantly bless your preaching of His inspired hymn book, the Psalms. May you be reminded that it is His Word. God has promised that it shall not return to Him void. He will honor the one who honors His Word. He will go before His Word and prepare hearts to receive it. He will stand beside His servants as they uphold it. He will attend His Word as it is preached. And He will come behind it and cause it to succeed in all that He desires for it to accomplish.

Let us be faithful to the Word.
Soli Deo Gloria.

NOTES

Foreword: A Recovery of the Psalms
1. Hughes Oliphant Old, *The Reading and Preaching of the Scriptures in the Worship of the Christian Church*, 7 volumes (Grand Rapids, MI, and Cambridge, England: Eerdmans Publishing Co., 1998, 1999, 2002, 2004, 2007, 2010).

Preface: Psalms for a New Reformation
1. James Montgomery Boice, *Psalms: Volume 1, Psalms 1-41* (Grand Rapids, MI: Baker Books, 1994), p.9.
2. *Ibid.*, p.10.
3. As quoted by Boice, *Psalms, Vol. 1*, p.388.
4. As quoted by C. H. Spurgeon, *The Treasury of David, Vol. 1b, Psalms 25-27* (Grand Rapids, MI: Zondervan, 1968), p.344.
5. Philip Graham Ryken, *City on a Hill: Reclaiming the Biblical Pattern for the Church in the 21ˢᵗ Century* (Chicago, IL: Moody Publishers, 2003), p.48.
6. Steven Lawson, *Holman Old Testament Commentary, Psalms 1-75, Volume 1 and Psalms 76-150, Volume II* (Nashville, TN: Broadman & Holman Publishers, 2003/2006).

Chapter 1 — Prepare the Heart
1. D. Martyn Lloyd-Jones, *Preaching and Preachers* (Grand Rapids, MI: Zondervan, 1971), p.9.
2. Richard Baxter, *The Reformed Pastor,* edited by William Brown (Edinburgh/Carlisle, PA: The Banner of Truth Trust, 1979 [first published 1656]).

3. Baxter, *The Reformed Pastor*, p.53.

4. Charles H. Spurgeon, 'The Minister's Self-Watch,' *Lectures to My Students*, First Series (Grand Rapids, MI: Baker Book House, 1977), p.4.

5. Martin Luther, an excerpt from the 'Preface to the Complete Edition of Luther's Latin Works' (1545), translated by Andrew Thornton from the 'Vorrede zu Band I der Opera Latina der Wittenberger Ausgabe. 1545' in vol. 4 of Luthers Werke in Auswahl, ed. Otto Clemen, 6th ed. (Berlin: de Gruyter, 1967), pp.421-28.

6. For further reading on this soul-searching subject of being religious but lost, read Matthew Mead, *The Almost Christian Discovered* (Morgan, PA: Soli Deo Gloria, 1996).

7. James M. Garretson, *Princeton and Preaching: Archibald Alexander and the Christian Ministry* (Edinburgh, England/Carlisle, PA: The Banner of Truth, 2005) p.33.

8. *Ibid.*

9. Charles Haddon Spurgeon, *Lectures to My Students* (Pasadena, TX: Pilgrim Publications, 1990), pp.18-39.

10. *Ibid.*, p.23.

11. *Ibid.*

12. *Ibid.*, p.25.

13. *Ibid.*, p.28.

14. *Ibid.*

15. *Ibid.*, p.29.

16. *Ibid.*, p.30.

17. Garretson, *Princeton and Preaching*, p.39.

18. *Ibid.*

19. Manuscript Lectures on Pastoral Theology given at Princeton Theological Seminary (hereafter called *L Pstl T*), 'Call to Ministry,' vol. 11, p.50.

20. Archibald Alexander, 'The Most Important Qualification for a Pastor,' *The Banner of Truth Magazine*, Issue 574, July 2011, pp.3-4.

21. Baxter, *The Reformed Pastor*, pp.61-62.

22. John Owen, as quoted by John MacArthur in *The MacArthur New Testament Commentary, 2 Corinthians* (Chicago, IL: Moody Press, 2003), p.40. Cited in I. D. E. Thomas, *A Puritan Golden Treasury* (Edinburgh: Banner of Truth, 1977), p.192.

23. As quoted by Philip Ryken in *Exodus: Saved for God's Glory* (Wheaton, IL: Good News Publishers, 2005), p.893.

24. Spurgeon, *Lectures to My Students*, pp.7-8.

25. John Stott, *Between Two Worlds* (Grand Rapids, MI: Eerdmans, 1982), p.181.

26. John Stott, *The Preacher's Portrait* (Grand Rapids, MI: Eerdmans, 1961), pp.30-31.

27. Lloyd-Jones, *Preaching and Preachers*, pp.171-3.

28. C. H. Spurgeon, *C. H. Spurgeon's Autobiography* (Pasadena, TX: Pilgrim Publications, 1992), p.268.

29. Ewald M. Plass, comp., *What Luther Says: An Anthology* (St. Louis: Concordia, 1959), vol. 3, p.1359.

30. *Ibid.*, vol. 3, p.1355.

31. *Ibid.*, vol. 3, pp.1354-55.

32. Thomas Watson, *Farewell Sermons of Some of the Most Eminent of the Nonconformist Ministers Delivered at the Period of Their Ejection by the Act of Uniformity in August 1662 to which is Prefixed a Historical and Biographical Preface* (Birmingham, AL: Solid Ground Christian Books, 2011), p.191.

33. John Gillies, George Whitefield, *Memoirs of Rev. George Whitefield* (Connecticut: Whitmore & Buckingham & H. Mansfield, 1834), p.474.

Chapter 2 — Embrace the Task

1. Ryken, *City on a Hill*, p.36.

2. 'Expository,' *The New Shorter Oxford English Dictionary on Historical Principles*, ed. Leslie Brown, vol. I: A-M (Oxford: Clarendon Press, 1993), p.890.

3. Lloyd-Jones, *Preaching and Preachers,* p.196.

4. *Ibid.*, p.97.

5. John Owen, *The Works of John Owen,* vol. VI, ed. William H. Goold (Carlisle, PA/Edinburgh: Banner of Truth Trust, 1977), p.245.

6. Merrill F. Unger, *Principles of Expository Preaching* (Grand Rapids, MI: Zondervan, 1955), p.33.

7. Walter C. Kaiser, Jr., *Preaching and Teaching from the Old Testament* (Grand Rapids, MI: Baker, 2003), p.50.

8. As cited by Alistair Begg, *Preaching for God's Glory* (Wheaton, IL: Crossway, 1999), p.9.

9. John Piper, *The Supremacy of God in Preaching* (Grand Rapids, MI: Baker, 1990), pp.9, 20.

10. J. I. Packer, as quoted by Iain H. Murray, *David Martyn Lloyd-Jones: The Fight of Faith 1939–1981* (Edinburgh/Carlisle, PA: The Banner of Truth Trust, 1990), p.325.

11. Murray, *David Martyn Lloyd-Jones: The Fight of Faith*, p.325.

12. *Ibid.*

13. R. Bruce Bickel, *Light and Heat: The Puritan View of the Pulpit* (Morgan, PA: Soli Deo Gloria Pub., 1999), p.19.

14. The following citations are taken from *The MacArthur Bible Handbook* (Nashville, TN: Nelson, 2003), p.156.

15. See the chart entitled 'Images of God in the Psalms,' *The MacArthur Study Bible*, p.762.

16. John Knox, *The Integrity of Preaching* (Nashville, TN: Abingdon, 1957), p.89.

17. Charles Spurgeon, 'Preface,' *Psalms Volume I* (Wheaton, IL: Crossway Books, 1993), pp.xiv, xvi.

18. John Calvin, *Commentary on the Book of Psalms*, trans. Henry

Beveridge (Grand Rapids, MI: Baker, 1971), pp.xliv, xxxvii.
19. John MacArthur, *The MacArthur Bible Handbook*, p.159.
20. *Ibid.*
21. Gordon Fee and Douglas Stuart, *How to Read the Bible for All Its Worth* (Grand Rapids, MI: Zondervan, 2nd ed., 1981), p.17.
22. Charles H. Spurgeon, 'Howling Changed to Singing,' *Metropolitan Tabernacle Pulpit*, vol. 39 (Pasadena, TX: Pilgrim Pub., 1975), p.235.
23. J. I. Packer, *God Has Spoken* (Downers Grove, IL: InterVarsity, 1979), p.28. John Calvin, the Genevan Reformer, stated, 'Preaching is the public exposition of Scripture by the man sent from God, in which God himself is present in judgement and grace' (As quoted by John Blanchard, comp. *Gathered Gold* (Darlington: Evangelical Press, 1984), p.238.

Chapter 3 — Acquire the Tools
1. Charles H. Spurgeon, *Commenting and Commentaries* (reprint, Edinburgh: Banner of Truth, 1969), p.1.

Chapter 4 — Overview the Psalms
1. James Montgomery Boice, *Psalms: Vol. 1*, p.9.
2. James Montgomery Boice, *Psalms: Volume 2, Psalms 42-106* (Grand Rapids, MI: Baker Books, 1996), pp.ix-x.

Chapter 5 — Select the Approach
1. Sinclair Ferguson, 'Exegesis,' *The Preacher and Preaching*, p.196.
2. Charles Swindoll, *Daily Grind*, 2 vols. (Dallas, TX: Word, 1988).
3. Warren Wiersbe, *Meet Yourself in the Psalms* (Wheaton, IL: 1986).
4. Ray Stedman, *Psalms of Faith* (Ventura, CA: 1988).
5. Ronald B. Allen, *And I Will Praise Him* (Nashville, TN: Thomas Nelson, 1992).
6. E. Calvin Beisner, *Psalms of Promise* (Colorado Springs, CO: NavPress, 1988).
7. D. Martyn Lloyd-Jones, *Spiritual Depression* (Grand Rapids, MI: Eerdmans, 1965, 1922).
8. F. B. Meyer, *The Shepherd Psalm* (Whitefish, MT: Kessinger Publishing, 2005).
9. Charles Bridges, *Psalm 119: An Exposition* (Carlisle, PA: Banner of Truth, 1977).
10. Thomas Manton, *Psalm 119*, 3 vols. (Carlisle, PA: Banner of Truth, 1990).
11. John Calvin, *Sermons on Psalm 119* (Audubon, NJ: Old Paths Publications, 1996).
12, James Montgomery Boice, *Living by the Book* (Grand Rapids, MI: Baker, 1997).
13. Jay E. Adams, *Counsel from Psalm 119* (Woodruff, SC: Timeless Texts, 1998).

14. Sinclair Ferguson, *The Preacher and Preaching*, (Phillipsburg, N.J.: Presbyterian and Reformed, 1986), pp.197-98.

15. *Ibid.*, p.198.

Chapter 6 — Understand the Types (I)

1. James Montgomery Boice, *Psalms, Vol. 1*, p.261.

2. I am deeply indebted to C. Hassell Bullock for his book, *Encountering the Book of Psalms* (Grand Rapids, MI: Baker, 2001), which I have used a great deal in this chapter. For further discussion of genre, see Gordon D. Fee and Douglas Stuart, *How to Read the Bible for All Its Worth*, pp.194-97; Bernard Anderson, *Out of the Depths: The Psalms Speak for Us Today*, 2nd ed. (Louisville, KY: Westminster John Knox, 1983); and D. Brent Sandy and Ronald L. Giese, Jr., eds. *Cracking Old Testament Codes: A Guide to Interpreting the Literary Genres of the Old Testament* (Nashville, TN: Broadman & Holman, 1995).

Chapter 7 — Understand the Types (II)

1. Charles Haddon Spurgeon, *The Early Years, C. H. Spurgeon Autobiography, Volume 1* (London: Banner of Truth, 1962).

Chapter 8 — Consider the Title

1. See James William Thirtle, *The Titles of the Psalms: Their Nature and Meaning Explained* (London: Henry Froude, 1904).

2. Willem A. VanGemeren, 'Psalms,' *Expositor's Bible Commentary*, ed. Frank E. Gaebelein (Grand Rapids, MI: Zondervan, 1991), pp.34, 19.

3. C. Hassell Bullock, *Encountering the Psalms* (Grand Rapids, MI: Baker, 2001), p.25.

4. Thirtle, *The Titles of the Psalms*, p.16.

5. *Ibid.*, p.66.

6. *Ibid.*, pp.70-74.

7. *Ibid.*, p.78.

8. *Ibid.*, p.86.

9. *Ibid.*, pp.126-27.

10. *Ibid.*, 172.

11. Derek Kidner, *Psalms 1-72. An Introduction and Commentary on Books I and II of the Psalms*, Tyndale Old Testament Commentaries (London: InterVarsity, 1973), p.17.

Chapter 9 — Make the Observations

1. John MacArthur, *Rediscovering Expository Preaching* (Dallas, TX: Word Publishing, 1992), p.172.

2. Quoted by Richard Mayhue, *How to Interpret the Bible for Yourself* (Ross-shire, Great Britain: Christian Focus, 1997), p.61.

3. For a further discussion of these features that follow, read C. Hassell Bullock, *Encountering the Book of Psalms: A Literary and Theological Introduction* (Grand Rapids, MI: Baker, 2001), pp.50-56.

4. J. C. Ryle, *Expository Thoughts on the Gospels* (Edinburgh: Banner of Truth, 1987), John 6:22.

5. D. Martyn Lloyd-Jones, *Preaching and Preachers*, p.76.

6. The Septuagint (300 BC) and Latin Vulgate (AD 400) treat Psalms 9 and 10 as one psalm.

7. Stephen F. Olford, *Anointed Expository Preaching* (Nashville, TN: Broadman & Holman, 1998), p.141.

Chapter 10 — Understand the Laws

1. John MacArthur, 'Insights into a Pastor's Heart — Part 1' (unpublished audio series). Transcript online at: http://www.biblebb.com/files/MAC/gty71.htm.

2. Merrill F. Unger, *Principles of Expository Preaching*, pp.164-65.

3. Bernard Ramm, *Protestant Biblical Interpretation*, 3rd rev. ed. (Grand Rapids, MI: Baker Books, 1970), p.123.

4. James Anderson, 'Introductory Notice,' in *Commentary on the Book of Psalms* by John Calvin (Grand Rapids, MI: Baker Books, 2003), pp.vii-viii.

5. John Calvin, *John Calvin's Sermons on Galatians*, trans. Kathy Childress (1563; repr., Edinburgh: Banner of Truth, 1997), p.136.

6. Walter C. Kaiser, Jr., *Toward an Exegetical Theology* (Grand Rapids, MI: Baker Book House, 1981), p.45.

7. *Ibid.*, p.106.

8. John Calvin, *The Epistle of Paul the Apostle to the Romans*, ed. David W. Torrance and Thomas F. Torrance (Grand Rapids, MI: Eerdmans, 1973), p.1.

9. John Broadus, *A Treatise on the Preparation and Delivery of Sermons* (New York: Harper and Brothers, 1926), p.33.

10. For further help, see Ronald L. Giese, Jr., 'Literary Forms of the Old Testament,' in *Cracking Old Testament Codes: A Guide to Interpreting*

the Literary Genres of the Old Testament, edited by D. Brent Sandy and Ronald L. Giese, Jr. (Nashville, TN: Broadman & Holman, 1995), pp.18-24.

11. *Ibid.*, 23.

12. John MacArthur, Jr., 'Moving from Exegesis to Exposition,' *Rediscovering Expository Preaching* (Nashville, TN: W Publishing Group, 1992), p.293.

13. Roy B. Zuck, *Basic Bible Interpretation: A Practical Guide to Discovering Biblical Truth* (Colorado Springs, Colo.: Victor Books, 1991), p.39.

14. Milton S. Terry, *Biblical Hermeneutics: A Treatise on the Interpretation of the Old and New Testaments* (Grand Rapids, MI: Zondervan Publishing, 1947), p.580.

15. Frederic W. Farrar, *History of Interpretation, Bampton Lectures, 1885* (Grand Rapids, MI: Baker Books, 1961), p.329.

16. Kaiser, *Toward An Exegetical Theology*, pp.44-45.

17. Robert Mounce, 'How to Interpret the Bible,' *Eternity* (May 1963), p.21.

Chapter 11 — Examine the Language

1. John MacArthur, *Rediscovering Expository Preaching* (Dallas, TX), pp.176-77.

2. John MacArthur, 'How to Study the Bible,' *The MacArthur Study Bible*, John MacArthur, author and general editor (Nashville, TN: Nelson Bibles, 2006), p.xxviii.

3. James Montgomery Boice, 'The Preacher and Scholarship,' *The Preacher and Preaching: Reviving the Art in the Twentieth Century*, ed. Samuel T. Logan, Jr. (Phillipsburg, NJ: Presbyterian & Reformed Publishing, 1986), pp.100-101.

4. P. Kyle McCarter, Jr., *Textual Criticism* (Philadelphia, PA: Fortress, 1986), pp.72-74.

5. Carl Armerding, *The Old Testament and Criticism* (Grand Rapids, MI: Wm. B. Eerdmans, 1983), 122.

6. William D. Barrick, 2005. 'Exegetical Procedure.' Paper presented at the Shepherds' Conference, Sun Valley, CA.

7. Kaiser, *Toward an Exegetical Theology*, p.49.

8. Robert B. Chisholm, Jr., *From Exegesis to Exposition*, (Grand Rapids, MI: Baker Books, 1998), p.33.

Chapter 12 — Find the Parallelism

1. C. Hassell Bullock, *Encountering the Book of Psalms: A Literary and Theological Introduction* (Grand Rapids, MI: Baker Academic, 2001), p.36.

2. Robert Davidson, *The Vitality of Worship* (Grand Rapids, MI: Eerdmans, 1998), p.5.

3. 'Biblical poetry consists of a distinctive type of sentence structure... It is called parallelism and is the verse form in which all biblical poetry is written... Parallelism is best defined as two or more lines that use different words but similar grammatical form to express the same idea.' Leland Ryken, *The Delight of Words*, 181. C. S. Lewis describes parallelism as 'saying the same thing twice in different words' (*Reflections on the Psalms* [New York, N.Y.: Harcourt, Brace and World, 1985], p.63).

4. John MacArthur, 'The Book of Psalms,' *The MacArthur Study Bible*, p.730.

5. Bullock, *Encountering the Book of Psalms*, p.36.

6. Gerald H. Wilson, *Psalms Volume I, The NIV Application Commentary* (Grand Rapids, MI: Zondervan, 2002), p.39.

7. Leland Ryken, *Words of Delight: A Literary Introduction to the Bible*, 2nd ed. (Grand Rapids, MI: Baker Books, 1992), p.181.

8. For the following examples I am indebted to Willem A. VanGemeren in 'Psalms,' *The Expositor's Bible Commentary*, p.53.

9. Ryken, *Words of Delight*, p.181.

10. *Ibid.*, p.182.

11. Allen P. Ross, 'Psalms,' *Bible Knowledge Commentary* (Wheaton, IL: Victor Press, 1985), p.781.

12. Ryken, *Words of Delight*, p.181.

Chapter 13 — Study the Grammar

1. Roy B. Zuck, *Basic Bible Interpretation*, p.68.

2. Kaiser, *Toward An Exegetical Theology*, p.98.

3. *Ibid.*, p.97.

4. *Ibid.*

5. *Ibid.*

6. *Ibid.*

7 *Ibid.*, pp.215, 217.

8. *Ibid.*, p.271; Charles Franklin Kraft, 'Some Further Observations Concerning the Strophic Structure of Hebrew Poetry,' in *A Stubborn*

Faith: Papers on Old Testament and Related Subjects Presented to Honor William Andrew Irwin, ed. by Edward C. Hobbs (Dallas, TX: Southern Methodist University, 1956), p.71.

9. Some strophe markers below come from Kaiser, *Toward An Exegetical Theology*, 214-17. See also R. K. Harrison, 'Hebrew Poetry,' in *Zondervan Pictorial Encyclopedia of the Bible*, ed. Merrill C. Tenney, 5 vols. (Grand Rapids, MI: Zondervan Publishing, 1975), 3:82.

10. Wilfred G. E. Watson, *Classical Hebrew Poetry: A Guide to Its Techniques*, 2nd ed., rev., Journal for the Study of the Old Testament Supplement Series, 26 (Sheffield, England: Sheffield Academic, 1995), p.162.

11. Kaiser, *Toward an Exegetical Theology*, pp.99-104, 165-81; *Malachi: God's Unchanging Love* (Grand Rapids: Baker Books, 1984); *Preaching and Teaching from the Old Testament*, pp.179-89.

Chapter 14 — Research the History

1. John MacArthur, *Rediscovering Expository Preaching* (Dallas, TX), p.178.

2. Stephen Olford, *Anointed Expository Preaching* (Nashville, TN: Broadman & Holman, 1998), p.113.

Chapter 15 — Study the Geography

1. John Broadus, *On the Preparation and Delivery of Sermons* (1870; repr., New York: Harper and Row, 1979), p.71.

2. Frederick J. Mabie, 'Geographical Extent of Israel,' in *Dictionary of the Old Testament: Historical Books*, edited by Bill T. Arnold and H.G.M. Williamson, pp.316-28 (Downers Grove, IL: InterVarsity Press, 2005).

Chapter 16 — Investigate the Culture

1. John Stott, *Between Two Worlds*, p.10.

2. John Broadus, *On the Preparation and Delivery of Sermons* (1870; repr., New York: Harper and Row, 1979), p.25.

3. Philip J. King and Lawrence E. Stager, *Life in Biblical Israel*, Library of Ancient Israel (Louisville, Kent.: Westminster John Knox, 2001), p.37.

4. John MacArthur, *MacArthur Study Bible*, p.822.

5. See Othmar Keel, *The Symbolism of the Biblical World: Ancient Near Eastern Iconography and the Book of Psalms*, trans. by Timothy J. Hallett

(New York, N.Y.: Seabury, 1978), pp.15-56 (Chapter 1, 'Conceptions of the Cosmos').

Chapter 17 — Discern the Figures

1. Zuck, *Basic Bible Interpretation*, pp.144-45.
2. Ryken, *Words of Delight*, p.160.
3. Merrill F. Unger, *Principles of Expository Preaching*, p.176.
4. Zuck, *Basic Bible Interpretation*, pp.145-46.
5. Ryken, *Words of Delight*, pp.166-68.
6. *Ibid.*, pp.166-8.
7. *Ibid.*
8. Zuck writes: 'A synecdoche is the substituting of a part of something for the whole or the whole for the part' (*Basic Bible Interpretation*, p.151).
9. Ryken, *Words of Delight*, p.177.
10. *Ibid.*, p.178.
11. *Ibid.*, p.177.
12. Zuck, *Basic Bible Interpretation*, pp.151-52.
13. *Ibid.*, p.149.
14. *Ibid.*, p.151.
15. *Ibid.*, p.152.
16. VanGemeren in 'Psalms,' *The Expositor's Bible Commentary*, p.25.
17. Zuck, *Basic Bible Interpretation*, p.151.
18. *Ibid.*, p.140.
19. Martin Luther to Eoban Hess (March 29, 1523) in Preserved Smith and Charles M. Jacobs, eds. and trans., *Luther's Correspondence*, 2 vols (Philadelphia, PA: Lutheran Publication Society, 1918), 2:177.

Chapter 18 — Connect the References

1 Thomas Watson, *A Body of Divinity: Contained in Sermons Upon the Westminster Assembly's Catechism* (London: Banner of Truth, 1958), 3.2; John Blanchard, comp. *Gathered Gold: A Treasury of Quotations for Christians* (Welwyn: Evangelical Press, 1984), p.25.
2. John Broadus, *On the Preparation and Delivery of Sermons* (1870; repr., New York, NY: Harper and Brothers, 1979), p.73.
3 Westminster Confession 1.9.
4. Quoted by C. A. Salmond, *Princetoniana: Charles and A. A. Hodge With Class and Table Talk of Hodge the Young.*

Chapter 19 — Craft the Outline

1. John MacArthur, 'Moving from Exegesis to Exposition,' *Rediscovering Expository Preaching* (Nashville, TN: W Publishing Group, 1992), p.295.
2. 'Plainly Teaching the Word,' unpublished message delivered to the Toronto Spiritual Life Conference, January 10, 1989.

Chapter 20 — Gather the Findings

1. D. Martyn Lloyd-Jones, *Preaching and Preachers*, p.211.
2. John Broadus, *On the Preparation and Delivery of Sermons* (1870; repr., San Francisco, CA: Harper Collins, 1979), p.120.

Chapter 21 — Integrate the Application

1. John A. Broadus, *On the Preparation and Delivery of Sermons*, 4th ed., rev. by Vernon L. Stanfield (New York: HarperSanFrancisco, 1979), p.165.
2. Lloyd-Jones, *Preaching and Preachers*, p.71.
3. John MacArthur, Jr., 'A Study Method for Expository Preaching,' in *Rediscovering Expository Preaching* (Dallas, TX), pp.217-18.
4. R. W. Dale as quoted by John R. W. Stott, *Between Two Worlds*, p.250.

Chapter 22 — Write the Introduction

1. C. H. Spurgeon, *Lectures to My Students* (1875, repr.; Grand Rapids, MI: Baker Book House, 1977), p.128.

Chapter 23 — Draft the Conclusion

1. John A. Broadus, *On the Preparation and Delivery of Sermons* (1870, repr.; New York, NY: HarperSanFrancisco, 1979), pp.108-109.
2. Martyn Lloyd-Jones, *Preaching and Preachers*, p.77.
3. Walter Kaiser, *Preaching and Teaching From the Old Testament*, p.188.
4. G. Campbell Morgan, *Preaching* (Grand Rapids, MI: Baker Publishing, 1974), p.87.
5. Richard Mayhue, 'Introductions, Illustrations, and Conclusions,' *Rediscovering Expository Preaching* (Nashville, TN), p.252.
6. *Ibid.*, p.252.
7. *Ibid.*
8. As quoted by Lewis A. Drummond, *Spurgeon: Prince of Preachers* (Grand Rapids: Kregel, 1992), p.223.
9. Lloyd-Jones, *Preaching and Preachers*, p.146.
10. Charles Spurgeon, *Lectures to My Students, Book Two* (Pasadena,

TX: Pilgrim Publications, 1990), pp.179-80.

Chapter 24 — Evaluate the Manuscript
1. Martyn Lloyd-Jones, *Preaching and Preachers*, pp.241-42.
2. *Ibid.*, p.223.
3. *Ibid.*, p.95.
4. *Ibid.*, p.90.
5. John MacArthur, Jr., 'Delivering the Exposition,' *Rediscovering Expository Preaching* (Dallas, TX), p.322.

Chapter 25 — Deliver the message
1. John MacArthur, *Rediscovering Expository Preaching* (Dallas, TX), p.321.
2. John R. W. Stott, 'Christian Preaching in the Contemporary World,' *Bibliotheca Sacra 145, no. 580* (October-December 1988), p.370.
3. Charles H. Spurgeon, 'Take Away the Frogs,' *Metropolitan Tabernacle Pulpit, Volume 59* (Pasadena, TX: Pilgrim Publications, 1979), p.82.
4. MacArthur, *Rediscovering Expository Preaching*, p.327.
5. *Ibid.*, p.299.
6. Charles H. Spurgeon, *The Metropolitan Tabernacle Pulpit, Vol. 34* (Pasadena, TX: Pilgrim Publications, 1974), p.114.
7. Lloyd-Jones, *Preaching and Preachers*, p.305.
8. *Ibid.*, p.324.
9. *Ibid.*, p.325.
10. Ryken, *City on a Hill*, p.48.
11. William Perkins, as quoted in Philip Ryken's *City on a Hill*, p.35.
12. John MacArthur, *Rediscovering Expository Preaching*, p.324.
13. *Ibid.*, p.325.
14. *Ibid.*
15. Kaiser, *Toward An Exegetical Theology*, p.239.
16. Richard Baxter, *Poetical Fragments*, 'Love Breathing Thanks & Praise' (New York: Gregg Division of McGraw-Hill, 1971), p.30.
17. MacArthur, *Rediscovering Expository Preaching*, p.323.
18. Stott, *Between Two Worlds*, p.275.
19. Lloyd-Jones, *Preaching and Preachers*, pp.91-92.
20. Phillip Brooks, *Lectures on Preaching* (New York, NY: Dutton, 1907), p.8.
21. Lloyd-Jones, *Preaching and Preachers*, 331.